The Recipe for Ecstasy

What Women Want:
Sexual and Relationship Satisfaction

Myrtle C. Means, Ph.D.

The Recipe for Ecstasy
What Women Want: Sexual and Relationship Satisfaction

Shari Nacson, Editor

ISBN 1502508591

In loving memory of a beautiful Black woman, my sister and friend, Carletta L. O'Neal.

Introduction

Part 1: Foundations of Love and Ecstasy

Part 2: Single Women

Part 3: Married Women

Part 4: Refining the Ingredients for Love and Ecstasy

Part 5: Understanding What Tastes Good, Bad, Exotic

Epilogue

Satiation 231

Appendices

References

Introduction

Hunger

On a bumpy unpaved road, I received my first lessons in love. From an early age, I knew that something was missing. This became apparent as I grew older and became an adult, an educator, a psychologist, a wife, a friend, a lover, and a mother. I was missing the kind of love for which I had always wished. I have always said that I wanted to be known as a lover: a lover of many things—most of all, life. Not just any life, but a life filled with love.

Per the definition, love should manifest as a strong affection and warm attachment to our first love: mother. Love is the one thing we all need from start to finish. It is an essential ingredient in our lives. With it you can do anything. Without it, everything is harder, much harder. Love is the sunshine and water we need to grow into a beautiful flower, a flower that can open up its petals and spread its seed. Now I have it and I want to share some of my life and love with you.

My interest in love dates back to September 5th, 1972, the day I was born to a teenage mother. I was raised on the eastside of the "D" (Detroit, Michigan). I grew up the oldest of four, but I was the one 'from another brotha.' The stepchild. Life was hard for me. In the hood, from the ghetto, with the drama! The drama of a mama who did not know what she was doing. Only 16, I wouldn't wish motherhood on anybody that age. My mother did not know much about love; it was apparent in her treatment of us. I don't blame her; her mother did not know much about love either. She was clearly still searching for love herself.

My interest in sexuality dates back well into my childhood. I remember sneaking into the living room to turn the radio down low, so I could hear bits and pieces of Dr. Ruth's talk show *Sexually Speaking*. In my adolescence, my interest continued to grow when

I became a peer educator for Planned Parenthood; it grew further, still, as I developed personally and professionally. I finally put pen to paper with these ideas when I began my dissertation in partial fulfillment of the requirements for a Ph.D. in Clinical Psychology. I chose as my research topic female sexual satisfaction. The final product, although tasty, was not what I had in mind. It was scholarly, full of theories and statistics. The most valuable outcome of my research was the identification of various factors (ingredients) that contributed to sexual satisfaction for specific groups of women. In addition, my research educated me about theories of development that also affect relationships and sexual satisfaction—more to the point, psychoanalytic (developmental) and evolutionary theory (mate selection).

In earlier literature, the topic of female sexuality was accompanied by uncertainty, ambiguity, and contradiction. Many theorists and writers have attempted to shed some light on the "Dark Continent;" ironically, their attempts have contributed to further confusion. After a thorough review of this literature, I developed a feel for what was missing—a practical framework for understanding the ingredients necessary for healthy, gratifying, joyous love and sexual intimacy. As I began to blend historic and modern theory and prose with my own ideas, I thought about women who are not going to do elaborate study. Women who are busy with their lives and want more health, satisfaction, joy, and connection in their love and sexual relationships.

♀

To help you digest all this information, *The Recipe for Ecstasy* will break it down into small, bite-size pieces. Using the aforementioned theories, I will shed light on this mysterious topic (female sexuality), including how to use this knowledge to improve the quality of your loving relationships.

As a woman who has come into the world with all the right parts, you are born with the necessary ingredients for baby-making (i.e., vagina, ovaries, fallopian tubes, and uterus). In addition to this biological readiness, there are innate properties that mature throughout the life cycle in preparation for having babies: the propensity towards intimacy and nurturance. According to, both, psychoanalytic and evolutionary theory, these factors exhibit a considerable influence on female sexuality. In most cases, the mother is the primary caregiver. Thus, a girl's first experience of intimacy and nurturance should be with her mother. According to psychoanalytic theory, the mode of satisfaction/gratification that begins at birth (parent-child interactions) remains as the core influence on sexuality and relationships throughout the life cycle. Sexuality develops in the context of relationships: one's relationship with the mother (or mother figure) and one's relationship with the external world.

The intense impact of this relationship formed the basis of my research: to explore the relationship between female sexual satisfaction and relationships with the primary caregiver (mother) and with the external world (the man/men of choice). Even though I used these seminal theories to add support to *The Recipe for Ecstasy*, this book is not dry or bland. It is full of flavor, is juicy, and has lots to savor.

♀

After my dissertation, I kept living, loving, and writing. I dated— you know, played The Game—for many years and finally found the love of my life: Martin Wesley Muhammad. Now that I have arrived at ecstasy, I have a mouthful of knowledge to offer, knowledge emanating from my personal experience of sexual satisfaction and love, my clinical work, my research data collected through graduate studies, and my time kicking it out with the girls— aka "The Family," the delectable ladies of Delta Sigma Theta Sorority (12 G.A.G.E.E.), and my girls from MSU. The most gratifying dishes came when I put it all together and mixed it up. I have prepped it, cooked it up, and now present to you a savory feast, one that I hope will linger with you, changing the way you live and love. The menu includes the process, the pleasure, the pain, and the power that come from ecstasy/true love

I am a firm believer that if you can read, you can cook—both in and out of the bedroom. I will provide the necessary ingredients and tell you how to put them together to create a delicious dish that you can savor. One might ask why *The Recipe for Ecstasy*? Why food and sex? This is where it all begins. Sex creates life; to sustain life we must eat. Once a life is created, it has to be fed. This is the responsibility of every parent, to feed his or her children a healthy diet, literally and metaphorically speaking. Chef hats off to those who took the time to teach their children about their bodies, sexuality, relationships, and intimacy—intimacy meaning true closeness. Not just physical intimacy, but emotional intimacy too. So if you get nothing else from this book, let me teach you about being close to one person at a time. Let me show you how it can excite you to "one-der-full" feelings of ecstasy. "One-der-full" is the experience of oneness and fullness that accompanies true intimacy

We begin collecting the ingredients for lifelong relationships from day one. Whether those ingredients amount to something savory, nourishing, fulfilling—well that depends upon what is offered to us and what we do with what we have been given. We learn our first lessons of love at home. According to Sigmund Freud, love and work are the cornerstones of our humanness. Our parents prepare us for life by teaching these fundamentals, or not! There are those who have been remiss in their duties, leaving their children hungry, or even starving!

A mother first shows love in the way that she cares for herself while carrying a new life into the world. Once born, a child is entitled to nurturance. Everyone should be fed. And if properly done, the child develops into an adult who then goes on to love. Can you imagine what it is like to feed someone, literally, with your mind, body, and soul? You mothers out there know what I am talking about, from the inside out, mother to child, and womb to world. Birth is where this story begins. When life goes on, love goes on, or at least it should, and it will if it is included in your diet.

We cannot exist on love alone. We must work. Work is an aspect of all that we do: educationally, professionally, personally, interpersonally and, yes, sexually. All love does not feel good, and all work is not productive. Therefore, we must be educated in the correct ways. These lessons are often passed down from generation to generation like a treasured family recipe. With this, I am opening up my treasured cookbook for all to see.

If you have been given love, then you know love. I have learned lessons about love and making love, some good and some not. But I have been working on perfecting this recipe for a long time. Although this has been my life journey, I will give you just the highlights. I will start with the love that I feel for my spouse and the love that I feel from him, mixed with plenty of sexual pleasure, yielding ecstasy. I took what I had (my ingredients) and he gave me what he had (his ingredients), and we put them together. Like the perfectly refined recipe, we put them together in a particular order and in just the right amounts. And out came something delicious: our love, our life together and our two beautiful children, Madeline

Grace and Marin Rae. All of which inspired me to this: *The Recipe for Ecstasy, What Women Really Want: Sexual and Relationship Satisfaction.* He gave me this and so much more.

In this book I have looked at relationships, love, and sex from several perspectives. I am currently writing from the perspective of a married woman who has children; I have been there and done that. I have been in the shoes of three of the four groups of women that this book will focus on: single without children, single with children, married without children, and married with children. Each group possesses unique characteristics that contribute to the list of ingredients for their respective recipes for ecstasy. Note that identification of the key ingredients came from my dissertation research. They were extrapolated from the narratives that these women wrote regarding their most sexually satisfying experiences. I call them savory soliloquies.

In the beginning there was hunting and gathering. This is how we once went about getting what we wanted. What do you do today to get what you want? Are you still hunting and gathering, reaping the fruits of your labor—a great self, a great other, a great life, a great lover? To eat we must work. For great sex we must work. Eating is just as basic as sex. They are both physiological functions, a need that craves to be met. To survive as a species we need, both, sex to create life and food to sustain it. This takes us back to our roots of sex and aggression, our basic instincts. Our proclivities towards love and work emanate from these basic drives. And it compels us to get out there to search for something to satisfy our appetites for love and sex.

Hunting and gathering at one time meant to hunt for the meat of animals to feed a family. Today it means to hunt the meat of a man to feed a woman and to gather the fruit and berries of a woman to feed the appetite of a man. This process is repeated, over and over, until she satisfies her appetite and until he satisfies his. These instincts are used for our very survival, the survival of the fittest.

To be fit we must have healthy bodies, minds and souls. For this we must also work. To have a healthy body takes proper diet and exercise. Work. We will take the gene pool for granted: Nature. Genetics gave you your looks, brains, and body (physical features, intelligence, physiology). But to have a healthy heart and soul you must be fed: Nurture. Work. We often take the seven food groups for granted. Have you been fed a balanced diet? Have your cupboards been stocked with the essential ingredients (love and work)? It is fine to compliment these healthy core ingredients with rare spices and specialty items (multiple orgasms and sexual abandon) Go gourmet! Although, there is no need for newfangled kitchen gadgets (vibrators and poles for dancing), it sure makes the cooking experience a lot more fun.

As you read this book keep these questions in mind. Did anyone teach you about love or making love? Have you had your recommended daily intake? Have you been fed the right ingredients? Do you know how to use your ingredients? Can you go out and select the right ingredients? Not just any ingredients, but beautiful, robust ingredients to complement your life? Will your ingredients add up to sexual and relationship satisfaction? Go ahead and review your diet but make sure that it is a balanced one: work and play, fantasy and reality, joy and sadness, self and other, satisfaction and dissatisfaction, subtlety and intensity.

Women have a number of challenges to overcome in their pursuit of sexual and relationship satisfaction. These challenges may include things like what we have learned about sexuality and love from our parents and/or society. For women especially, there may be limited knowledge of our body parts and how they work (anatomy and physiology). And these challenges can lead to other obstacles, such as fear of intimacy or inability to reach an orgasm. Some challenges are specific to Black women, and may be associated with the legacy of slavery—a time when we were ripped from the arms of our men, taken to be used and abused, even sold! Made to bear children that were not to be nurtured or loved, but instead were prematurely put to work, when they should have been nurtured. These things from our remote past, passed down from generation to generation, may affect a woman's sense of individuality and self-worth. This legacy also affects the availability and eligibility of the Black man. While other challenges (e.g. having an inadequate love object (mother)), are more general and affect women across all races, *The Recipe for Ecstasy* will address challenges that linger, particularly, for Black women—with the hope of helping women overcome these challenges.

I will also identify the role that our personal history and various aspects of development affect what we know about love and making love. In this way, it is suitable for all races and both sexes, though I admittedly have given it a 'chocolate flava.' Therefore, it will have special appeal to the Black woman and man. It will show you how to reach the highest level of relationship and sexual fulfillment—ecstasy. It's what we seek, two great pleasures of life: eating (learning) and loving (making love).

To make love is to cause the experience known as love to exist or occur. We can make love occur in both the physical and emotional sense. Love, a key ingredient in the recipe for ecstasy, is a difficult thing to define because we do it in so many ways, because it feels different to each of us. For our purposes, love will be defined as a strong affection, warm attachment, and attachment based on sexual desire. It will also be broken down into three components: intimacy, passion, and commitment. Identified by Sternberg as the *Triangle of Love,* I used these elements to quantify love in my research. Like the perfect slice of pie, the three sides connect to form a gratifying treat: love.

Sexual satisfaction is something we each personally define. This is why I have asked women to tell me *in their own words* what makes them feel full, what has made them lick their plates clean. There will be some ingredients that are universal to all women, such as orgasm. If you are preparing a dish, you don't serve it before it is done cooking. Women want orgasmic pleasure; it is vital to *The Recipe for Ecstasy.* For those women who have yet to indulge in this delicacy, let me be the first to introduce you to unadulterated pleasure.

The first intimate conversation about sex should take place with parents, someone who ideally has your best interest in mind. This ostensibly enables you to have that one-on-one with 'the' one, when the time is right. You can openly discuss things like: expectations, preferences, fears, fantasies, and techniques. Even under ideal circumstances there may be some things missing from your pantry of knowledge. And more to the point, under conditions of neglect and abuse, certain things will be missing (your cupboards may be bare). So if you never had that first conversation with the folks, or even if you did, this book is for you. This book is for those who didn't get that intimate talk. And for those who want a refresher course, here it is with a twist. Here you will find an opportunity for relearning, unlearning, and for some, just plain old learning. Chew on this before you go out there and stick your fork into something worth eating, digesting, living and loving.

My personal goal is to feed my children enough so that they grow to love themselves enough; that they love themselves enough so that they can love and be loved to satiety. So, I thoughtfully feed them. My professional goal is to feed you enough, so that you grow enough to love and be loved to satiety. So, I will thoughtfully feed you, as well. If this book does nothing else but make you think about who you are, what you have, what you were fed, and what you crave, then I have done my job. In the process we will have created a great meal!

If you want the ingredients, here is the list: intimacy, passion, commitment, orgasm (multiple even), newness, variation (in the sex act), his focus on her/ attention (mindfulness), nature of the relationship, sexual abandon, awayness, quality of relatedness (mutuality), arousal, love, technique, orgasm intensity, setting, mood (safe, playful, romantic, relaxed), self-regard, and intensity of physical and emotional response. Put it all together and you get this dish (food prepared in a particular way): *The Recipe for Ecstasy, What Women Want: Sexual and Relationship Satisfaction.*

Bon appétit!

Part 1
Foundations of Love and Ecstasy

Chapter 1
Prep Time

Any great meal begins with thoughtful preparation. You need the key ingredients, the appropriate tools and supplies, and an atmosphere conducive for creating your masterpiece. Think about your preparation for loving relationships. What was in your daily diet? Were you properly prepared to give and receive love? Ask yourself these questions: Were you nurtured or neglected? Were your parents attentive or abusive? Did someone talk to you about your body and sexuality? Did you have the opportunity to witness loving relationships?

The Chef and The Sous Chef

Our preparation for lifelong loving takes place from birth. Our love capacity starts with the love that we received from our primary caregivers. "It means that something goes on between an ordinary baby and ordinary mothers and fathers that creates and ensures the capacity for love in infancy and in later life. It tells us that love and pleasure in the body begins in infancy and progress through childhood and adolescence to a culminating experience, 'Falling in love,' the finding of the pertinent partner, the achievement of sexual fulfillment" (Fraiberg, 1971). For many of us, our first love is the center of the universe known as "Mother." Although Father is an important piece of this pie who we should not discount, his role is usually secondary to the role of Mother.

A father is responsible for encouraging a girl's attempt at femininity. He responds by setting the appropriate boundaries so that she can remain safe, as well as by offering reinforcement in terms of appropriate displays of affection. A good father makes sure that his daughter knows her worth. He treats her with the value and respect that she deserves, so that she knows better than to let anyone mistreat or mislead her. He loves her like no other man will, but a man is welcome to spend his lifetime trying. Together, the chef and sous chef create love to be served at every meal. Mothers and fathers occupy many roles in the lives of their children (teacher, friend, preacher, enemy, etc.), but none more important than the role of 'lover'. We will explore each parent's role as it relates to individuality, sexuality, and relationships.

Poor Nutrition

To "make love" you need to be able to create an experience of strong affection, warm attachment, and attraction based on sexual desire. A mother provides these key ingredients by way of nurturance. Once we are born we need to be nurtured. If this need is not met it is like being starved to death. Death is the extreme consequence of emotional deprivation, neglect, and abuse. We often think of death as a physical ending of life. However, the death I am referring to is emotional.

So, now that I have your attention, let us talk about the more common consequence of neglect: failure to thrive. This is a condition that is characterized by delayed physical and emotional development. It has many determinants, is often the result of medical problems, malnutrition, neglect, poverty, or abuse. For our purposes I will focus on the emotional stunting that occurs and manifests as a result of neglect and abuse (poor nutrition). Poor nutrition can lead to poor self-esteem, feelings of inadequacy, poor body image, and immature sexuality. The individual fails to develop a sense that they are worthy of love and the feeling that they are able to give love. When a girl is malnourished she will be insecure, feel inadequate, and have low self-esteem. Thus, she grows into a woman who acts out of desperation. She is unsure of herself and this uncertainty leads to poor mate choices and unstable relationships.

The Bun is in the Oven: Pregnancy

We need food to keep us alive: the nourishment of our mind, body, and soul. I mean this literally and figuratively. Literally, a mother feeds a baby before it is even born. A mother's care manifests in how she provides for herself and, subsequently, the unborn child. This is her first act of love and nurturance.

Think about what you know about your experiences in the womb. Did you have a balanced diet while you were growing in-utero? A diet consisting of protein, fruits, vegetables, dairy, vitamins, and minerals? You know, the stuff that would provide a strong physical foundation. Proper nutrients would offer an opportunity to grow into a healthy adult. Or did your mother eat foods high in fat, drink alcohol, use recreational drugs, smoke cigarettes, and/or fail to take prenatal supplements? This kind of diet creates a foundation that is unstable and full of cracks. A child enters the world with a deficit, some of which can never be recovered.

The Bun is Done: Birth

What kind of start did you get? Once born, the feeding continues, mother to child. Can you imagine what it is like to feed someone, literally, with your body? You mothers out there know what I am talking about: those breastfed babies whose mothers make an additional sacrifice so their child can be strong, healthy, and protected. The nutritional value of breastfeeding goes far beyond a full belly. Breast milk is the gift of immunity, the gift of a higher I.Q., the gift of decreased health problems. Most of all it is the gift of intimacy. "In breast feeding, the infant is cradled in the mother's arms. Pleasure in sucking, the satisfaction of hunger, intimacy with the mother's body, are united with recognition of her face. The baby learns to associate this face, this mother's face, with an enjoyable and comforting experience" (Fraiberg, 1971). The bond that is created between a loving mother and a child during this process is unparalleled. These feelings of nurturance grow over time, providing a sense of being loved to the child who develops into an adult and then goes on to love. First, the seed is planted; if fed we grow and blossom into the most beautiful flowers—flowers who will continue to spread their seeds.

The Good Enough Mother: Parenting

A loving mother provides love, warmth, structure, discipline, guidance, comfort, and a sense of value. Passed down to us like grandmother's recipe for peach cobbler, mother gives us the first ingredients in our recipe. It is the sweetest gift. Every mother's goal should be to provide the necessary ingredients to produce a person who feels special, valuable, confident and, most of all, loved. When a person knows their value from birth, it is obvious. It manifests itself in self-esteem and self-worth, in confidence and hope. It might start with make-believe. For example, young girls and boys pretend to be princesses and superheroes, respectively. An emotionally healthy girl matures into the woman who demands to be treated like a queen; the boy becomes the hero who wants to honor and protect his most valued treasure.

I have been talking about the "good enough" mother. That is the mother who tries her best. She loves with intention, but has her flaws and, at times, she disappoints. Unfortunately, there is another kind of mother: the insufficient mother, who neglects, deprives, and abuses. She is harsh, cold, distant, inconsistent, and unavailable. She too passes down the family's recipes. But the outcome is much different. There are no sweet smells to savor. Rather, an offensive odor lingers into our adulthood: shame, insecurity, anger, low self-worth, anxiety, fear of intimacy.

Good Enough Parenting

An important aspect of parenting is teaching. Ideally, parents teach their children many things, including how to love, manage feelings, cope with difficult times, develop and maintain relationships. Sexuality is often avoided, disregarded, or ignored. Why, when it is as normal as eating and sleeping? Some people bring all their anxieties and fantasies into the discussion. While anxiety and fantasy will not be ignored, it will not be the focus either. Now is the time to look at the reality of sexuality and find the pleasure. Isn't sex supposed to be fun?

Did your parents teach you about sexuality? Did you have a discussion about your body, its development, and its sexual appetite? Did anyone talk to you about intimacy, both physical and emotional? If the answer to any of these questions is no, you are not alone. Open discussion of sexuality is an important aspect of the learning process. Observational learning is also an invaluable tool. Parents, by way of their interaction with each other, have ample opportunity to show their children how to appropriately express their sexuality (i.e., hugs, kisses, caresses, flirtatious eyes).

Sex happens in a variety of contexts. For some, it is a one-night stand; for others it is a part of a lifetime commitment. This book will focus on sex in the context of a meaningful adult relationship. At the same time we will look at the other context (casual relationships) in which sexuality is expressed and experienced. While reading, consider the effect of your personal development in your current relationships; focus on how that relates to your experience of sexual satisfaction. Ask yourself: Was I deprived, maintained, or nurtured?

Deprivation destroys, maintenance maintains, and nurturance nourishes.

Stocking the Pantry: Personal Ingredients and Preferences

Before you go out looking for the person you want to share your life with, you must make some important decisions. What are you looking for? Make a list. Just as when shopping for groceries, you don't usually look for things that you already have, unless it is something you can never have too much of, such as kindness or intelligence. So check the refrigerator and pantry; do a personal inventory. This helps to make informed decisions. It can save a lot of time, energy, money, and heartache.

Here's my personal inventory. I am bright, sexy, and stylish. I got a mean shoe game. I am a good cook, with a big butt and strong legs (this according to my husband—something I should have known given that I tear it up on the dance floor every chance I get). I love to shop. I have nice teeth and long, pretty hair. I love to eat. Sex is a hobby (an important one). I'm bossy, exacting, demanding. I like nice things. I am a great listener who has lots to say. I love to have fun, fun, fun. People love to talk to me, especially about sex.

According to Beyoncé, I'm a "Diva". A diva is the female version of a hustler. I make things happen. Whatever I want I go after. I wanted out of the ghetto. I wanted to be a doctor. I wanted a family. I also knew what I wanted when I was looking for my husband. I wanted a man who was tall and rich and chocolate. I don't mean to make this process sound easy; it was not. I went through a considerable amount of trial and error. More error. There were many unsavory mixes before I found someone just right for me, but knowing exactly what I was looking for surely made things easier.

Black women, especially, have some hurdles to jump when it comes to selecting a partner. Topping that list of challenges is the task of finding an eligible man. Notice I did not say "eligible *Black* man." Sistas have different tastes; going outside of the race gives you more options from which to choose. Be mindful, however, that mixing flavas complicates your recipe. Whatever your preferences are, know them. Know the things that your recipe for ecstasy cannot do without, as well as the things that you could substitute or sacrifice. For example, when making meatloaf you can use milk, water, or apple juice. You could even do without the breadcrumbs. But you cannot make a meatloaf without meat! So if you don't want a mate with kids, don't date a man with kids. If you would prefer a mate who doesn't drink at all, but could tolerate a social drinker, be honest about it. First, be honest with yourself. Then, be honest with him before you stock your pantry with his items.

If you don't eat pork, you don't buy pork chops; if you prefer fresh veggies, you don't stock your pantry with canned goods. Don't bring into your kitchen things that you ultimately don't want to eat. Skip the sales, the buy one get one free—shop for quality and for taste. Some people shop at the local chain grocer, while others prefer the specialty markets. Wherever you choose, just remember: where you shop dictates what you bring home.

These are the ingredients I had in mind. I wanted him tall and handsome. This ain't no cliché either! I like 'em fine—fine as wine in the summertime! For some, physical attractiveness is not a priority as long as the person is not too hard on the eyes. And if that is what works for you, that's cool. But I like 'em fine. And I was not willing to compromise what was on the inside, either. This is why people thought I would never be married. Too choosy. He had to be smart. I like to talk and sometimes I like to get deep. I needed someone who could go the depths. He had to be ambitious, if not already a success. I like nice things. Kind, loyal, and loving. I wanted someone I could share my life with: a friend, a lover, a husband. I wanted all these things. Most of all I wanted a partner for life!

For me, a partner fits all of the following definitions: (1) a persons with whom I will dance through life as a spouse; (2) one who plays on the same team as the other (might have different roles, but with the same goal); and (3) one of two persons contractually associated as joint principals in a business (marital contract for the business of love and sharing one's life).

You need to understand that people have preferences. It is okay if a person is not interested in you because you do not tempt their taste buds. Don't take it personally. How can it be personal when two people have just met? Although it may feel like rejection, it is not necessarily so. Think of it more as an expression of their preference. If I don't like fish, it doesn't matter how it is served. I don't want it.

People have the right to send a dish back if it is not what they ordered or if it does not appeal to their palate. So, go ahead take another look at the menu. You just might find the right dish this time.

This brings me to another one of the difficulties associated with seeking a partner, dealing with disappointment and frustration. There has to be a tolerance for these emotions, as it is rare that you will find that special someone the first time out. It happens; but it is the exception, not the rule. Get ready to put in some time and effort (work). Be prepared to take a few bites of something and want to spit it out. It will all be worth it when you stick your fork into something you really want to eat. I'm talking about savoring: enjoy the presentation, lift it to your lips, let it rest in your mouth, chew slowly, swallow, feel good, go back for more. Don't be fooled by imitations. You may have difficulty finding "the real thing." He may only have bits and pieces of what you hunger for. He is a friend, but not a lover; he is a lover, but not a friend. Don't settle for saltines when you want Ritz or for instant mashed potatoes when you like them from scratch. Know what you want and take the time to figure out if he has the right stuff.

So, we go back to your shopping list. Take some time and think about what should be included. I have provided my list and my husband's list to give you some ideas. When creating your list, think about what you *must* have versus the things you can live without. Your list could be broken into three categories: need, want, and splurge!

Grocery List

My Grocery List	His Grocery List	Your List
Tall	Sweet	
Handsome	Smart (but not arrogant)	
Smart	Highly educated	
Successful	Spontaneous	
Ambitious	Appreciative	
Loyal	Love to Party	
Kind	Income Earner	
Loving	Traveler	
Curious	Sex, sex, and more sex	
Best friend	Lover of music	
Good Lover	Ride or Die Chick	
Traveler	Warm	
Fun	Physically attractive /Sexy	
Swagger	Stylish	
Nice teeth	Frugal	
Body	"Foody"	
Booty	Tolerant	
Partner	Good cook	
Adventurous	Open	

Canned or Fresh: Casual or Serious?

What are you looking for, taste and a full belly or a lot of substance and satisfaction? This goes not only for the characteristics of the person, but also for the nature of the relationship. I believe that, as you mature, relationships fall into two categories: casual or serious, i.e. fucking or dating. Like fruits or vegetables, they can both be good for you. But depending on where you are in your own life, one might be more appetizing than the other. No matter who you are, I believe that everyone wants to be with someone. However, each person gets to that place when they are ready for it. For some of us, that time happens early in life (twenties or thirties), while for others it is later in life (mid-forties or fifties); for some it is never.

Being mature is a state of mind. It is a place I hope you get to experience, if you are not there already. It is when you are ready and willing to make choices in your life. It is when you take responsibility for your own happiness. It is the time when you say, "I want _____," and you take the necessary steps to get it. Whenever that time is, I believe that when you get there, either you just want to have fun or you want to see if this could be "the one." The one you spend the rest of your life with, the one you love, the one who loves you, the one who makes you scream out his name, the one you create a family with, the one and only one. Where are you? How did you fill in the blank? Canned or Fresh?

If you are looking for love, don't shop for sex. And if you only want sex, don't tell them that it is love. Love is not a part of all sexual relationships. Some sexual relationships are casual and fun. There are no expectations other than pleasure. But it is still a relationship, unless of course, it is a one-night stand. You have a casual sexual relationship with the person on the other side of the booty call: the fuck buddy, the maintenance man, the friend with benefits, and the pipe layer. Sex is how you relate to each other. Simply put, you can take the sex out of the relationship, but you can't take the relationship out of sex.

For the romantics out there who are looking for love, you need to be honest with yourself and the people you get involved with. You want a serious love relationship that will take you there, take you to a point of ecstasy physically and emotionally. Your shopping experience might be a bit more challenging. You are not looking for something that solely tastes good, but also something that is good for you. So you have to read the labels more closely and see what ingredients he or she possesses. Will they be a great love and a great lover too? Some people make such poor food choices. They choose something because it tastes good. But what tastes good is not always good for you. No matter what is on the menu you have to consider the context, the nature of the relationship. So let's look at the different types of relationships out there: from talkin', fuckin', kickin' it, hangin' out, to dating, co-habiting (shacking up), being committed, becoming engaged, and marrying.

Keeping in mind the nature of the relationship, remember that different dishes call for different ingredients. Canned or Fresh? When you start to look for the items on your list, take your time. Pick the most fresh, firm and flavorful. Squeeze it, smell it, look at it closely. Is he or she really what you want? Go back to your list; don't ignore it. You wrote it, so pay attention to what you are craving. Let us start shopping!

Chapter 2
Menu Planning

There are lots of items on the menu, so stay focused. If you are just dating, and you are not sure what type of dishes you like, it is a good idea to get a sampler platter. That means you don't jump into exclusive dating. See what's out there. Learn about your preferences. There are some people who go to a restaurant and select the same thing every time. Now, either they like it just plain old vanilla or they are just too scared to make themselves vulnerable and choose something new. But this is the only way to find out what you really like. Try a little caramel with nuts!

Dating is supposed to be fun; it can be frustrating too. You have to be prepared to deal with the variety of emotions that will come along with the experience: excitement about all of the possibilities, fear of rejection, hope for the future, and disappointment in the dating process.

Appetizers: Some Initial Thoughts About Dating

The first days of dating are like an appetizer (a bite-sized amount of food that is served before the meal to whet or excite the palate). Keep it light; don't fill up on this course. The appetizer is just to stimulate interest. And like most things that are for excitement, it wears off over time. Dating requires vulnerability. You must let your guard down to let someone in. This does not happen quickly. It is slow as molasses.

Don't inhale your food. Take your time; chew it slowly so you can actually taste the flavors. Getting to know someone is a gradual process that happens over time. As two people get to know each other, they should become more comfortable sharing. Communication is an integral part of getting to know each other. Words bring clarity to confusion. So, ask direct questions and tell truths. Nothing tastes worse than a belly full of lies. This brings us back to those intentions and to your grocery list. Be honest with yourself when dating. What do you want? Friendship? Love? Sex? Companionship? All of the above?

Ask questions and pay attention to the answers—the real answers, not just what you want to hear. Don't read between the lines; don't try to decipher hidden meanings or assume you know what a person means. Ask direct questions and let him tell you who he is, what he likes, what he wants and whom he wants. This is how you get to know someone. The same goes for the sex. If you want to know how to light someone's flame, ask him or her for the match, and then strike to achieve a burning hot flame. That is assuming that the person that you are dealing with is honest and forthright, that he or she is not interested in playing games. Good luck with that!

Researching Key Ingredients

Asking questions has always been an important part of the process. This is a fundamental piece of one of the most intimate relationships that exist: the relationship between a mother and child. It is a dynamic that occurs over and over again. All children use questions to get oriented to the world. Children have to ask questions because the world is a mystery to them. Think about this when you are trying to get to know someone. Their world is a mystery to you. Why do we stop asking questions? Because sometimes we don't want to know the answers. At times, we prefer to live in the realm of fantasy and "what if." But you need to allow yourself to see reality, "what is", if you are going to create a recipe for ecstasy.

Focus on "what is." Being able to deal with reality is what helps us develop fully. Don't stop asking questions when you are trying to get to know someone (just like when we were young, trying to join the world). And be sure to ask questions of yourself, as well. What do you have a taste for tonight? Do you want a snack, just something to hold you over? Or are you looking for someone to hold you all night, every night—a meal that will fill you up?

Verbal and nonverbal communication of your needs is a key ingredient to sexual and relationship satisfaction. We develop from uncivilized to civilized; from smiles to coos; from grunts and babbling to words.

"During the first six months the baby has the rudiments of a love language; there is the language of the smile, the language of vocal sound-making, and the language of the embrace. It's the essential vocabulary of love before we can yet speak of love. (In 18 years, when the baby is grown and 'falls in love' for the first time, he will woo his partner through the language of the smile, through the utterance of endearments and the joy of the embrace)" (Fraiberg, 1971).

Grunts and babbling are to babies what words are to adults. Hugging and kissing, while very basic, are essential expressions of love. We should never abandon these intrinsic ways of communication. Despite adult maturation, this innate way of communication can still be an effective way of expressing your feelings. Mmm, ahhhh, oooh, oh yeah baby, that feels so good...

Life is all about evolving, or at least it should be. From girl to woman, from boy to man, a mother teaches a child how to love. But when you find that special someone, s/he has to fill in the gaps with the specifics and teach you how to love him. Only the individual knows how s/he wants to be loved. Men and women need to teach each other. Use your words to help things develop in a mature, civilized manner.

Now, don't forget about the unspoken forms of communication: body language. Hugs, kisses and embraces communicate vital information about a person and their ability to be affectionate. People communicate who they are and what they want in many ways, not just words. You have to pay attention to body language and actions. I am a firm believer that people tell you who they are in, both, direct and indirect ways. Pay close attention. For example, how does he respond when you ask direct questions? Is he evasive or open? If he says he will call at 8:00 p.m., does he? Is he curious about you and your life, or does he just want to know if you are wearing panties? How does it feel when he looks at you or touches you? It's all information.

Many men find it hard to believe that women are capable of having casual sex. Surprise! We are and we do. Just like you. That's not to say that all men are only interested in a two-piece dark (legs and thighs... for those who don't know). It is in a woman's nature to want more. The nature of women is to get emotionally involved and desire intimate relationships. We are often described as the emotional ones. In general, this is true. Research has suggested that the brain differences between males and females affect how we process language, express feelings, and interact socially. Women seek intimacy. This being true does not negate the fact that sometimes a hearty one-night stand will do. Therefore, there is no need to sugarcoat things.

For you men out there, if you know your intentions when you begin to pursue her, don't lie when the truth will do. Give her the opportunity to make a choice. Don't choose for her by way of your deception and omission. There are plenty of women who are willing to hit it and quit it. All relationships are not a full course meal. Sometimes you just want a quick bite to satisfy your appetite. If the appetizer is all that you want off of the menu, don't bite off more than you can chew.

Snack on This

There is a difference between being in like, in love, and in lust. You should know what you are in, and what he is into.

The Three C's:
Chemistry, Connection, and Commitment

Before you can determine if a person can satisfy your appetite, there must be chemistry. Dating activities like *Quick Spark, Just Lunch, Play Date, and Dinner for Eight* tell us that it does not take that long to determine whether or not you and he have chemistry. These dating tools are used to facilitate and expedite your choice. People meet strangers at public places for dinner or five-minute conversations to see if there is any chemistry. Either you feel it or you don't. Unfortunately, this is one of the drawbacks associated with online dating, texting, and any other impersonal forms of communication. There is an illusion of intimacy that distorts the dating process.

To determine if you have chemistry, you have to experience the reaction between you and another person. Chemistry cannot be cooked up over the Internet or across cell towers. To mix ingredients one needs to place them in the same bowl and then use a utensil to help them blend. Chemistry requires face-to-face contact—getting the ingredients on the same prep station. That is what you get when you sit down for a meal. This is why I think dinner is a great first date. It might not sound all that exciting, but if it is done properly, it can lead to dessert, and who doesn't like having a sweet treat to eat? Therefore, if you have a hearty appetite, and want more than just one-night, after the appetizer, order the main course, and don't forget to leave room for dessert.

I can't tell you how many times I have heard, "He is a nice guy" or "She is a sweet girl." But does he or she do it for you? I am talking about chemistry. Chemistry is that instant mutual connection. It's a feeling, a vibe. You can't fake it. Either it's there or it's not. People need to have chemistry in order to be sexually good together. Chemistry doesn't develop over time. It must be there from the start and is subject to titration: it can grow or diminish over time.

It is important to understand this, because many people erroneously believe that attraction will come. I am not trying to be superficial. For long-term sexual and emotional satisfaction, chemistry is essential. When this ingredient is present there is a strong mutual attraction on many levels, not just sexually. There are internal qualities that also attract, such as intellect, romanticism, sophistication, humor, and confidence. Chemistry is that initial spark, it gets things hot, it lights the flame.

There are other things that will keep the flame burning such as vulnerability, intimacy and passion. Hot, hot, hotter! These things are the ingredients of connection. In this instance, a *connection* is a relationship in which a person is linked to someone else. Unlike chemistry, connection develops overtime, and is the product of sharing one's thoughts, feelings, hopes, dreams, fears, values, time, etc. You might ask the important question: How long does it take to determine if there is a connection? That depends on the quality and the quantity of the sharing.

An even more important question might be: What are the ingredients that can take you from chemistry to connection to commitment? Commitment is a choice. It involves making a pledge or a promise. Loyalty. Obligation. So think clearly and choose carefully. Be sure that when the two of you are together sparks fly—chemistry. Once you have had those initial bites to whet your appetite, then you can decide on the main course. Allow yourself to be vulnerable so that you can give and receive in equal parts—connection. If the meal is satisfying you just might want to become a regular—committed.

Main Course: More Thoughts on Dating

The first three to six months of getting to know someone are often experienced as somewhat ideal. The time frame may vary depending on how often the two people see each other. Everyone is on his or her best behavior. Everything has a little sugar added. This can, and should, only go on for so long. The idealized phase needs to transform into something real. A relationship that is transitioning from the ideal to the real may be rather disquieting for some. When things get real, flaws become apparent. Up until this point he or she is damn near perfect for you. You are mutually attracted, share common interests, have fun when you are together, think about each other when you are apart, have long conversations on the phone, text back and forth constantly. But now you are disagreeing (politely), noticing flaws, and welcome schedule conflicts every now and again. Need a little space?

While it comes with some challenges and disappointments, the real phase in a relationship is where the meat is. It is during this phase that people really get to know each other. This is where she begins to wake up without the makeup, literally and figuratively speaking. Now that you are past initial fears of abandonment and rejection, you can relax a little and stop working so hard to impress each other. It's time to really get to know who is underneath that pinch of sugar.

This is a particularly important phase for those of you who are looking for something long-term. Because from this point forward, what you see is what you get. You need to pay attention and accept the realness of the qualities that are being exhibited. Everyone has assets and flaws. The strengths are relied on in the beginning days of a relationship; then things begin to shift. Humans are flawed. It is realistic to expect to see these flaws as time passes. The key question is: Can you live with the flaws or are the flaws deal-breakers for you?

For example, my husband is a "pile maker." Piles are the product of procrastination, when you fail to deal with things (i.e. mail, problems, chores, errands) as they come to you and in turn, you create a "pile" that becomes too overwhelming and you keep putting it off. And there begins the vicious cycle. I, on the other hand, am pretty particular when it comes to housekeeping. That's the nice way of saying that I am a "neat freak." While his piles work my last nerve, it is something that I am willing to live with because he is worth it.

This is important not only as it relates to being able to tolerate flaws, but also as it relates to dealing with conflict effectively. Because it is this aspect—the differences between people—that causes conflict. Many people deal with conflict as if it were an ingredient that causes an allergic reaction. Avoid, avoid, avoid. But it is my contention that conflict is an invaluable resource when it comes to intimacy. Any effort directed at resolution has the potential to bring people closer. If it is done right, he will learn something about her and she will learn something about him, and hopefully they reach a suitable compromise. In this case, I watch my husband's piles grow, and when I can't stand it any longer, one of us cleans it up. And the process starts all over again. Nothing is perfect. You just have to keep moving forward, making progress.

When it comes to flaws, you need to know what you can tolerate. Go back to your grocery list and see if this is a must have or a deal-breaker? Be careful not to err in the opposite direction either. When you find that one key trait, don't hold on to it too tightly (fun, smart, ambitious, attractive, great lover, big dick, big ass, stack of dollars), and forget to look at the rest of the list. You may only want to see the strengths; but one ingredient does not a recipe make. Even though the real phase illuminated some flaws that need to be considered, a person may still hold on to hope, using denial to guide the way. You see what you want to see. Yes, things can be worked on. People grow over time. But how long do you wait for a person to grow? It's not a good idea to fall in love with someone's potential.

You need to know what you are getting yourself into. If you are not sure, go back to your list. Ask yourself: Is this the person I have been looking for? Does he or she posses the right ingredients? Don't get fooled by what is on the surface. Skim off the fat so you can get to the stock that is underneath. And once you figure out what's in the pot, don't keep reheating the soup. If it does not taste right, stop stirring the pot. There comes a time when it is done, overcooked even, and the only thing left to do is toss it out!

Dessert: Getting To Know You

Consider getting to know someone to be like biting into a three-layer double chocolate cake. The top layer is covered in icing (chocolate of course). It is where all the sweet stuff is. Some people like to eat it first. Beneath the icing is the first layer of cake. Here are your good qualities. These are the qualities that you display openly. On the second layer, there is even more of you, the good and the bad. This middle layer is separated from the top and bottom layer by a thin layer of icing. The icing is to keep things sweet as a person gets to know your flaws.

Finally, on the bottom layer lies the core of you. Here is your foundation. The bottom layer is full of history. It is the last thing you get to when you are sharing your just desserts with someone. It is where the family drama and dysfunction lies. It is where your unsuccessful past relationships reside. The bottommost layer is full of your insecurities and fears. "The ugly." It cannot be forgotten, for it is the core of you. Then there is the past that you have somehow managed to enact in your current relationships because it is all you know. It is sure to follow; you might feel wary as this bottom layer is tapped, for it will surely differ from the ideal.

The flavor turns from sweet to bitter. You try to tell yourself something, anything to bring back the sweet taste of double chocolate. But, the man is struggling to be a man. He has insecurity because there was no one to teach him how to be a husband or father. And the woman feels like a little girl: she does not quite know how to be a woman, lover, friend—let alone a wife or a mother. With the sweetness gone, is it time to try something new from the menu—or do you continue to chew?

Some things are just for display; they are not meant to be eaten. Think about when the waiter walks around with his tray of would-be desserts. Wait until you find the real stuff before you sink your teeth into it. A person can't just look at something and know if it tastes good. You have to take a bite, but you don't have to swallow. If it doesn't taste good, spit it out. Once you get to that real phase, use the information that you have to make the best decision for yourself. No one knows better than you about what will satisfy your appetite. Some people wait too long before deciding, "This isn't what I ordered". Send that shit back! Interesting how as kids so many have been forced to eat something that doesn't taste good—no wonder we wind up in adulthood not knowing how to discern what we want or how to get up from the table when the meal is done.

It is important to understand that some flaws are minor, like being messy or tardy. But there are some monster flaws out there, too: alcoholism, financial instability, explosive temper, disloyalty, physical abuse, baby mama's drama, insecurity, baby daddy's bad credit. Baggage. Issues. We all have them, some more than others. And only you know what you can or cannot live with until death do us part.

When it's wrong it's wrong. And the opposite is also true: when it's right it's right. A relationship can go from gourmet to garbage. And on some level you may sense it. The question is: Are you going to allow yourself to know? Know it, so that you can do something about it? Or are you going to live unconscious, staying in a state of denial? Denying your reality only leads to denying yourself pleasure and fulfillment. Denial prevents you from knowing what you want and thereby interferes with having it.

When you get past the clouds of denial there should be a keen awareness of what you have kept in your pantry beyond its expiration date. For some it is that one thing that you are hoping will become more, but it never does. People hold on to the temporary, but immediate, gratification that comes along with great sex, fun, excitement, and good conversation, while at the same time ignoring the obvious red flags: meanness, undependability, addictive tendencies, dishonesty, jealousy, etc.

Angela Henry (2006) put it best when she wrote, "Most of my past relationships had had the shelf life of a milk carton left sitting out on a countertop. I usually held onto them past the expiration date, pretending I didn't notice the smell when it went bad." All it takes is a whiff. You can smell spoiled milk the moment the top comes off. But some people just ignore it. Why, when the worst that will happen is that you will have to toss it out and go buy some more? It is okay to be disappointed, frustrated, sad and maybe even lonely. These feelings are temporary realities—just as long as you don't let them stop you from going after the satisfaction that you desire and deserve.

Kitchen Clean Up: The Break-up/Moving On

How do you like your kitchen, nice and clean, everything in its place, cookbooks accessible? Are your pots and pans in the right place? The kitchen is where the cooking takes place. No one likes to cook in a dirty kitchen. So clean it up after you make a mess. You can only do this if you can see the mess. If you have numbed yourself to your internal and/or external reality, you cannot keep things in order. So pay attention. Yes, that means noticing the painful, distasteful, and messy things, too. You have to go through it to get to the other side; thus it is inevitable that you will get some of the mess on you. Some dishes require that you roll up your sleeves, dig in and get your hands dirty. Just clean up when you are done. Grieving is a part of this process.

Tending to your kitchen is a part of the cooking process. Some cooks wait until the meal is done and clean the giant mess at the end, while others clean as they go. The emotions of heartbreak are something that we should be able to tolerate and recover from. So, go ahead use all of the pots and pan at your disposal. Splash tomato-sauce on the wall; you can clean it later. I tell my clients all the time, "They are just feelings and they go away. You are able to live through the pain and discomfort." Most of us do, but it is how we live through it that matters. Will you recover from loss and sadness with hope and excitement for the future? Or will you wallow in it, and make an even bigger mess of things by acting out, sleeping around, marathon shopping, drinking, overeating, isolating, self-loathing?

Now don't get me wrong. I do believe that there is nothing like "new dick" to help you get over a breakup. It is like driving past Kripsy Kreme and seeing the "Hot Now" light on, stopping and getting a fresh batch, a little dough and some nuts. New dick: a true creature comfort. But new dick has its limits. It is only a temporary *dickstraction*. Your mind is still cloudy and the wounds are too fresh to be ready for something with substance. You might have to sit down and have a few bad meals before you find your favorite dish, something that sticks to your ribs.

A big part of kitchen clean-up is being able to deal with your own mess. This is what allows you to deal effectively with the mess created by others. Some people live unconsciously, which means that they are guided by internal conflict, fear, insecurity, anger, guilt, and shame, leaving them vulnerable to unpredictable and inappropriate behavior that manifests at inopportune times. It's like cooking with your eyes closed. You know how that dish will turn out: a hot mess! Those of us who live consciously are guided by our hopes, dreams, desires and decisions. The key ingredient to true intimacy is getting to know oneself before one can get to know someone else. You must know what you want and be willing to ask for it. Use the breakup as a learning experience. Take from it only what you need for your next meal.

What do you bring to the table? If you are a hot mess, get cleaned up so that you can come to the table feeling put-together. Define yourself. What are your personal characteristics, good and bad? Remember we all have flaws, and they are a part of the dish, so don't leave them out, especially when you are dating and trying to get to know someone. You have to be honest with yourself and then decide if you can meet their needs, and if they can meet yours. Can you satisfy each other's appetites?

One of the things that I have learned is that you have to tidy your kitchen before the ingredients are put on the counter. If the first key to tidying up after a break-up is to know yourself, then the second asset is acceptance and love. No matter your flaws, despite the trauma, after the loss, love yourself, so that you can love someone else. It might sound cliché, but it is true. You can't love another if you don't love yourself. I would extend this idea to acceptance, as well. Accepting oneself means flaws and all. Loving oneself means being good to oneself in thoughts, actions, choices, and relationships. If you set the precedent, then you will expect and demand it from others. And you won't sit around wasting time when you figure out he does not make you salivate.

Have you waited long past the expiration date? What happens if you digest food/drink that has expired? You get sick; at worst, you will get food poisoning, which can be a very violent physical experience. Why subject yourself to emotional food poisoning, when you don't have to? Why waste your time on something non-nutritive that doesn't suit your palate? Choosing to stay in an unsuitable relationship is choosing to make yourself sick—when you could be out there making better things happen.

Now, you might be wondering, how long does it take to find out that s/he is not the one? One date? Ten dates? If you follow this recipe, it won't take long. Have hope and don't stop cooking. Just be sure to clean up the kitchen before you start again from scratch.

Chapter 3
Acquired Tastes

We all have our preferences or tastes for things. What satisfies my palate might offend yours. Dating is the process of learning your own palate and then seeking out what satisfies it. At first it is a quest for information. If you are asking the right questions, you will know if this is the person for you. The questions come from your grocery list (Chapter 2). Some things will be obvious; he should be: handsome, smart, successful, kind (these things are on my list). But there are others that you will need to ask about: personal history, job history, health, sexual partners and sexual health, hobbies, financial priorities, children, interests, goals, plans for the future, etc. If his ingredients don't satisfy what you crave, then keep it moving.

When a woman is hungry for sexual and relationship satisfaction, "anything" just won't do. In her own lifetime, what meets her needs at one phase of development will not satisfy the same as when she, herself, is in a different phase of life. Women have different needs depending on where they are in their lives. My dissertation research helped me identify essential ingredients to sexual satisfaction that were specific to women depending on their marital status. Single versus married; it's like comparing apples to oranges. Both sweet, but knowingly different. To complicate the recipe, you can add the sweetest and most valuable ingredient to the mix: children.

In today's society, many of us have children or are planning to have children. We are trying to make babies, find time alone without the kids, are too tired because of them, or are looking for the right father to raise them. They can't be left out unless you, of course, have previously decided that you are not shopping down that aisle. Therefore, children must be considered. Thus we will look at single and married women with and without children.

In my research, I interviewed 105 women. Of these, 53 were single and 52 were married. Among single women, 51% were childless and 49% had children. Among married women, 50% were without children and 50% had children. More complete demographic information on the women is presented in Table 1. In response to my interview questions, these four groups of women identified the ingredients that contributed to their most sexually satisfying experiences. As the researcher, I looked for common ingredients, as well as for secret ingredients that might bring culinary ecstasy to other women—women like you.

Our appetites are unique and may change over time for various reasons. So, we go shopping, again and again, sometimes revising our grocery lists... looking for the ingredients for our recipe for ecstasy.

Table 1.
Demographic Characteristics of the Entire Sample

Demographic Variable	F	%
Race		
African American	60	57.1
Caucasian	43	41.0
Asian	2	1.9
Marital Status		
Single, never married	37	35.2
Divorced	14	13.3
Widowed	2	1.9
Married	52	49.5
Number of Children		
0	52	49.5
1	20	19.0
2	22	21.0
3	7	6.7
4	3	2.9
5	1	1.0
	M	SD
Age	35.32	10.13
Education		
High School or General Education Diploma	9	8.7
Associate Degree or Trade	31	29.8
Bachelor Degree	32	30.8
Master Degree	24	23.1
Ph.D./M.D.	8	7.7
Occupation		
Unemployed	13	12.5
General labor	22	21.2
Skilled trade	19	18.3
Management	9	8.7
Professional	41	39.4

The Origin of Taste Buds

We all come from what psychologists call a symbiotic relationship—the relationship between mother and child. This relationship is characterized by a unique closeness, a oneness for a period of 40 weeks, 10 months, or however long it takes until that baby popped out of the oven. This once-in-a-lifetime experience sets the stage for future romantic relationships. We are constantly looking for a relationship that feeds us all the nutrients we need, while at the same time protecting us and loving us. It is who we are. At the very least a woman wants to feel close to someone, even if it's solely physical. Don't skimp on the physical aspects of closeness, either. Sex is a biological drive that is equally important as eating or sleeping. An important need, sex is restorative, a hunger that must be fed.

Strictly Self-Gratifying Meals: Single Women Without Children

Let us start with the woman who has the time to focus on cooking it up without the distractions and disruptions of a husband and kids. Single without children, the truly unattached. These women are living phat-free. Ah, to be single again! She gets to eat what she wants, when she wants, with no consideration for anyone else's appetite but her own. She can dash off to the gym, have a skinny latte with the girls, stay out all night, pick out a new ride, jet set around the world, and she doesn't have to think of anyone else. There is no one else to take care of but herself. Those were the days...

This task is a big one. If she is doing it right, the single woman without children is honest with herself, she is good to herself, she knows what she wants, and she expects to get it. Wouldn't it be nice if this were true for you? Unfortunately, not every single woman has it together. She is not honest; she is not good to herself. She does not know who she is or what she wants, so she will not get it. I hope this is not you.

Tailgating: Embracing "The Game"

Now, of course, being single comes with its downside as well. She is left to fend for herself. She is the only one responsible for getting her needs met. Dinner for one can be lonely. If you are anything like I was as a single woman, getting a steady piece can be a chore.

It's feast or famine. When it comes to dating, there are all sorts of obstacles in her way. These obstacles include, but are not limited to: a shortage of eligible men; limited exposure to environments that are conducive to dating; fear of rejection; and "The Game."

When I say eligible I mean honest, gainfully employed, straight (not on the down low), and single (for real). An inadequate dating scene—the lack of a place to go to actually meet an eligible bachelor—keeps many single women behind closed doors, almost as much as fear of rejection. Looking at one's list of desirable ingredients is a helpful tool to finding places to meet men who are realistic potential mates. Even with such resourcefulness, it can be hard to find that one someone. The inability to find the desired ingredients in one person has women collecting men like they do shoes.

The biggest and baddest obstacle out there has got to be The Game. The games that people play when they are on the prowl. A game is defined as a competitive activity that has rules. It is something that is played for fun. In the world of dating, The Game is characterized by the chase between a man and a woman, whose objectives may be very different. He might just want to get laid, so she ends up getting played. Or she might want a little cash, but he hits it and makes a dash.

To be in The Game, you've got to know the rules, roles, and the plays.

In The Game, there are specific roles that must be occupied. There are, of course, the ones who have come before us, the retired like me. I'm coaching now. There are the starters, and the bench-riders. There are the 'playas' and the ones that get played. Know your position, and play it. Play it well! If you are in it, be in it to win it.

What team are you on? A, B, C, or D? The A team is that **A**t home dick. Big Daddy. The one you will do anything for; the one you like to serve. "He's mine. Don't touch. Don't even *think* about it."

The B team is striving for the **B**est that can be. If he falls short the B is for Benchable! That is, no matter how hard a man may try, he will always have limits. Therefore, he can only play for so long and will inevitably end up on the bench. So make it good. For me it is big, black and beautiful. That's the best that you can be for me.

For my sorority sister "Motown," it is **C**ash. And that means that you are on the C team. Don't leave home without it. For some women, he is called: Suga Daddy. He is the guy who pays the bills and if he is truly sweet then he may get to stay and eat. Most Suga Daddys are only good for their money. However, some get the benefit of nuts and honey!

And the D team: I **D**on't need you. These are the losers that you just put on the curb. They can't even ride the bench. In this game there has to be a loser. That's just how it is. You want to win, so someone has to lose.

Snack on This

Remember that people are single for many reasons and at various points throughout their life. Depending on the timing (20's, 30's, 40's, 50's, 60's on up), one's needs change, and so does the baggage that comes along with them. But the game stays the same. Some women have been there and done that. They have been married and divorced more times than they care to admit. All they are looking for is someone to keep them company, real good company... like a pint of double chocolate ice cream. While other women are still trying to catch their first taste of something sweet.

Whether he is company or companion, one thing is for sure, she wants to cum. Women in their mid-thirties to mid-forties are in the prime of life. Many of us are at our sexual peaks. Hopefully, your man is not slowing down sexually. You know he hit his prime in his early twenties. That refractory period (the period after an orgasm where a man is physically incapable of becoming aroused) can ruin everything. Yuck! There is nothing worse than being all hot and bothered and not being able to get your freak on.

When you are single, this can be a real challenge. But I digress. Back to The Game.

While games are typically fun and exciting, The Game can be very painful and disappointing, especially if you are in it and don't even know that you are playing. Single women (men, too) beware of The Game. It is real. If you are playing in it, play smart, or you are sure to come in last.

I know you have heard it said before, "He's a playa". But what does that really mean? In short, he is a liar and a cheat. But it is so much more than that. The Game has been evolving. You know—with the advent of the Internet, texting, twittering, facebook, etc. Single ladies, use the right strategies, because he is sure to have a playbook.

Maybe men are clever or more proficient at The Game and disguising unappealing characteristics—the lies, the late night phone calls (booty calls), the unrequited love, the flowers you never see, the doors that are never opened. These are all signs, but a lot of women fall for it anyway: the banana in the tail pipe. A man who does not take the time to set the mood, make you "wet," excite you to intense orgasms, and make you feel beautiful and loved; well this guy probably won't commit himself or his resources to a relationship. Men give the clues, but some women still can't solve the mystery.

From the first moments of dating, a man shows a woman his capacity to be a boyfriend, lover, husband, and father. It's all in his approach. Is he a gentle, kind man? A man who will call and ask you to dinner and dancing, who shows up with flowers and is actually on time? If he is willing and able to do these things, it increases the odds that he will put in effort in the boardroom and the bedroom. He will pay bills, cut the grass, change diapers, dress the children, and make passionate love to you. He will show you the money, and then tickle your fancy with the taste of nuts and honey.

Now, it's been a long time since I have been in The Game. And I am sure it looks a little different from how it once was, back in my day. But there are some things that just don't change: lying and cheating. Lets consider lying and cheating to be the staples of The Game, the poisonous pair. Now this might seem a bit confusing to some of you playas out there, who "let them know from the j-u-m-p what's up." He says, "I'm not ready for a relationship." That means, "I just want to fuck." There is the illusion of honesty because it's clear that you are not "the one." But when he is with you, you feel like the one or you tell yourself that you do.

So, most of the lying and cheating that is taking place is within you.

You are lying to yourself about what you want or what you are getting, and at the same time you are cheating yourself out of having it. Don't sound appetizing to me. Why would you want to fuck with leftovers, when there are so many new and enticing entrees from which to choose?

Of course there are exceptions to every rule. There are the casual sexual relationships, where everyone is mature enough to voice their intentions and accept the limitations of having a friend with benefits (a fuck buddy, a booty caller, a pipe layer, a maintenance man, a tenderoni, a sugar daddy, a flavor of the month, or whatever hits the spot when you get hungry). You just might want these sloppy seconds. But be clear: a friend with benefits gives you limited coverage. Emotional support is not included in the benefit package.

So how do you know if it's "game" or if it's real? Let's see. Single, but dating. Not just sex. It should be grounded in something. What? The anchor is getting to know each other well enough to make an informed decision and answer the question, "Are you right for me?" If the answer to this question if yes, then you will make love. True love does not need games and schemes; it is enough. Trust in it and you can create a recipe for ecstasy.

Taste Tests: The Dating Game

Dating is like wine tasting. According to *Wine for Dummies*, wine tastings are events designed to give enthusiasts the opportunity to sample a range of wines. Just like wine tasting, dating can range from simple to sophisticated. It is most satisfying when done enthusiastically—even if there are some samples that don't match your palate. Dating is designed so you can sample the wide range of prospects out there. When tasting a new vintage you should make use of all of the senses. First look at it, and then smell it. When dating, a person should be interested in making a good first impression. You should look good and smell good. If something doesn't look or smell good, don't go any further. You will not be interested in hearing or touching, let alone tasting. It is not shallow to judge by appearances—the package does matter when it comes to satisfying your sexual and emotional hunger.

According to evolutionary theories, women seek out mates who can be good providers; men seek out women who can reproduce and be good mothers. The theory of mate selection also tells us that men compete for the attention of women and women do the choosing. This is probably how it is *supposed* to go down. I think men stopped competing a long time ago. I believe that the availability of women—in terms of population and promiscuity—has decreased the need for competition. Men don't work as hard as they should to get you—because they don't need to. Now this availability is partly due to the fact that women out number men. But it is also a result of the value that women have placed on themselves—very little. Pussy is a dime a dozen. Despite the ratio of men to women, women could and should make themselves less available. Don't be so eager to give of yourself physically or emotionally. Slow down… don't chew so fast! Let him work for it. Let him compete for you. Let him "put a ring on it" before you begin those wifely duties.

It is like the law of supply and demand. If a desired commodity is scarce, the demand is high and the price goes up. Consumers have to pay more and/or work harder to get it. So, treat yourself as a fine wine with limited distribution. Make him earn a taste. Now careful, I am not talking about solicitation. I am talking about being deserving of you. Some women are fixing plates, fucking, and financing the whole meal. Acting like a wife, feeding a man all of you, while he is tossing you crumbs. A fuck buddy, a girlfriend, a friend with benefits—that is not a wife.

Think back to the days of hunting and gathering. Remember, men like to hunt. They are aggressive creatures by nature. Women are the gatherers. We like to browse around and take our time picking nuts and fresh berries. Men, on the other hand, want to expose their teeth and dig their claws into the meaty flesh. Men want to feel like they have earned their prey, this is why men love "bitches". You are worth the effort; don't be *too* available. This is when it comes to approaching a man, going out, changing plans, and having sex. Be open, but not wide open.

Again, think wine tasting. When the cork is popped off of a new bottle of wine, the wine first needs to breathe. Don't be in such a hurry to pour. The first pour is a sip… just enough to catch the aroma and sample the flavor. Then, the wine pours out.

I believe in equal opportunity initiation, but women must be careful when they step to a man. Show him that you are interested, but not too eager. That's a turnoff (a clear sign of desperation). Be confident, but not too aggressive. Men want assurance that a woman is into him, so let him know that you are interested and open. Not wide open, unless you are hoping for sex in the next two hours. If sex is all that is on the menu, then go ahead take charge. However, if you want something that you both can savor, then encourage him to take his time with this fine wine. Get to know each other. Let him smell, swirl and sip—slowly introduce him to your flavor, and then he will savor it.

What do you see when you look at this fine wine? Good health and emotional stability? Does she take care of herself? Is her esteem on high? Does she have impeccable taste? Clues often come in the first interactions. Be mindful of what you project and perceive.

Personally and clinically, I'm big on personal hygiene and grooming—indicators of how a person tends to and takes care of his or her self. Of course, these are not the only indicators, but they are important when it comes to the first impression. What are the hallmarks? You know, nice teeth, clean nails, fresh breath, and a clean shave (ladies, you too). Anyone interested in dating should do these things, the bare minimum. But, it should also be taken a step further. Ladies, take the time to dress nicely, put on make-up, polish your nails, put on a little smell good etc. Don't run out in your favorite sweats with a baseball cap on. This look might be okay if you are lounging around the house, but if you are in the market for a man, don't even run to the corner store in those sweats. *Always* be ready for an opportunity.

I am not saying put on your Sunday best; this could be just as much of a turn off. He might think that you are high maintenance, desperate, or that you have exquisite and unaffordable taste. Wear something that says who you are: fun, sexy, confident, mysterious, conservative, easy-going, sophisticated.

Whatever the outfit, be your best self.

The same goes for the fella. He also needs to attend to himself if he wants to get chosen. Does he appear successful or stable? Got Swagger? Or is he staying in his mama's basement? For men, a tailored suit or fancy car might indicate his level of success. You cannot stop there. Looking and smelling, alone, won't tell you if this fine wine is for you. Ask questions. Take a sip. What do you taste? Reluctance, openness, generosity, kindness, self-centeredness? Is he driving a rental? Is that a weave? Hey, people should get what they ordered, the real deal, no imitation.

Be mindful that you will be on both side of observing eyes, as an observer and as a person who is observed. Early dates are all about getting to know each other, thus requiring mutual disclosure. Be careful that neither of you greedily hog the conversation. Share the experience and learn about one another. It is the sharing that makes this process productive. Pay attention to what he shares, how he answers your inquiries; these words hold valuable information that will help you know if this is part of The Game or if you've met someone with whom you can move past games and dig into fine dining.

Hopefully, the person engaged in this tasting with you is being honest about who he is and what he wants. With all the different forms of communication available to us today, there is no reason why a person should have trouble communicating openly and honestly. Face-to face, sign language, text messages, emails, voicemail, snail-mail, telegram, twitter, facebook, skywriting, Morse code... Pick one; any one. Just be honest. Live in reality.

A person must first reside in reality before inviting someone to share in it.

Why would someone be dishonest? Fear, guilt, and shame. Dishonest people don't know themselves and they do not want to know reality. This makes it hard to get to know them, because a person can't teach what they don't know.

What are the red flags? Time together, but you don't know much about him. They are the guys who tell lies. Get caught up in The Game. When asked very important questions, they give the wrong answers. This throws the recipe all off. Don't lie when the truth will do. She should decide if she is going to give it up (her body or all of her); and this decision should be an informed one.

Pay attention to your taste buds. Is something a little bit off? Something missing? Too much of something else? Did you request a sweet wine and you got one that is dry, bitter, not wine at all? If it's going well, you will be able to describe your first knowledge of this wine... and he will be able to describe you. You should walk away feeling like you really know something, even if it's only a sample of what is to come.

After the sip, there is the swirl, "chew," and swallow. Keeping in mind the purpose is to decide if this is something you might want to have more of—a glass, a bottle, a case, a cellar's worth, enough to last a lifetime. Hopefully, talking will awaken a thirst in you. And wouldn't it be nice to find someone who could, both, quench your thirst and wet your whistle?

After your tasting, if you have decided that you don't want to invest further in this person, be honest, but kind, and move on. You don't have any time to waste. It is what it is, and it won't become something it is not. White wine will not become red wine. Chardonnay will not become Merlot. If you decide that you are interested in another sample, say that too. Say it not only with your words, but also with your actions. There should be cool enthusiasm in your interactions. Call, e-mail, text to say hello, let him know by way of your interactions that you are interested. But don't be a stalker. Don't make yourself too available. Don't appear desperate. Remember: *cool enthusiasm*. Fine wine is not for gulping. Savor the sips, taking note of whether or not your palate desires more. Continue to take your time as you have this glass of fine wine before dinner.

Part 2
Single Women

Chapter 4
Down Home Cooking: Introduction to Single Women

Time to Dine: The First Bite of Dating

As a single woman you get to make all the decisions. What's for dinner? Beef. Who's for dinner? Beef. I often hear that it is easier to be single. To some degree, this is true. There is no consideration, no consultation, no communication, no compromise, no compatibility, no conflict resolution, and no commitment. There is also no companionship. While being single is easier, it can be lonely and, at times, not as much fun. When you put a whole woman and a whole man together they make something better. Like dipping strawberries in chocolate, of course they are good separately, but together, um, a delectable treat.

When I was looking for a man, as a single woman without kids, I could take my time and peruse the menu. I could have a sampler platter, intended just for fun and variety, without any ties or expectations. While exciting, this got old and tiring because, in the end, I still wanted something to satisfy my hunger. I had an appetite for love. And I was willing to do the work.

Dating is like a part-time job. It requires time, attention, and a stomach for disappointment. No one knows better than the single woman the disappointments that come with this process. Dating gone wrong leaves a bad taste in your mouth, a bite that lingers long after you have spit it out. After any meal you should brush, but especially after a bad one. Clean your palate to prepare for the next morsel.

When you find someone who makes you want to swallow instead of sip, remember that the recipe for ecstasy is not a hurried one. If you are considering a serious relationship, I suggest that you put the big hot pot on the back burner. Don't rush into sex too fast. If this is something that is going to last, the sex can wait.

"What am I waiting for?" You ask. You are waiting to get to know each other a little better, until there is a foundation that can withstand the vicissitudes of emotions that are sure to come soon after you cum. Slow down; don't eat too fast. Take your time and chew, or you might find yourself choking on your third marriage.

On the other hand, all men are not a full course meal, some are just meant to snack on. This is for those of you who: are unconcerned about what happens when he's not behind your closed door; are not worried about him walking out the door; or have been starving and waiting too long since someone walked through the door at all. Here are your cooking tips.

Be sure to remember there is the correct "before the pussy behavior" and "after the pussy behavior." Before the pussy he will pursue you with all the vigor and intention that he can muster. Before pussy, it is about the conquest. Men like the hunt and capture. After the pussy, he is a different man altogether. His motivation might decrease significantly, especially if he is not that into you.

The Game is ubiquitous. An unfortunate, but necessary, evil in dating. The best anyone can do is play well and play safe. So whether he is a snackmate or full course meal, use the same strategies. He should still be honest, respectful, and kind. Ladies, be sure to protect yourself: heart and health. Always wrap it up—use condoms!

Just One More Bite: More Thoughts on Dating

In the beginning days of dating, be reasonable in your expectations. Busy women tend to want to microwave all the time, but some things need to go into the slow cooker. Don't expect security, love, trust, or commitment to cook up like a bag of popcorn. These are all things that come with time. Remember, in the beginning you are looking for mutual attraction (chemistry), common interests, a good time, easy conversation, the chance to get to know each other, and lots of fun.

As you progress from the ideal stage to the real stage, expect some disappointment. As you get to know each other better, flaws will become apparent and you have to decide whether or not these flaws are deal breakers. Remember no one is perfect. You want to collect enough information to decide whether or not he can satisfy your palate. To answer that question you need to know what you are in the mood for: something fun and fast like the drive thru; or love, sweet love, like fine dining at a five star restaurant. If the taste test is successful, then you decide to take things to the next level; if not, then there is the breakup.

Of course, a breakup can take on various forms. The cussing and fussing type. The emphatic or apathetic text message. The Dear John letter. The soft landing: the break-up that lingers like garlic in your mouth. It was good on the meat, especially with the wine, but the aftertaste is horrible! Yuck! Take it off the menu; get him out of your diet.

I know it may be difficult to say goodbye, especially if the dick is good, so go ahead, and have just one more bite. But, after this you have to start that diet. If you find that this person is not the one for you, you can't keep putting the break up off for tomorrow, you have to move on. Spit it out. Now, of course, this is easier said than done.

Time to Cleanse your Palate: Getting Over a Bad Meal

The experience of disillusion is painful, yet necessary. Across our lifespan it helps us to identify what we do and do not want in a partner. Just keep in mind the importance of being honest with oneself when these disappointments occur, and to allow time for recovery.

Depending on how long you have been dating, the grieving process may be a little longer and a little more difficult. That is a nice way of saying that it will hurt like hell, like picking up a hot pot without gloves. You just want to drop it. But, grieving takes time. Take time to clean up the mess so that you can go back to the menu and make another selection. If you do not, that bad taste will linger and it will be sure to ruin your next meal.

In dating there is something to be said for efficiency. The sooner you determine whether or not this person is for you, the better. It will save time and heartache. Yet, moving on from this type of situation will be difficult for different reasons. It will be difficult because of your mental timeline for life, that you 'just knew' you would be married by now; or because you have to come up with a gentle way, hopefully, of saying, "Thanks but no thanks."

However it goes down, the same rules apply: If he does not choose you and if you do not choose him, it is not your last supper. You will not starve. Clean up your emotional kitchen and start from scratch. This is where many people get stuck. They don't clean up, they don't allow themselves to grieve so that they can make room to try again. It's sad but true. Be honest with yourself. Accept reality, he did not choose you. Deal with your disappointment, grieve, and move on.

If we accumulate baggage after every failed attempt at love, it becomes a lot to carry around. Periodically, go through the fridge and pantry to discard the expired ingredients. You do not need to keep a stockpile of the fear, anxiety, inability to trust, and low self-worth that may result from unsuccessful attempts at love. These things take up space and might accidentally be used in a later recipe, ruining the whole dish/relationship. That's not to say you should totally disregard your past relationships. Use those experiences as information to help you make better decisions in the future. Take a personal inventory. Be sure you are using the right ingredients.

When your last meal was a huge disappointment, you need to have the courage to try something else on the menu. Continuing in the dating process after disappointment or rejection requires *vulnerability*: being without adequate protection, susceptible (open to being affected). A state of being in which a person's guards are down, vulnerability leaves us open to various possibilities, some good possibilities, some not so good. Despite the risks, vulnerability is the only condition that allows for intimacy and growth. If the worst that will happen is that you will be left with a bad taste in your mouth, then go ahead, take a bite, and see if you like. If you find yourself disappointed, just spit it out and order something else.

When I tell my clients "You need to grieve," they often ask, "How do I do that?" "What does that mean?" Allow yourself to be sad. Sadness is the natural response to loss; if you fight that response, then it will fight you back—and it will win. Feelings must find some mode of expression. Either feelings will be expressed appropriately with our knowledge and awareness (thus allowing us to influence when and how they are expressed). Or, if fought against, feelings will come out at some inopportune time in some inappropriate way that solely interferes with the good things in life (e.g., depression, anxiety, overeating, binge, drug use, retail therapy, promiscuity).

Be patient, tolerate the pain, and give yourself a chance to recover. Grieving involves being sad. Of course, no one wants to do it, but it is required to make room for what comes next: HOPE. Hope is the other side of loss. It is the part of grieving that people often don't consider or even know about. To move forward in life we must have hope. Don't focus on what life could have been, think about what life can be, and get to work.

Tears and sharing are always good ways to deal with sadness. Find comfort, lots of comfort. Find things that make you feel good, even in retrospect; not things that feel good now and make you feel horrible later, like excessive drinking or shopping. Talk to a friend, write in your journal, take a hot bath, listen to some soothing music, watch a funny movie, pray, exercise, meditate, get some couch time (therapy). See the Appendix F for a playlist of my favorite break-up/make-up jams to help to ease the pain and keep it moving.

My personal favorite form of comfort is new dick. There is nothing like new dick to help you get over old dick. It's exciting and fun. This may only be an option for women who are capable of casual sex. And you have to be mindful of the purpose, "dickstraction," not commitment. It is what it is… don't lose track of what you came for. Look, but don't touch. Touch, but don't taste. Okay, okay, taste, but don't swallow. Remember new dick is just for fun. Like having something sweet to eat.

Chapter 5
Microwave Dinner: Single & Child-Free

From the Kitchen of: Single and Child-free Women

The Ingredients for Sexual Satisfaction

Setting	58%
Arousal	50%
Love	46%
Nature of Relationship	42%
Intimacy	38%
Mood	38%

recipe card #1

In my study, 26 (25%) of the 105 women were single and child-free. For the purpose of making things simple, all the single women are clustered into one group. It doesn't matter how you came to be single: never married, separated, divorced, widowed, manslaughter. This recipe applies to you.

To be single is to be searching, seeking, or looking for something to satisfy your appetite. I know there are women who will disagree. The *I-don't-need-a-man* kind of woman. I believe everybody wants to be with somebody. Living without a man is like cutting out one of the food groups; any nutritionist will tell you that is not a good idea when you are trying to maintain a healthy diet. It is in our nature (the nature of a woman) to seek companionship, even more in our nature to seek intimacy. So, without further ado, single women:

Here is a recipe especially for you! (See Recipe Card 1)

Setting: Rustic and Creative

Fifty-eight percent of the single child-free women I studied identified setting as the key ingredient. One might wonder, why setting? Who cares where the sex takes place? Clearly these women do. *Setting* is defined as the time, place and circumstance in which the sexual act takes place. It includes those private encounters only meant for two and those public encounters that are open for all to view. For 15% of single child-free women, there was either an audience present or audience potential. The audience potential speaks to the carefree nature of these women. Therefore, two ingredients were actually identified, setting and audience.

More specifically, these women had sex outdoors. For example,

The most sexually satisfying experience of my life was when I made love in the rain at a park. It was a warm summer night and everyone was out. I think the best part was knowing that people were watching us. I felt like the queen of the freaks.

Clearly, this is a woman without a care in the world. She can have sex whenever, wherever and with whomever she pleases. She is not thinking about what's for dinner or if she needs to stop and pick up diapers. It is all about fun and excitement for her. This is one of the upsides of being single, living phat-free.

A single woman has plenty of options; she can choose when, where and how it all goes down. Listen to this:

Yum, yum, at 135th and Lennox, kind of in the hood, which kind of added to the debauchery of it all. On the third floor, in a 300 square foot apartment, with the windows open, and the rain coming down. Lying there butt-naked, with that fuckin hair [of his]. I am going to have this mutha' fucker fuck me all over this house.

Can't you just picture it? Set the scene; the actions will follow.

Single women are free to experiment with their recipe. They can spice it up and substitute ingredients just to see how things turn out. Another woman wrote, *"I had sex with this guy, standing up, in broad daylight in his backyard."* She goes on further to explain that this experience was so satisfying because of *"the excitement of not being caught or being seen."* Another woman told me that she had sex *"on a golf course."* She likes to do her cooking outdoors because it is *"fun, exciting, and mysterious."* For other women, the settings included various locations such as, *"sex on a stairwell, on the table, on the floor and couch"* or *"the Mackinaw [Island] Bridge support beams."* Talk about exciting!

These women got downright creative when putting together their masterpiece. And if you can have sex on a support beam on the Mackinaw Island Bridge, you are just a talented woman. It is easy to see that single women are free to try new and exciting things. They don't refer to the nature of the relationship at all. In one of the recipes the partner was referred to as *"this guy."* His name doesn't matter as much as his role: the maintenance man, pipe layer, friend with benefits, suga daddy, play thang, tenderoni, etc.

Setting: Awayness

Everyone knows that vacations are all about fun. What you might not know is that sex while on vacation can be simply delicious. Location, location, location! Away from work and the everyday routines of life, we have the opportunity to use a new or different place as a venue to create our perfect dish.

Setting is also captured in the ingredient "awayness" (the circumstance or state characterized by being physically and/or emotionally away). Of the 26 single child-free women, 13% had significant amounts of "awayness" in their recipe. One woman responded, *"We were on vacation in Florida and we were on a beach."* Another woman wrote, *"We had sexual intercourse as soon as we arrived at a condo on the ocean when we were vacationing."*

Setting sometimes enhances the sexual experience by increasing the level of arousal. Take the woman who got cooking as soon as she arrived at the condo. *"The new environment and the adventure of a new place and the excitement about the trip"* were essential ingredients to her recipe for sexual satisfaction.

For some women getting hot, aroused, or excited is not about what you do, but where you are (physically and emotionally). Take this next savory soliloquy, where the woman makes time and space for a good meal:

We had plans to get together one day to relax and watch T.V.

Well, I had other things on my mind. Before he arrived I moved all the furniture to one side of the living room, therefore leaving an open space. I put a blanket on the floor, had candle lit, and a cold bottle of wine. I also had on a sexy nightie. When he arrived he had Chinese food in his arms; we had an indoor picnic on the floor. After eating, I couldn't control myself. I removed his clothing and caressed his body; he kindly returned the favor. Then we made love on the blanket. The session was very intense and wonderful. Afterwards he cuddled [me] until we fell asleep. It was a great evening; however, we still never managed to watch T.V.

Can you feel things heating up? That's because the next ingredient on the list is arousal.

Arousal

Arousal means to stir up, excite, or stimulate. I refer to it as being a little hot under the collar. Think of how exciting one can get when just thinking of their favorite dish, spicy sausage. It might just cause you to salivate or, better yet, lubricate. Operating on, both, an emotional and psychological level, arousal was identified as a key ingredient by 50% of the single women without children. Like the dials on a stove, arousal has several levels of intensity.

Snack on This

This is probably a good time to introduce the phases of the sexual response cycle, with arousal, also known as excitement, being the first phase. According to Masters and Johnson (1966), the sexual response cycle has four phases: excitement, plateau, orgasm, and resolution. Take into consideration that Masters and Johnson have focused only on the physiological aspects of sexual stimulation. Sexual expression and responsiveness, however, is likely to reflect the interaction of several things including hormones, individual personality, psychological development, and psychosocial context. The sexual response cycle is as follows:

continued...

Excitement is the first phase of the sexual response cycle, which is characterized by a number of responses common to both men and women. It may vary from one minute to several hours. Although the stages of the sexual response cycle are the same for men and women, there is a significant difference at the beginning and end of the cycle.

The excitement phase is where women warm up. The early physical changes include vaginal lubrication, vaginal expansion, and swelling of the external genitalia. This phase is also characterized by muscle tension, increased heart rate and blood pressure, engorgement of sexual anatomy, and sex flush—pink or red rash on the skin, usually the chest or breasts. Sexual arousal is also characterized by a subjective experience of sexual excitement and pleasure.

Plateau is the second phase of the sexual response cycle, in which sexual tension continues to escalate until it reaches the peak (i.e., orgasm). The oven just gets hotter and hotter. You can go from baking at 350 degrees, to roasting at 500 degrees, and you can even broil. Hot, hot, hot!!! It is difficult to distinguish this phase from the excitement phase, because there are no clear differentiating signs. This phase lasts a few seconds to several minutes. Prolonged sexual tension during this period may result in greater levels of arousal and more intense orgasms. The heart rate and blood pressure continue to rise, the breathing rate increases, sex flush and coloration of genitals becomes more pronounced, and muscle tension continues to build until orgasm is achieved. When I cook in the oven, I use a timer, and it goes off when the dish is done. Ding, buzz, moan, sigh, scream, cry, oh yes, oh no, oh shit, mmm huh, big daddy, please, Jesus... there is no limit to the myriad of expressions used to alert you to your dish being done.

Orgasm is the shortest period of the sexual response cycle, usually lasting only a few seconds. But for some of us lucky women it can go on... and on... Male and female orgasms tend to differ in a few ways: ejaculation, length, and multiples. Most women don't, but some women are able to ejaculate. They tend to be in the minority, just like men who have the ability to have multiple orgasms. The female can produce another orgasm immediately following an orgasmic experience. Did I hear someone say seconds, thirds, multiples? Female orgasm usually lasts longer than male orgasm. However, the subjective experience of orgasms for men and women are indistinguishable. This phase is characterized by a climax of sexual pleasure variously associated with rhythmic contraction of the perineal and reproductive organ structures, cardiovascular and respiratory changes, and a release of sexual tension. Increased levels of oxytocin (a pituitary hormone) may be implicated in orgasm intensity.

continued...

Resolution is the final phase of the sexual response cycle, characterized by the return of the sexual systems to a nonexcited state. If no additional stimulation occurs, resolution begins after an orgasm. Most men enter a refractory period, a time in which they are unable to achieve an orgasm. The refractory period may range from minutes to days, depending on factors such as age and health

Women, however, are capable of reaching orgasm at any point during the resolution phase.

If the dish is done, turn off the oven. For you women out there who can't get enough, you are ready to start baking all over again.

Like fine wine, that gets better with time, as a woman's body matures it becomes more sexually responsive. This includes an increased libido and an increased ability to achieve orgasm. This level of responsiveness changes throughout the life cycle. It is initiated by increased sex hormone production. More specifically, an increase in levels of circulating androgens has been demonstrated to have a powerful effect on eroticism in both sexes (Rutter, 1971). Androgens are a class of hormones that, among other things, influences sexual motivation in both sexes. (Crooks & Baur, 1993).

Okay, back to the good stuff. Hot, hot, hotter! One woman identifies the intensity of arousal (something constituting a heightened level of arousal/excitement) as the outstanding component of her sexual experience. She wrote,

What truly made this experience so satisfying is that this is the first person I have met that I was instantly attracted to. Here is a good example of chemistry. So, that first night I was extremely aroused.

I was totally attracted to him. Everything about him turned me on. I have never felt this way about anyone before. That is one of the things that really aroused me.

In this woman's recipe it was pure chemistry that created the increased level of arousal.

Arousal: Oral Stimulation

There can be many ingredients that make a woman hot. Try the new oral sex for example: talking. I can't tell you how many times my husband has made love to me with his words. We started our relationship with words, as we worked oh-so-hard to get to know each other. Communication, both verbal and nonverbal, is an invaluable ingredient when it comes to both sexual and relationship satisfaction. More specifically, it can enhance a person's experience of arousal.

Developmentally, the ability to communicate is one of the very first lessons that a child learns. Children first communicate with their cries. Soon after a child is born, the mother begins to get to know her baby by listening intently to its cries. It is common for a mother to be able to distinguish a hungry cry from a sleepy cry, or an angry cry from a scared cry. But, one day these wails must give way to words. For, it is words that truly bring clarity to confusion. We use words to orient us to the external world and to organize our internal worlds (thoughts and feelings). Therefore, it should come as no surprise that effective communication is a key ingredient to sexual and relationship satisfaction.

Note that I said effective communication, like the difference between brown sugar and white sugar, they are both sweet but, one is healthier than the other. I am not talking about cussing and fussing, screaming and yelling. These are not the tools of understanding, conflict resolution, or compromise. I am talking about listening with the intent of understanding, so that you can excite and be excited. Take this information and use it to create the life that you want and the love that you want.

What we are taught about communication depends on early interactions between a parent and child. This experience of learning facilitates the process of growth and development. It will take a person from savage to civilized, from confusion to clarity, from actions to words.

I remember my one year-old daughter (Marin) banging on the table, as she demanded to be fed right away, if not sooner. And I listened to the grunts and moans of satisfaction as she devoured the food that was placed before her. "Yum, yum, yum, yum, yum, yum, yum." For the longest time, she ate with her hands, with very little interest in using the proper utensils that have been designed for eating. In that moment the need for teaching and evolving was all so apparent. And my role in that process was clear, crystal! Teach her to speak, to delay gratification, or my job would remain difficult. I would have to interpret her actions and grunts, and respond as quickly as possible to avoid the screaming that would soon ensue as a consequence of impatience. It is my job to socialize her and to civilize her.

My older daughter, Madeline, is very articulate and has been since she learned how to use words. My husband says it is because of the mental battle of words that takes place between the two of us. He calls it mental sparring. She is proficient in conversation because she gets a constant workout with mom. I am her personal trainer, the head chef. We share a lot of words in a given day, and therefore we are close. There is nothing closer than the intimacy of a mother and child. Carried inside the body, on the hip, wrapped in a sling, I feed her many things. The use of words is paramount when it comes to mental organization, conflict resolution, development of intimacy and understanding. But it is also an invaluable tool that helps to create arousal and affect sexual satisfaction.

Talking is one of the first tools we acquire, and for some reason people stop using it. Talking is the new oral sex. It helps people to learn about each other, in the most intimate of ways. A woman could just use her words, or she could use the moans, groan, oohs and ahhs to let you know when she is good and hot, nice and wet.

Listen as this woman clearly articulates how the level of communication facilitates the process of arousal.

We lay awhile, just stroking and talking. We ended up having a long, intimate conversation about sex. We shared personal histories, laughed, and reassured each other that what we were doing now was fine. We kept stroking and asking each other, "Do you like this?" "How does this feel?" Pretty soon I was telling him that it felt really good— we were looking into each other's eyes—how's this? Soon he was exploring my labia, clitoris, and entrance to my vagina—still looking and still asking. Each advance, we went slowly and checked in, always feeling and talking with our eyes and faces. I began to feel incredibly aroused. When his penis came in me we went slowly, still checking, although part of me wanted to go wild. We ended up making love for a long time, still checking with each other every time we tried something new.

Here is a woman who knows how to ask for what she wants, and fortunately, she has a partner who cares enough to give it to her. They were both seeking and giving information. It sounds so basic, yet many people fail to do it. Everyone knows women use more words than men. We have an innate need to communicate; it is what we do. Maybe he might consider talking more if he knew how hot it could make her.

Take it from Will Downing who says:

'Cause if you need it
You need a little more affection,
Not just plans of undressing
Baby, I'm open for love suggestion.

If you really
(You want a real connection)
A real connection
(Romance and a little passion)
Some passion, girl
That's what you want
I wanting your
(Love suggestions)

Whatever's on your menu
Right away, baby, I'll serve it up
And if I can't get through
No worries, please, I'll save it up...

So baby I'm listening
All the things or spots I'm missing
Talk to me, no guessing
I need your love, love suggestions

A woman should always feel safe enough to ask for what she needs, and if her man is capable, willing to work, and loves her, she should get it. What a perfect combination: love and work! He would be willing to do the work, and not complain that you are nagging or never satisfied. At the same time, a little begging might make things sizzle. *"He touched me between my legs and whispered in my ear, you are so warm and so wet. I began to tingle and begged for him to put it inside me. I was so hot!"*

Arousal: Foreplay

One thing that women have been talking about for years is the need for more foreplay. And if you have not heard it, then you are just not listening. *Foreplay* is the key ingredient to arousal. Remember it takes a woman longer to get heated up for sex. And for many women, the temperature begins to rise before she ever hits the bedroom. You wouldn't put chicken in Crisco before it gets hot, so don't let him put his meat in before you are hot and ready. This means he will take his time with you, making sure to fulfill your desires. I know that every time you eat it cannot be a full course meal. But you should at least try to have something from all the food groups. Make sure that there is kissing, rubbing, caressing, spanking, sucking, and then fucking!

An important aspect of picking a good partner is making sure he is a competent lover. Women should know what it takes to get them turned on. Do you like kissing and caressing? Do you want him to suck, fondle, or pinch your nipples? Stroke your hair or pull it? Do you want him to eat with his hands or face? How do you like your dish served up? Make another list and be sure to tell him what's on it.

All women want to feel secure, special and desired. Sexual arousal can lead to several feelings. You will feel special when your lover, friend, husband, man, boyfriend attends to your needs. Don't assume that he knows those needs, especially if you have just started to date. Tell him. I can give you a few tips that will help you in the kitchen of life and love. Outside of the bedroom, he should be nice, make you feel like he is thinking about you: call, text, send flowers, compliment you, be honest. He should not show up late, forget to call, get off and leave you hanging… I know you want to cum, too. These are the kind of things that can get you hot and bothered before he even touches your body. It is about how he makes you feel.

Engendered feelings are feelings that result from the mixture that he stirs up. The mixture might include feelings such as sexy, desirable, loved. He should show you how much you mean to him by taking his time to get you in the mood; use his technique to focus on her. Communicating his desire for her by taking the time to seduce her, undress her, touch her, no caress her. Surprise her! Make her feel like she is all that and a bag of chips. You want her, and she knows it. She can feel it deep in her soul. She wants to be cherished. She wants you to make her feel like making love.

Foreplay was not identified as a discrete ingredient in the narratives but it was inferred. Foreplay is an aspect of technique. It includes feelings that are engendered through actions. These actions may start outside of the bedroom with a salacious text, a game of cat and mouse, a look, a touch, a kiss.

Arousal: Technique

I am a firm believer that if you can read, you can cook, both in and out of the bedroom. But the recipe for ecstasy is not just about being able to cook, it is about taking ingredients and making something that tastes great. For this, you need technique. Technique is the roasting, braising, grilling, brining, whipping, poaching, sautéing, and boiling of lovemaking. It is how we do what we do. A woman's level of arousal can be enhanced by *technique* (the manner in which the sexual act is performed, with the consideration of skill).

Technique takes things into account such as a person's endurance, intentionality, and self-control. Think of how he wields his instrument. Is he like a true professional, a chef, or more like a side-order cook? Will he give you some good take-out or room service to order? A man who is truly interested in pleasing his woman will allow her to order what she wants from the menu. He won't get bent out of shape when she tries to tell him just how she wants her dish prepared. He will whip it (that pussy) up, and bring it, right, to you!

There may be many cooks standing in line to stir her pot, but she wants the one who has just the right technique to hit the spot. One woman preferred *"the slow repetition of strokes inside [her] vagina,"* and another woman wrote that,

One of the main things was he said and did all of the right things. He just knew how to touch and caress me. I didn't have to tell him 'no, not that way,' or 'do it this way.'... I also loved the way he would look into my eyes and tell me how attracted he was to me— overall, how special and needed I was to him.

Two other women wrote about technique during specific acts that created intense levels of arousal. "Stimulation of the clitoris and vagina" produces a physiological response that represents excitement (i.e., vaginal lubrication) or, as this woman put it, "the juices were flowing." This recipe leaves a lot to the imagination, because there are several ways to stimulate the clitoris and vagina. However, the woman reporting this experience was describing oral sex. The author's interpretation and imagination yields the face and hand technique. That is, stimulation of the clitoris with the face, especially the tongue, but let's not limit the possibilities (e.g., nose, cheeks, and eyelashes) while the fingertip strokes the opening to the vagina and the area commonly referred to as the G-Spot. After all, who consumes any good meal without the use of face and hands? The other woman wrote, *"He ate pussy good as hell."* Good technique leads to high arousal. Now I know there are some nay-sayers out there, but my suggestion is that you tell him "don't knock it until you've tried it." Like 50 Cent (2007) says, "It tastes so sweet, that sticky cotton candy."

The next group of women tells us that if you mix things up just right, she might get so hot that she is in a daze or excited to other levels of consciousness. *"I felt excited, vulnerable, and stunned by the feeling of pleasure."* *"Very electrifying."* These are examples of the subjective experiences that may be associated with an orgasm. It is a powerful experience, and for those who haven't had the opportunity to partake, you have been deprived of one of the great pleasures of life. But hopefully, that ends here, with *The Recipe for Ecstasy.*

There are many different adjectives used to describe the subjective experience of orgasm. Remember that everyone's experience is different. It's like taking a bite of something, it tastes different to everyone, but it always taste good, real good. An orgasm can be explosive, overwhelming, earth-moving, wonderful, off the hook, powerful, mind-blowing...

Love

Surprisingly, the third most identified ingredient for this single group of women is my personal favorite, *love*. Love is such a hard thing to define. In my study I used the Sternberg Triangular Love Scale to measure love. Sternberg (1986) defines love as the combination of intimacy, passion, and commitment. These dimensions are defined as follows:

Intimacy is mostly emotional and encompasses those feelings that promote closeness, feelings of oneness, and the sense of warmth in a relationship.

Passion is that aspect of love that involves physical attraction and that precipitates the desire for merger through sexual fulfillment.

Commitment is the part of love that acknowledges the presence of love for another, and involves a decision to preserve that love. (Sternberg, 1987).

This ingredient, love, was identified as the key ingredient for ecstasy by 46% of single women without children. For example, one woman reported that the feelings aroused during the experience were "connectedness and love." Another woman, when asked the same question of what made her sexual experience so satisfying, simply responded, "Love." Of these 26 single women, 67% identified love as an essential component in their consideration of whether or not to have children with this partner. They wrote comments such as: *"He's a good man and I love him," "I really did love him and I wanted to marry him," "Because we have a solid, loving relationship, I want to be old with him,"* and *"I love this man more than I have ever loved anyone."*

Remember, these are single women talking. Although they have the freedom to have sex outside a loving relationship, many of them identified love as a key ingredient to their most sexually satisfying experience. It is what we all crave. You know when a meal has been prepared with love—it just tastes better. Love makes everything tastes better. Why does love improve the quality of everything? When you love something (or in this case someone), you give it your all. You work and commit to making things turn out right, even if it takes all night. You won't stop until the flava pops.

Nature of the Relationship

The fourth ingredient, *nature of the relationship* (N.O.R), was a key ingredient for 42% of single women without children. Relationships take on many different appearances—from casual to committed to many things in between. He could be the flava of the month or the cream of the crop. Some relationships are smoking hot, while others are lukewarm. Why would this affect a woman's experience of sexual satisfaction? Context is created when you consider the nature of the relationship. If he is a casual sex partner there may be lots of passion, but no intimacy. The reverse could be true if he were a committed partner. These two ingredients manifest themselves differently in a sexual experience.

Take a fuck buddy for example, how well do you know each other? How well do you want to know each other? Is he someone that you can let your guard down with? Are you comfortable telling him what really turns you on? I don't know about you, but for many women a fuck buddy is not the most trustworthy person you are going to share your bed with, and the smart women out there won't share much else. Remember: you can take sex out of the relationship, but you cannot take the relationship out of sex. From casual to committed, the nature of the relationship can affect how good things really get.

Of this 42% of single women without children who identified N.O.R. as an essential ingredient, 82% pointed to the N.O.R. in response to the "big question:" *"Have you ever considered having a child/children with this partner? If you answered yes, why? If you answered no, why not?"* Remember, we are not just talking about any partner; we are talking about the man with whom they had their most sexually satisfying experience. The women who "did consider having children with this partner," wrote responses such as, *"I have considered having children with this person as we plan to get married one day,"* and *"Yes, because marriage was discussed at some point in our relationship."*

The women, who did not consider having children with this partner, wrote comments such as: *"No, because he is living with someone else,"* or *"This partner was a fling."* Note that 70% of single women without children reported that their most sexually satisfying experience took place in a casual relationship. The remaining 18% of the responses regarding the nature of the relationship were directed at the experience itself, such as, *"sex with current boyfriend,"* and *"we were monogamous,"* responses which speak to the level of commitment in the relationship. Listen as the nature of this relationship shifts from tepid to hot, from mild to spicy, from lust to love:

It was three months since we had sex (my partner and I). We were not serious; actually, we had sort of gone our separate ways. I was not open to him sexually before this night. For the first year of our relationship I wasn't very into it. He was great, but I didn't know enough about sex. Well, we had started dating again and we went out this night to a party. All night we danced all over each other, arousing us both, exciting. Well, I went to his place afterwards and spent the night. Of course we had sex. It was the first time in three months and I felt that I was now experienced and wasn't scared to let my feelings go. I also felt my partner was relaxed because that was the first time we both wanted to experience different positions and ways (oral sex). It wasn't the same old sexual way (top and bottom) experience, but the first time I experienced love.

Intimacy & Mood

The fifth or final ingredient has two parts, because two ingredients were identified with the same degree of frequency for these single women. First, *intimacy* was identified in 38% of these narratives. Intimacy is defined as the condition of being intimate, which is marked by closeness or pertaining to one's deepest nature. It ranges from *connectedness* to *boundarylessness.* Connectedness represents the act of joining or the state of being joined, a union. For example, a woman wrote, *"I felt we made a connection of the soul and body."*

Boundarylessness represents a degree of closeness that assumes no boundary or limits, such as *"feeling connected heart to heart with the innocence of our beings interwoven."* Another woman wrote, *"It was the first time I'd gazed into my partner's eyes while making love."* For one woman, intimacy served as the catalyst for her introduction to the smorgasbord of sexuality: *"Before I had intercourse with my first boyfriend—my first sexual experience—we held each other and he told me deep, personal feelings."* She went on to say that *"He was honest"* and *"sincere;" "I trusted him and had compassion for him."*

Mood was also present in 38% of the savory soliloquies. Setting the mood for ecstasy might be like setting the mood for an intimate dinner. Put out the silverware and the good china. Make sure the champagne is on ice. Add a touch of candlelight and some soft music, like the tunes listed on my romance playlist (See Appendix G). The rest is up to the chef: fill the air with the aromas of something tantalizing, like the smells of a woman and a man.

Now the mood is set. She's hungry and I bet he is too! Mood is a temporary state of mind or feeling, as evidenced by the tendency of one's thoughts. The moods identified by these women ranged from *romance* to *satiety*. Love, affection, and/or enthusiasm characterize romance. Let this women set an example, *"My partner and I connected intentionally to have a romantic evening."*

For one woman, a romantic evening went like this:

We bathed, had candles burning and romantic music (our favorites) playing. We played a romantic game that was titillating and built tension. We made love, had dinner, made love again, and talked 'til morning on and off while we cuddled.

This might be something to strive to.

Have you ever been so full after a meal that all you can do is sleep? Gratified beyond the point of satisfaction? In the *Recipe for Ecstasy*, satiety captures this experience. I believe that the experience of satiety cannot be entirely appreciated without a description of the events that preceded and contributed the mood. Therefore, the following narrative has been chosen to make this point explicit:

My partner and I had candles lit and were lying in bed talking and caressing each other. He looked into my eyes and told me how much he loved me, and began kissing me. We became immediately passionate and held tightly, kissing each other. He then went down on me and made me reach orgasm two times. I begged for him to put it inside me. He put himself in my mouth and I sucked it until he came. He stayed hard and began fucking me hard like we both wanted. He rolled me over on my side and entered from behind. He then told me to reach for my vibrator and put it on my clitoris while he fucked me. After I had another orgasm, he told me to reach for the lubricant on the nightstand. He put it all over me, and took me anally. As he stroked gently in and out, we both had orgasms several times. We ended by holding in exhaustion and feeling like we could do anything with each other. We talked about how wonderful it was and held tight for some time.

In the above narrative satiety is captured by the idea that they *"ended by holding in exhaustion."* It is also captured by this woman's description, *"I fell fast asleep afterward and slept well."*

Mood also includes descriptions such as "Fun, exciting, mysterious," and "I felt warm and calm." Just as the right mood can arouse a burning inferno, the wrong mood can snuff out even the biggest flame. Single women without children can focus on such things as fun, excitement, and mystery, without the worry of a crying baby in the background or being stood up by the babysitter. There are some single women out there who have to work hard to get in the mood; they are lucky if they have a person to share that mood with when the feeling hits. These single women give us the next group of recipes. They are hard pressed for time, energy, money and sanity. So, preparing some elaborate meal may not be on the menu.

Chapter 6
Take Out: Single & Mothering

The pursuit of a mate for a single woman with kids is different from the pursuit of a single woman without kids, as is her pursuit for sexual satisfaction. She might only have time for a fuck buddy, but she really wants someone who provides emotional support and companionship. If done properly, being a parent is difficult and time-consuming. This is true even when both parents are involved. Therefore, when there is only one parent, the workload can feel like a greasy heavy meal just sitting on your stomach. All you want to do is lie down.

These women got it hard. They have to play by a different set of rules no matter what they have a taste for. Motherhood comes first, or at least it should. And to be a good enough mother, who is also dating, means that you have limited time and money. A dating single mother has different, crucial, objectives. If she is looking for a serious relationship, she has to make sure he will be a good partner and a good parent: a good parent to a child that he did not father, thus requiring him to be generous and fair with his resources (physical, emotional, and financial). While a good father and a good husband have some overlapping ingredients, there are some elements that are specific to each role. A good husband is honest, dependable, kind, and loving. A good father sets limits with love. He is a teacher, a disciplinarian, and a role model.

Within this context if sex is on the menu, it is usually take out. Either pick something up on the way home or hit the drive-thru. That is, sexual hunger must be fed around daycare, babysitters, bedtime, Dad's weekend (if you are lucky), laundry, cooking, homework, bills, etc. This might mean that a booty call or friend with benefits is on the menu. Single women with children often choose to keep their "friend" anonymous when it comes to the kids. It is prudent not to expose children to the smorgasbord of men who might come and go while dating. Single mothers should not expose their children to the uncertainty and impermanence inherent in dating—kids only meet someone who Mom truly believes will stick around. To that end, I can't say it enough—babysitter, babysitter, babysitter!

A single woman who has kids may feel lonely, overwhelmed, vulnerable, and unprotected. The awkward experience known as dating becomes more complicated if she is looking for a partner who could also be a good father. This is a dish of another flavor altogether. Now she is not only looking for a friend, lover, companion, but also a caregiver. He needs to possess some added ingredients, which we will discuss later.

Now, into the meat of the meal. For single women with children, ecstasy is all about efficiency. Makes sense, given the context. Single women with children opted for the sampler platter of sexual satisfaction. A little bit of this, a little bit of that—and she is sure to cum across something that she likes (See Recipe Card 2).

From the Kitchen of: Single Women with Children

The Ingredients for Sexual Satisfaction

Variation in the Sex Act	70%
Newness	52%
Nature of Relationship	41%
Positive Self-Regard	41%
Mood	37%
Orgasm Intensity	37%
Setting	30%

recipe card #2

Variation in the Sex Act

For this group of 27 women, variation in the sex act was the main ingredient, identified in 70% of the narratives. Variation in the sex act, for single woman with children, included accessories, anal sex, oral sex, and a variety of sexual positions, for example, *"when my partner oiled me all over, kissed my back, neck, oral sex, and tried anal sex."* In the following narrative the guy dressed his meat before he ate it:

> *I had gone over to my partner's house. He decided to try something different, so he blindfolded me and laid me on the bed. He spread my legs and began to shave/trim the hair in my vaginal area. After he cleaned off the shaving cream, he began to lick my private area until I had an orgasm. Then he took a vibrator and moved it in all the right ways and I reached an orgasm again. He took off the blindfold and held me upside down while he fucked me to my third orgasm.*

In the next narrative there are several components to the sexual experience, including foreplay, mutual gratification, orgasm responsiveness, different positions, various sex acts, and accessories. For this woman it was important to be well accessorized. But the most salient feature of her erotic experience was the variety. Variety is the spice of life; without it things get stale, like a bag of chips open all night. Watch a little porn, add a splash of fantasy to your reality, a dose of doggy style to go with the moans and the groans. No one desires chicken every night of the week. So where is the beef? Maybe this woman has it:

> *My most satisfying experience occurred approximately one month ago. My boyfriend and I were giving each other backrubs on the living room carpet. We turned the satellite channel to "New Age CD" and slowly began to give each other backrubs. After he rubbed my back for approximately 15 minutes, he told me to just relax and enjoy the music. He started to rub my leg down by the calf and he slowly worked his way up my thigh. He continued to tease me for about 10 minutes. He then flipped my body over and began to perform oral sex on me. I reached my first orgasm in about three minutes. He then began kissing me (which in itself makes me so horny). I worked my way down to his penis and performed oral sex on him. We then began to have intercourse in a number of different positions. I know I had at least three more orgasms. Our final position (which is my favorite) was when I was on my knees and he entered me from behind while holding my hips. He reached orgasm and exploded inside me. It was great!*

As you can see, this woman has a healthy appetite. Her body is very responsive, allowing her to achieve many orgasms during one sexual experience. She likes it doggy style, which is on all fours and from the back. In this position, he can reach deep inside and hit the spot, like a tall glass of lemonade on a hot summer's day. Don't you get thirsty just thinking about it? A good cook is flexible. She can tweak a recipe with a slight substitution, and *voila!* from "doggy style" to "lazy dog." Add this, subtract that, a slight variation, and you have created an entirely new, scrumptious, recipe.

I can't say it enough: foreplay, foreplay, and foreplay! Remember the sexual response cycle and that oven which needs to be preheated before you get to cookin'? It takes a woman longer to get sexually aroused than men. She takes fifteen to twenty minutes, where he might take only five. She is not even warm yet, and he is ready to dive right in. So even though he may be ready, it does not mean that she is. Good things cum to those who wait, so take your time, eat all the food on the plate.

A number of these single women mentioned the variety came in the form of *foreplay*. Foreplay involves the activities directed toward arousal, which take place before intercourse. In the world of recipes, foreplay is akin to time spent with the sous chef. So, how do you train your sous chef to work in your kitchen?

Tell him about your body and how it response to his touches, kisses, and caresses. Educate him about the signs of arousal in women. They may be a little harder to detect, vaginal moisture and expansion are not as obvious as an erection. Make sure that he checks your temperature with his fingers to make sure that you are hot. Before he sticks his meat in the oven, preheat it, while the meat marinates. It will be more flavorful and juicy when it is ready. It gives you both time to long for that first bite. The sexual tension will build as you both anticipate the climax. Most women attribute their overall sexual satisfaction to the prep time involved: foreplay.

Kissing, hugging, touching, rubbing. Talking? Yes talking. Talking can be one of the most stimulating acts of foreplay. And I am not necessarily referring to talking dirty, although this works too. I am talking about intimate sharing; there is nothing like getting personal to put a woman in the mood for getting personal. I know this is not what your man wants to hear: more talking. But if you tell him, "talking will facilitate intimacy, and if I feel like you are into me, the possibilities are infinite", I'd bet that he would oblige. Yes, sometimes you might opt for the quick solution to vaginal lubrication by using some over-the-counter product like KY Jelly or my personal favorite Astroglide, but it's nothing like the real thing, baby. Tell him to take his time; better yet, show him how to take his time by taking your time with him. The hotter you get the more responsive you will be, and that just makes it gravy for everybody.

This woman agreed, *"A lot of foreplay, kissing, talking, and love-making, oral, vaginal and anal sex for three hours off and on."* Another woman wrote, "All the foreplay that he does and oral sex that he does." In short, if you want him to hit your spot, he has first got to make it hot!

Newness

Can you remember the last time you tried something new off of the menu? You know how mundane eating out can be when you always choose the same thing: chicken. Try something new. It just might be the best decision made in a long time; it just might blow your mind. *Newness:* a condition and/or state that is characterized by recent origin; having existed only a short time. This ingredient was present in 52% of the recipes.

Newness can manifest itself in many different ways. In the experiences reported, the women were having sex with a partner for the first time; engaging in a particular act for the first time; and/or experiencing feelings, such as an orgasm, for the first time. For example:

The most satisfying experience of my life was when I was first introduced to oral sex. This experience was so satisfying because I didn't know that experiencing an orgasm that way could be so wonderful.

Oh, she has been missing out on some really good eating. "Do you know what a Cinnabon is? It's bread! And frosting! And cinnamon! They heat it up! Really hot!" (Seinfeld, Steinberg, Hickner & Smith, 2007) A nice little treat for the mouth.

And then there is new dick: *"It was the first time with this person."* Oh, what a treat! Think of it—all the anticipation and excitement that comes with having someone inside you for the first time. New dick is like eating fondue; it's just for fun. It has no nutritional value. Be careful, because if that new dick is good dick, it can be very disorienting. You will forget to set limits and before you know it, you will be binge eating until it is time to purge.

For this next woman there are different aspects of newness. It was a new relationship and he brought something new to the table, a bib, which he used to catch the juices that flowed from inside of her.

One weekend I came home from school and my fiancé and I were hooking up for a sexual encounter before I headed back. This was during our dating. I was so excited every time we got together. It was a new relationship for me. He began to perform oral sex on me. This was the first time he had done this to me, so that made it all the more fun. What really turned me on was when I looked down at him, he had a towel tucked in his shirt like a bib, and it was suppertime.

When asked what made this experience so satisfying, she noted that this was the first time she was *had* for supper, and she wrote:

"The towel he wore around his neck like a bib, and the fact that this was the first time he performed oral sex on me. He was being freaky and I liked it."

And so do I.

Nature of Relationship & Self-Regard

Third on the list of ingredients was one part Nature of Relationship and one part *positive self-regard*. Nature of the relationship was identified by 41% of these 27 women; 45% of the comments were in response to the "big question:" Would you consider having children with him? Most of these women responded "No," for reasons such as, "He's a player;" "Because our relationship was only about sex, no love. And I believe that considering children is a big step. There must be much more to it than sex;" and, "I feel he's selfish and I don't want any more children without being married, and he's not the man I want to marry."

So what kind of man is the marrying type? Of course you want to marry a man who knows how to satisfy your sexual appetite, but there are some other ingredients that need to be present if things are to go beyond that one night. Let the married women tell you what other ingredients should be on the menu.

The other 55% of the savory soliloquies that included N.O.R as an important ingredient simply described the relationship in which this sexual experience took place as casual. These responses ranged from:

"It was just a sex thing. You know, a booty call when either of us was in heat;"

to

"A man who painted my car one time. His name was [John]. We grew up in the same neighborhood and went to the same school."

As I mentioned before, single women with children have to consider what type of partner and parent a person would be. For many, when thinking back on their most fulfilling sexual experiences, sex was the only thing on the menu worth having.

For some women a love triangle prevented them from considering having children with their partner. There were just too many cooks in the kitchen. The first woman wrote, "No, because I'm in love with someone else and at the time we were going through some problems." The next woman wrote, "No. It would never work; he has a live-in girlfriend of 14 years."

The above recipes also bring up another important consideration for some of the women who are dating: the other women. I don't know how or why some men would choose to deal with more than one woman at a time, especially when some of us can be pretty high maintenance. Sometimes we want the money and the honey; it is usually just enough for one. There is definitely not enough to go around. Someone will get neglected—left with the hunger pangs of an empty stomach.

To avoid starvation and deprivation, a woman needs to be open and honest about her expectations, and hopefully he will do the same in return. But everyone dating must be mindful that they are not the only choice on the menu.

Here are some questions to ask him that might narrow down your selection and help clarify the nature of the relationship:

Are we dating exclusively?

Are we dating others, but only having sex with each other?

Are you having sex with all of the women you are dating?

Are we dating or just fucking?

No matter the nature of the relationship, a woman likes to feel special, but don't' be unrealistic with your expectations. This means that if it's just about sex don't expect to be treated like a girlfriend. He may not buy you flowers or take you out dancing. However, he can and should still be nice. I'm not talking about lying or pretending that the relationship is something that it is not. I am talking about basic decency, courtesy, and respect. He should call and cum when he says that he will. Be nice! This is not gourmet cooking. I am talking about the basics, peanut butter and jelly. Women let him know that you are a "big girl" who can handle the truth, even if that means he is just not that into you. Even if he does not adore you, he does not have to abhor you.

Women like to feel um-um good. *Positive self-regard* is the ingredient that captures this experience. It describes how a woman experienced both herself and/or her partner during the sexual act. This ingredient was present for 41% of these responses. The first woman did not need an "S" on her chest to feel *"sensual, sexy, and seductive."* As previously mentioned, women want to feel cherished, as in: *"very sexy, desirable, naughty, uninhibited, and satisfied."* Another lady wrote, *"The feelings that I experienced were wonderful. I felt good about myself and my partner."* One woman had indulged in plenty satisfying meals and she stated she was "100% confident re: my body size (weight, 320 lb.)." That's what we want to hear. Feel good in your own body. Hey, I ain't mad at her, big girls need lovin' too, the meatier the bone the better the bite.

Some people like to trim the fat, like this next woman, as she cooked up a lean lovemaking cuisine, she wrote:

I was a bartender; he had his own auto body shop and was deep into Herbal Life and had lost 90 pounds. So I got on Herbal Life with him and lost about 40 pounds, and for some reason he started to look so good to me I just wanted him in a bad way. So one night he invited me over to some white friends' home for drinks. They had a new hot tub and we all got in naked. I was so proud of my body that I just didn't care that we had no clothes on in front of strangers. After we got out of the water he and I had sex all night long in a bedroom downstairs.

During her experience she reports feeling *"strong and very beautiful."*

There are many ways to make a woman feel good, both, in and

out of the bedroom. Depending on the nature of the relationship, it could vary from sending her a text to say, "I'm thinking of you," to a bouquet of flowers. My "Big Daddy" tells me how special I am when he says that he knows that he chose right. He says, "Being with you is like hitting the lottery". Of course that could be said butt naked or fully clothed, in private or said publicly. No matter how you slice it, I always come out on top. That's how he makes me feel when he loves me and when he makes love to me.

Mood & Orgasm Intensity

The fourth ingredient also has two parts, one part *mood* and one part *orgasm intensity,* each representing 37% of the responses for these 27 single woman with children. In terms of mood, 40% of the women had a dose of romance, as evidenced by a *"remote location, romantically staged,"* and 30% had a dose of *"total relaxation."*

It is not surprising that the two most identified moods, out of all the possible moods, were romance and relaxation. These are two moods that are hard to come by for a single woman with children. Romance? Who has time for that when you have children to raise and bills to pay? Characterized by loving feelings, romance is a commodity that may be hard to come by in a casual dating relationship or with a fuck buddy. My suggestion for you single women out there who want a dose of romance is: *create it.* That is, fake it until you make it. If he is not the one for you, but he *is* the one for now, you take on the responsibility of creating a romantic mood. Put on your slow jams, light some candles, provide your favorite treats, and set the tone.

Be mindful that this works even if you are alone. Even more so, because you should not have any trouble creating a loving atmosphere for making love to yourself. Yes, this is also something single women have to keep in the pantry. Masturbation, self-pleasuring, rubbing one out, stroking the kitty—whatever your pleasure. It does not matter what you call it, as long as it feels good. I like self-pleasuring, pun intended. Self-pleasuring is not just for single women, it is for all women who want to learn about their bodies, teach their partners about their bodies, get off, and spice things up. In my study, however, the most common reason reported for self-pleasuring was absence of a partner. Therefore, one might conclude that women prefer the real thing. No imitation meat for us, that is, unless the real thing is unavailable.

Now there are orgasms and there are orgasms. With a man or alone the objective is always the same, to get full on pleasure. The women who identified orgasm intensity, as an ingredient didn't just cum—they had memorable pleasure. The kind of pleasure you have after eating something good, real good. There are several different types of orgasms: multiple, local, full body, clitoral, vaginal (g-spot), and combined. For a long time people considered clitoral orgasms to be inferior to vaginal orgasms. Let me first start by saying, I don't know how any orgasm could be inferior. Orgasms are like candy: everybody likes it. Who do you know that doesn't like candy? It comes in many varieties, and I guarantee you everybody has a favorite. And if you don't like candy, just as with orgasms, you just ain't had good candy yet. I don't care how you get it, who gave it to you, how long it lasted, how many there were, how big it felt: an orgasm is a good thing.

According to The National Health and Social Life Survey, only 29% of women *always* experience orgasm during sex with a partner, as opposed to 75% of men (Hyde & DeLameter, 2006). For 80% of women achieving an orgasm, it involves some sort of clitoral stimulation. In terms of intensity, orgasm can vary from local to full body. A localized orgasm involves rhythmic contraction of the inner third of the vagina, uterus and pelvic floor. While a full body orgasm is just that, you feel it all over your body, from your head to your toes. You know, the eye-rolling, toe-curling kind. Some single mothers described their orgasms as *"explosive," "breathtaking,"* and *"earth-moving."*

Now, that's a pretty powerful orgasm!

Setting

Setting, ranging from a "living room carpet" to "my partner's office" played a key role for 30% of the single mothers in the study. Some settings include a sprinkle of *awayness*:

A weekend getaway, focusing just on each other, with baby oil, hot tub, wine, and multiple orgasms.

This woman had "nothing to worry about," "no phones, pagers," just sexual satisfaction.

Surprisingly, setting appeared as a key ingredient in the recipes for each group of women. The order of importance changed relative to parental or marital status. But, make no mistake, setting is meaningful for women when it comes to sexual satisfaction. I believe it mostly affects a woman's mood. We need to be in the mood. The mood sets the tone for everything that is to follow. So look around you. Has the right mood been set, to hit the spot that will get you hot?

Cooking to Taste

It is important for a woman to know her personal desires before she can communicate them effectively to her partner. Take your time to think about what you have a taste for and the ingredients needed to create your own special recipe. Think about the hottest sex you've ever had or dreamt of having. Use these fantasies to help fill in the gaps of your reality to create a complete culinary masterpiece. Whatever the nature of the relationship, set the mood, imagine the place, see yourself in those various sex acts, tell him how you want to feel, show him how to arouse and excite, and work together to create a recipe for ecstasy.

Part 3
Married Women

Chapter 7
The Seasoned Palate:
Introduction to the Married Women

In my study, 52 (49.5%) of the 105 women were married. Meaningful relationships can happen in and out of wedlock. Not all relationships are a full course meal; some are just a quick bite to eat, something to tide us over. Whatever the legal status, most of the same dynamics apply. Now, if it is a long-term relationship—that is, over a year—then there are rules and roles. Therefore, if you are in a long-term, committed, monogamous relationship, dinner for two is what's on the menu.

I have heard many people say that marriage is overrated. They just ain't doing it right! How is your marriage rated? Are you in a marriage that is rated R, X, XX? Best... as in good, better, best? Or is it rated like Cold Stone Creamery: like it, love it, gotta have it? What works in my relationship might not work in yours. However, when it comes to marriage, there are some fundamental truths that apply to all.

All kitchens should have pots and pans. This is, of course, if you plan on cooking in it. There is a right way to do things. When you have more than one person in the kitchen of life and love, you need a cookbook to help maintain order. You can free style when you are a solo act, but the more cooks in the kitchen, the greater the need for a system. Marriage is an institution, and all institutions have some sort of system. Why should marriage be any different? It is not.

Marriage is the foundation of family. Family civilizes man. It shifts the focus from self to self and other, from independence to interdependence. Family requires that we learn how to put others first and not be governed by raw desires. While marriage is a part of the family system, it is also very separate. Marriage is a relationship between man and woman that is governed by law. It has established practices and rules. There is a license; there are vows; and there are rings and things. The wedding is a symbolic, yet legal, ceremony that represents an eternal union. It is full of plans, hopes, and dreams. The wedding cake, with its symbolic layers, gets more and more intimate as you reach the top, until you reach the man and woman, face to face.

The ring, depending on your taste, can be quite an expense. Diamonds, the hardest of the gemstones, are considered the most valuable. If you have one you know why. They are beautiful. When I first got mine I would just gaze at it, admire its' beauty.

My husband told me that my wedding ring was his biggest and best investment. He viewed it as an investment in our love for each other and our life together. This was a secured investment because we both wanted something real, something that would last, and something we could depend on. Something satisfying. Let us not forget the vows—those all-so-important words that men and women exchange to pledge their love and life to each other. For those of you who are not married, but in long-term relationships you might refer to the concept of vows as mutual expectations or promises. No matter what you call them, they exist, and they govern our behaviors—or at least they should.

Just as in dating, there is an ideal stage of marriage: the honeymoon stage. Ah, to be a newlywed! This stage is longer for some than others. However long the period, the honeymoon comes to an end at some point and real life begins. In the honeymoon phase it's all love. Or at least it should be. With real life comes work. That's right, marriage is hard work. It is the essence of love and work operating together. Depending on how you work it, life together can be sweet or bitter. I prefer the former.

For things to taste sweet, a system should be in place. Just as with a recipe, put things together so that the relationship turns out right every time. In this system there are roles. Depending on the nature of the relationship, the roles could be very traditional. The man is the head of the house, thus he makes the money and the decisions. The woman stays in the house, thus she makes dinner and babies. He tends to the outside of the home, while the she tends to the inside of the home. He hangs with the boys. She hangs up clothes.

Evolution would tell us that the man goes out and earns, while the woman stays in and tends to the home and children. In today's world, the scripts might be flipped. In a contemporary relationship the wife might be the one who earns the main income. That may or may not alter other parts of the role distributions. No matter what model you choose to follow, just be sure that everyone is on the same page. Wouldn't it be a hot mess if you are reading from one recipe and he is reading from another? Talk about the kind of relationship you desire. Be it old school (traditional) or new (contemporary), the two of you should decide together. It is important that both individuals contribute to the establishment of the system of marriage.

Although marriage is a union that bonds and binds two people together, individuals enter into the relationship. This individuality is an important aspect of *The Recipe for Ecstasy*. Know thyself. Know what you bring to the table. You need to be a complete person who possesses self-awareness and self-love.

Ostensibly, two people create better than one. Two heads think more and two hearts love more. What happens when his chocolate bar meets my peanut butter cup? Something sweet! If we take a Reese's Peanut Butter Cup, for example, the chocolate and peanut butter don't blend together. They are two distinct ingredients that stand alone, but together, at the same time. This sweet treat symbolizes a true union, one in which two people stand together in their individuality.

Sometimes in relationships it is necessary to put someone else's feelings, needs, dreams, desires first. In order to do this without losing one's self requires self-awareness and inner security. People can and do lose themselves in relationships. This is more likely when the self is fragile, undefined and insecure… when a person is selfless. To be self-aware is to know who you are, where you come from and where you wish to go. The self-aware person is capable of creating something made to order, the life and love that he or she wishes to have, without the worry of losing oneself.

Now that you got your man, what do you plan to do with this life that you have decided to live together? As long as you both are in the mix, the dish will be sure to satisfy. Planning, prepping, cooking, presenting, and enjoying a meal is all about teamwork. Teamwork and love: the cornerstones of humanness.

My husband and I make a great team. People look in awe and wonder at what we accomplish together. The work of life—career, family, interests, obligations, home, and friends—we do it all together. No, we do not spend every moment together. Far from it. Our schedules keep us apart during most of the week, but when we are together we feel that we are truly together. We spend quality time doing the things that make us feel good, keep us close and happy, and feed our friendship. When we are apart, *we keep each other in mind* and hold each other in our hearts. One might find it cliché, but the truth, is my husband is my soul mate. He completes me. Literally, at times he completes my thoughts. And I don't mean he finishes the sentences that I start. He completes a thought in my mind. He gives me the answer when I haven't even asked the question. No, this is not some magical thing the "universe" granted us. *Our love is something we created.* Something we made. He is my soul mate because we share our lives with each other, right down to our very souls.

As much as we share in common, we have very distinct differences in our tastes. It is these differences that sometimes bring about conflict between us. Together we work hard to prevent our differences and disappointments from destroying our dish. It is no secret that people get divorced too readily, like sending back a disappointing entree and ordering another item off the menu. Take your time; scrutinize the menu, so that you can choose right the first time.

A favorite quote of mine, "True love is your soul's recognition of its counterpart in another" (Abrams, Levy, Panay, & Dobkin, 2005). Sound appetizing? I can hear it, see it, smell it, touch it, and taste it. Can you? Have you found the ingredient that completes your recipe for ecstasy? If not, keep reading; keep looking; keep wishing. If so, now that you have found true love, how do you keep it? By periodically adding new items to the menu from which to choose. Keep sharing your ideas about life, love, and making love so that no matter how long you have been cooking things stay new and exciting.

Chapter 8
Dinner for Two: Married & Child-Free

From the Kitchen of: Married and Child-free Women

The Ingredients for Sexual Satisfaction

Mood	58%
Nature of Relationship	50%
Setting	50%
Newness	46%
Intimacy	42%
Intense Physical/ Emotional Response	42%
Love	38%

recipe card #3

For a dish that can be savored for a lifetime, you need to take the time to put it together and do the work to keep it. What are you, as a couple, going to put together, *together* being the operative ingredient in the recipe? Your ingredients need to be mixed with his ingredients to create your masterpiece. Titrating the mix, tasting it, and making adjustments to it—well that requires thoughtfulness, deliberateness, patience, investment. Conscious commitment, through marriage or other promises, helps us keep focused on the mix, even when the world provides an array of stressful distractions.

Being married comes with expectations. I can't tell you how many times I've heard, "I'm looking for unconditional love." Well, if you are a grown-up, you can give up on that fantasy right now.

Unconditional love is for children. It is something that you get from your parents. And if you didn't get it, then you won't have it. The desire for unconditional love is just something else you need to grieve, because adults have conditions, expectations, demands, requests, promises, honey-do lists. Whatever you want to call it, it ain't unconditional.

Fifty-two married woman, regardless of the presence of children, share the same top three ingredients: mood, N.O.R., and setting. This is no accident. A good wife might find herself tired, frustrated, or overwhelmed after cooking and cleaning, shopping and planning, working and organizing. With all the conditions a wife is expected to meet, it might be necessary to put her in the right mood to facilitate sexual satisfaction. How better to get in the mood than a sense of connectedness and an exciting venue?

Mood

Mood was the main ingredient for the 26 married women without children, making up 58% of the recipe. There are many moods to choose from, and even more items to help set the mood. Moods can range from romantic to sneaky, and many things in between. Moods as different as sweet and salty, like the difference between a big bag of Better Made Hots and a Snickers bar.

Intimate. Romantic. Safe. Playful. Relaxed. Nasty. Satiated. Sneaky. Freaky. Take a minute and think about what you are in the mood for, so he can get it just right. Do you need soft music and dim lights? Or does your appetite call for a blindfold and handcuffs? Whatever you desire, make sure you have all of the ingredients that you need. Remember, a little sugar and spice makes everything nice!

Your man could take you out or keep you in for a gourmet dinner, complete with candles and wine, a little "Luther," and a late night stroll under a full moon. All this, right before he lays you down to caress your body. You know, romance. One married woman responded, *"It was not routine and seemed very romantic. I felt my partner was very sensitive and was wanting to please me. I was aroused by the romance."*

There is another type of woman who could care less about candlelight, unless the candle is being used to drip hot wax all over her ass. Some women like it down and dirty. Sneaky freaky, where he might kiss you deeply in your in-law's bathroom, on top of the sink, during Sunday dinner, then he takes you right then and there. You both get to feel like you are in the wrong, while at the same time feeling so right, so sneaky.

One woman, stuffed to capacity after her climax, wrote:

"It was as if I were flooded with a relaxing serum. I was overwhelmed by the heat that rushed through my body and the feeling of satiation which followed. I didn't want to move for several minutes following."

Not one more bite! She was not the only woman who felt *satiated* after her sexual experience. Twenty-percent of these twenty-six married child-free women were beyond full, all the way to satiety. To be left feeling *"totally relaxed."* Now that sounds like a recipe for satisfaction!

Many women want to feel safe and secure in their relationships. One woman wrote, *"I felt secure in myself and in my partner's respect and affection."* I read that and think about the flip side. What is the alternative to what she felt? Feeling afraid and insecure? Feeling safe and secure in an intimate relationship dates back to the mother-child relationship. A mother provides a "holding environment" for her child to grow in (Winnicott, 1960). A holding environment is a psychological and physical space provided by the mother to the infant so that the baby feels safe and protected, allowing for optimal growth under the circumstances. A holding environment makes you feel taken care of, protected, understood, loved, and held in such a way that your consciousness (which at the beginning is unformed, fluid, and changeable) can grow spontaneously and naturally on its own (Almaas, 1998). This feeling of safety leads one to develop into a secure adult, with self worth and a strong sense of self-efficacy. An adult who is capable of producing love as good as a gourmet meal. A gourmet life.

In a marriage, the feeling of security allows for vulnerability, which helps the relationship grow to actualize its possibilities. Are you the kind of woman who wants to be held (before, after, or instead of sex)? I know that I am. Do you spoon with your man to get to sleep? Is he there when you need him? Does he come when you call? This is your physical holding environment, when your husband greets you with hugs and kisses because you are his Mrs.

Emotional atmosphere, a product of consistency, trust, love and work, might be a little more difficult to create. *Remember, deprivation destroys, maintenance maintains and nurturance nourishes.* If you neglect your relationship, it will spoil, just like food left out too long. This is not how you keep leftovers. You would not slave in the hot kitchen all day to create a meal and then leave it out all night. That does not make sense, does it? Nor does neglecting your relationship.

Cheating and lying—health hazards—will ultimately close a kitchen down. I mean all the way down. These ingredients leave a woman feeling many things (sadness, anger, fear, shame, humiliation, guilt); feeling secure doesn't come from this. In my clinical practice I have seen several married couples who don't have sex at all! These relationships are dripping with insecurity. Why buy the cow, if you can't have the milk? There is nothing like feeling safe with your man, especially when it comes to exploring and expressing your sexuality. Maybe this is why 40% of these women specified that the mood was *safe*.

Setting

The second ingredient has two parts, one part *N.O.R.* and one part *setting*, both appearing in 50% of the married child-free recipes. Often it was the setting that elicited the mood. For example, *"My spouse and I took the whole evening to explore each other and be together. We had low lighting and soft music and did not rush to complete intercourse."* This woman was clearly hungry for romance. And he gave it to her good, by setting the tone.

Within setting, many women found that being viewed a certain way increased arousal. Many women are exhibitionists of one kind or another. Girls like to be seen, looked at, and adored. From a very early age young girls like to play dress up and adorn themselves with fancy dresses, jewelry, and make-up. This continues well into adulthood. Just look around and think of the women in your life. No matter what she is into (Afrocentrism, couture, hip-hop, bee-bop, business, mod fashion, or classy chic), the girl dresses up. Yes, I know many women dress up for themselves. We like to look good because it helps us feel good. But, let's face it, the booming world of fashion and plastic surgery didn't sprout from nowhere. Women like to be seen.

Thus, it is not surprising to discover that 62% of the setting-influenced married women without children reported that the presence or potential of an audience was part of their most satisfying sexual experience. This finding was noteworthy with single women without children, too. These women reported having sex in "unique" or "intimate" places such as *a romantic setting outside while camping," "balcony of apartment," "on a beach,"* and *"in the forest".* What is it about being seen—or just the potential for being seen or heard—that turns women on? It is full of excitement, taboo, and yields tons of fun. For many people the idea of doing something forbidden creates arousal. The world is your playground; dine outside if you can.

Nature of Relationship

Having a companion on this journey called life is very important. The N.O.R. was key in 50% of the responses of women who were married without children. Fifty-four percent of these responses were directed at the question: "Would you consider having children with this man?" In contrast to the single women without children, all of these women responded "yes." That is because these women experienced their most sexually satisfying experience with their husbands or in the context of a serious relationship where marriage was a consideration or possibility. One woman wrote, *"Yes. He's my partner for life; family expansion/growth; love."* Another woman wrote, *"Yes, because I will only have children by my husband and he will be my husband very soon."*

The other 46% of the responses that identified N.O.R. as an ingredient while indicating that they would not consider having children with their partner/spouse spoke to the sexual experience itself and why it was so satisfying. For example, *"security, friendship, and love"* and *"the commitment between me and my husband."*

The next savory soliloquy, although from a married women, uses ingredients from a past sexual experience to describe ecstasy. It may be helpful to those women who are trying find novel ways to add spark to their marriages, to think back to the days of being single and free.

Sample this tantalizing treat that uses a mixture of N.O.R and setting to intoxicate:

I had been waitressing at a country club to work my way through grad school. There was a manager there whom at first I did not notice. Over time I started noticing how cute he was, how warm and friendly and easy-going he was, how he always had a nice warm way of handling/responding to the guests, how even with wait staff he was easy-going, but could communicate what he needed. I really like that— that he was nice. I knew he was younger than I, but I didn't know by how much; so I lusted after him for a while (two months). Eventually, I think he could tell I was noticing him. We eventually started talking and I discovered he was six years younger than I was (I was 27, he was 21— that felt like a big difference then). So we kind of tried to ignore each other, but I think we both just got more and more interested even though (or maybe because) we felt we shouldn't. It culminated one night when I called him late at his club just before he got off. Even though I was conflicted and hung up, he knew what I wanted, and a half hour later (2:30 a.m.) he pulled up at my house. I was still up thinking about him. He never even made it in the house. We made love on a couch on a screened-in front porch. It was really sweet and exciting, felt like it was outdoors, but it felt private. We had both wanted each other for a long time. It was slow and long, lots of kissing each other's bodies, oral sex, but not to orgasm. I'm not sure we actually had intercourse and I don't think I had an orgasm. But it was so intoxicating and otherworldly to finally be with him. It felt like we shouldn't be doing this and it felt secret, but it felt like we just couldn't hold ourselves back anymore. He also brought a bottle of the most expensive wine the country club had. It was great. We drank from that, and at one point he poured it all over my breasts and licked and drank it all from me. Somehow that was exciting, too. Somehow at the time it mattered that it was a very expensive wine that he was willing to use that way in lovemaking. Somehow the whole night was probably the most exciting and intoxicating of my life.

There are several other ingredients (sexual abandon, arousal) in the above recipe, including a pronounced sense of longing, which is especially tantalizing when there is something new you have been waiting to stick your fork into. Can you remember the last time you waited all day salivating over the thought of it? Can you remember feeling parched, so thirsty that you couldn't wait to take that drink? Or so horny that you could not wait for your first bite? Or was it that rare sweet treat that you waited all week to eat? Whatever your pleasure, there is nothing like that first taste, that first bite, that first sip, that first swallow after waiting and anticipating. And if it is *something new,* that makes it even better.

Newness

Newness was identified in 46% of the narratives by married women without children when remembering their most satisfying sexual experiences, which range from *"something new with partner"* to *"when I had sex with my first love."* Another woman listed the sole ingredient of her peak experience as *"the newness."*

It is never too late and one is never too old to try something new. As one woman wrote, good sex might take someone to unexpected heights:

"It was new, long in coming... almost my first total expression of love, and it was late in life. I had been committed to celibacy for 19 years and this was so intimate... the event was so hot and new,"

The resulting orgasm, she states, *"was like flying... total explosion; not used to it; very NEW, NEW feeling."*

Now I believe that there is nothing better than new dick. But, as you know, when you are married there is no such thing. Or at least there shouldn't be, unless this is in your cookbook. Speaking to the women out there who are in open relationships. So, how do married women keep things on and 'poppin'? They have to be creative and spontaneous to add a little spice to their love life: a new position, a new room, a new attitude, a new role-play, a new toy, a new city, a new piece of lingerie. Ladies get your man something new too. Get him some sexy Ed Hardy's or Calvin Klein boxers, briefs, or boxer briefs (my favorites). Whatever your flava, keep it sexy chocolate. Keeping things new means variety and spice, think Cajun. No one wants meat and potatoes all the time. Chicken, again? No thank you. I like sushi. I'll take my meat raw... R-A-W!

Intimacy and Intense Response

The fourth ingredient is a combination of intimacy and intensity of the physiological and/or emotional response, appearing in equal parts at 42% in the narratives of twenty-six married child-free women. It is all about how you feel when you are with him. Mmm, Mmm Good! On the inside and out. Titillating. Wonderful. Amazing. Fantastic. Ooh-wee! Beautiful. Loved. Desired. Special. Can you imagine feeling so close to someone that cumming brings tears to your eyes? This next woman doesn't have to:

My first "true" orgasmic experience. It started out with my partner and myself lying on a couch watching television. We began rubbing and kissing and soon I was lying on top of him with my back to him. I removed my pants, but he was still fully clothed. He began to gently rub my clitoris and soon I felt as if I would explode. The sound of him breathing heavily in my ear even though I wasn't doing anything to him made the moment even more exciting. Eventually I came, so hard it brought tears to my eyes.

And for her this combination yields an intimate recipe: *"I felt complete trust, well-being. I felt excitement, but also contentment."* Intimacy can be substituted for closeness. But be careful not to mistake other ingredients for intimacy. It cannot be substituted for great sex, fun, excitement or powerful orgasms. To get there, a person has to be vulnerable, open up and let the other come in. Like a hot fudge sundae, an intimate relationship is so close it is hard to tell where one begins and the other one ends. Don't forget the cherry on top!

Intimacy: the stuff that real relationships are made of. Take time to smell the aroma, as these women cook up recipes for intimacy:

We went away for the weekend to a convention and lay naked by each other in our room on a king-sized bed. We cuddled, hugged, and made love and watched horror movies all night.

The next woman places emphasis on feeling, not just physically but emotionally:

My spouse and I took the whole evening to explore each other and be together. We had low lighting and soft music and did not rush to complete intercourse, but instead removed our clothes and lay and talked and touched and explored, not only with our hands, but with various other tactile experiences: foods, various materials, lotions, etc. When, after a long period of foreplay, we moved on to intercourse, it, too, was slow and interspersed with explorations of positions, talking and taking time to "feel." It was enjoyable because we took the time to feel what our bodies were experiencing, as well as to listen and learn what the other was experiencing. It was not just orgasm with our bodies; our minds were involved as well.

Like the relationship between a mother and child, true intimacy takes place between two partners. Each person should have the experience, no matter how brief, of being the one who gets the full attention of the other—a time when someone is so connected that they know things about you that you don't even know. So close that they know your needs before you communicate them. So close that it is difficult to tell where you end and they begin. It is this connectedness that is first apparent in the mother-child relationship. This intimacy lays the foundation for the mature union of man and woman, husband and wife. Many people are ill equipped for intimacy. If you did not have that symbiotic relationship with mother than adulthood intimacy can be challenging and for some impossible.

In marriage, true intimacy transcends the good, the bad and the ugly. You partake in all of the meal, or you have none of it. You desire to be so close to your mate that you share everything, including their sadnesses and losses. Therefore, when it is good, marriage is very good; and when it is bad, it is the worst. The true measure of a healthy marriage is that things are good most of the time.

Even the greatest of chefs get it wrong sometimes. But just keep cooking, you are sure to get it right eventually, especially if you follow this recipe for ecstasy. Remember, don't forget the intimacy. It is key.

Love

The recipe for ecstasy for married women without children is incomplete without a little love, 38% to be exact. Love is the ingredient that is, I think, taken for granted in a marriage. Yet, for some married couples it doesn't even exist or it has been dying due to starvation. Love feeds us from the day we are born. And if handled correctly, it provides us with a never-ending supply of nutrients.

For one married woman, the presence of love created an experience so satisfying that it was the only ingredient she needed. When asked what made the experience so satisfying, she simply responded, *"Love."* Another married woman wrote, *"I felt and saw love in my partner's eyes. I felt beautiful and exciting. I felt my partner was attentive, experimenting, and full of love."*

Simply put, love can stand alone; it doesn't need a garnishment or condiment. It is what it is, and that is all it needs to be.

Love is something that everyone has an appetite for; it is the one ingredient that we all crave. Once given love, we have the opportunity to do and be whatever our hearts desire. Love is the most powerful of the ingredients that you will find listed here. It is the love that is first given to a child from its mother that begins the cycle.

Everyone comes into the world as a lovable person. Just think about it, all babies are lovable, even with their cries, spit-ups, middle of the night feedings, poops, and demands. They are so easy to love unconditionally. Some may think that only a mother knows this kind of love. Ideally, we all should know it, because we have all had mothers, at least biologically. Unfortunately, we all don't get the chance to grow in a holding environment; we don't all experience unconditional love as infants or as children. But, it is never too late to learn. That is what this book is all about. Stay hopeful that one day you can find someone to call your baby. Someone that you can love and who will make you feel loved, so that you can continue to give love, receive love, and make love.

Chapter 9
Family Dinner: Married & Mothering

One might think that this group of women has it all. They found the man, had the babies, and life is good. Well if you know what I know about being married with children, life is hard. It is especially hard for the marriage to maintain its flava when you add children to the mix. And it can be even harder to hold on to your individual flava once you have become a wife and a mother. If you are anything like me, you feel attached to little people all the time, and many women feel like being married is like having another little person to attend to. No disrespect fellas, but some of you are pretty high maintenance. But the little people who demand so much of our time and energy are the true focus. Right now it is all about growing them up and getting them off the bankroll. Despite all this giving, other priorities—like my marriage and my sex life—need to be attended to.

While children are an absolute miracle, they can blow out the hottest flame. Think baby crying right in the middle of foreplay. Think cooking and cleaning. Think homework. Think carting the children around all day for sports, dance, tutoring or whatever. It is important to understand that the marriage is a separate, but integral, part of the family. It is equally important to understand that the person, the woman, the individual, is also in the mix.

Like the added ingredients that commingle in your favorite marinade—the rosemary, raspberries and basil—you should be able to discern each nuance. If your palate is sensitive and you are aware than you can taste the part that is *I*, she can taste the part that is *he*, and together can taste the part that is *we*. What do you taste? All of she mixed with all of he? That will yield a complete recipe for ecstasy.

Is that basil and raspberry that I taste in this sauce? Life can become so busy and hectic that there is no time for you or for your marriage, no time for noticing the subtle flavors in the recipe that you created. Don't get lost in the sauce. Take the time—no, make the time (time is not your friend, it is always passing)—for your marriage.

To hold on to your individuality, you must remember who you were before marriage and family. What were your interests and hobbies? Who were your friends? Where did you spend your time? How did you have fun? To hold on to your marriage and keep the flames burning hot, remember when you fell in love, and ask yourself the same questions. Ask yourself a few more questions. What turned you on/off? How did you take your beef? Did you like it doggy style? Are you a romantic? You might find yourself with the same old appetite or find yourself craving something new.

Our appetites are unique and may change over time for various reasons (emotional, physical, financial, spiritual). When you go shopping, looking for the ingredients for your recipe for ecstasy, think about your answers to the above questions. As you read what the married women in my study had to say about being sexually satisfied, see if it matches or clarifies the things on your list.

From the Kitchen of: Married Women with Children

The Ingredients for Sexual Satisfaction

Mood	77%
Nature of Relationship	46%
Setting	46%
Variation in the Sex Act	42%
Newness	38%
Arousal	35%

recipe card #4

According to my findings, all married women have similar taste when it comes to feeling sexually satisfied. Both groups, with and without children, identified the same top three ingredients: mood, N.O.R., and setting.

Mood

Mood was identified in 77% of the mixture. Some of these women identified the mood as *"relaxing."* A person, place, or thing can produce relaxation. One woman's mood was connected to being *"on vacation with my husband—relaxed,"* while another woman received a massage from *"head to toe;"* relaxed.

When you are a married woman with children, being relaxed takes on special meaning. Unfortunately, the more children you have, the more you need to feel relaxed, and the less likely you are to get it. Children, while they are the greatest gift, require an inordinate, unquantifiable amount of time, attention, love, energy, patience, money, discipline, direction, comfort, support, tolerance, and understanding. Providing all of this—well, it is the antithesis of relaxed. Thus, it makes sense that these women appreciate the mood when it is set on relaxed. So, tell your man, if he really wants to see you hot, here's how to get you primed: clean the house, cook the dinner, make the decision, and take the children for the day. This will give you time to relax and think about something else for a change: hot sex on a platter.

Married women with children have also learned a thing or two from their kids, who just want to have fun. Being a wife and mother, while it can be fun at times, it can also be a lot of work. All "good enough" mothers know about the never-ending, revolving, perpetually not-done to-do list. "You can't be hungry; I just fed you" "C'mon, I just cleaned that!" "We're out of that again? I just bought four the other day." Momma is always working. Momma wants to stop work and just play sometimes. Twelve percent of the recipes crafted by married and mothering women called for a youthful and/or playful mood. For some, fun might be role-playing, for others it could be a pole dance. However you choose to have fun, be sure to use your "head," for it is a sure bet.

Play is regression in the service of the ego. It takes you back to lollipops and ice cream cones. Makes you want to see how many licks it takes to get to the center of a Tootsie Roll, pop! Sexual abandon + play = unlimited pleasure. Sure, I said that marriage and family requires structure and systems, but every now and then you have to let that system go to the wind and just do it. Do it real good!

Whatever the flava, make it fun! If you are not having fun, you've got to ask yourself what are you doing in this 'til-death-do-us-part?

What are you going to do, be together all that time and blow each others shit?

For all you wives and mothers out there, I hope that you have not forgotten how to enjoy things. If you have forgotten or just never knew how, read what others have done; you'll get some ideas. For example:

Over the course of several encounters we had lots of time to play and privacy, lots of baby oil, back rubs, shared showers, chocolate frosting (all over). He even shaved my pubic hair once. That was interesting.

Remember all the fun you and hubby used to have before you had one, two, three... other mouths to feed. Whatever you pleasure, hold on to it. Don't sacrifice the spontaneity and the spark.

Snack on This

Date Night

Don't stop doing things together, especially the things that got things cooking from the jump. Dating is a characteristic of new relationships, the falling in love stage. The difference between falling in love and being in love is the degree to which two people are involved. In the falling in love stage, people are, or at least should, be very involved: the phone calls (that last for hours), texts (all day long), and dates (that last for days). How is it that when people get married, they become less involved?

Dating also keeps things fresh in an old relationship. When it is new you always want to be together, talk until 3 o'clock in the morning, make love all the time. This will change as you move from fantasy to reality, from infatuation to commitment. But you still have to maintain the connection. Don't remove the date when you are no longer dating. Once when I was out for date night (married with two kids), my husband said to me, "We have fun, and look good doin' it". Do you have the image? Do you look good doin' it? Do you do it at all? Many couples have made date night a regular part of their relationship's diet. If you haven't, you should. It may help reignite a fire that is barely burning.

Nature of Relationship & Setting

N.O.R and setting make up the second ingredient, at 46% each. For the first time in this study, only two women identified the nature of the relationship as a factor in response to the "big question:" Would you consider having children with your most sexually satisfying partner? This means that, for this group of women, the nature of the relationship contributed to the pleasure alone. One woman even responded, *"No. I love my husband very much and I have children with him and wouldn't want it any other way. That relationship was just for fun."* For this group of women, the nature of the relationship (in this case the casual nature of it) was an essential aspect of the sexual experience.

The next woman keeps the recipe short and simple, but sweet. *"It wasn't just sex. It was with someone I really loved."* Research suggests that the quality of the relationship facilitates orgasm responsiveness (Ozeil, 1978). In a romantic relationship, where a woman can openly communicate her sexual needs and desires to her partner; she can experience orgasm, maybe even ecstasy. This type of openness is facilitated by vulnerability.

There was really no particular setting identified by these 26 married mothering women, but setting was certainly deemed important. The settings ranged from *"in a shower with my husband"* to *"making love outside under the stars at a campground."* Note that this recipe includes a dash of awayness and a splash of audience potential or presence. The thought of being seen can be exciting for women who are exhibitionists. But for many mothers, who feel like they have to sneak and get it between naps, errands, and playtime, there is nothing exciting about the possibility of being seen. So, for the women who don't yet have to consider the whereabouts of children, or anyone one else for that matter, have some fun for me.

Awayness

It is always great to take a plane, train, or automobile to get away. Sometimes getting away means using your imagination. This one is particularly appetizing: *"I actually got into the bathtub and opened my legs and ran medium to high running water in between my legs."* If you notice, this married woman's most sexually satisfying experience was dinner for one. I can appreciate the satisfaction that comes with being able to eat a meal without having to fix four plates before you get to sit down to yours, lukewarm at that. She made sure her dish was hot and she didn't have to share it with anyone. Now that sounds satisfying! I know that you can't trust everyone's cooking, but this woman swears it was *"the best experience ever. Try it."* It is important to mention that zest was added to this recipe by the *"pressure from the water,"* and also from her fantasies about *"one person whom I loved."* This woman let Calgon take her away. And it is a sentiment that I know many married women with children can appreciate.

When a couple has children, vacation takes on a whole new flavor. Getting away might make one feel like a kid in a candy store. Therefore, it is no surprise that married and mothering women put a sprinkle of awayness in their dishes. When parents get away from their children they should take full advantage of the opportunities that present themselves, and I am not just talking about sleeping in. On vacation, sex could be on the menu every time you sit down to eat. That is, sex every day, and if you are really hungry, several times a day. Eat up!

Of course, being on vacation with kids can be a very different experience. You are lucky if you even have a chance to sleep in the same bed. Depending on the age of the child/ren, vacations can be very demanding. Our first trip to Miami (with the kids) was a memorable one for many reasons, one being that our entire day was planned with our seventeen-month old's sleep schedule in mind. No joke! On top of that, I was in a room with one kid and he was in a room with the other. Sex was not on the menu. So, you can best believe that when we are away from the kids, it is all you can eat; we feast on each other.

Variation in the Sex Act

Life as a married woman with children should be characterized by structure and consistency. Children need it to create a safe environment in which to thrive; parents need it to keep them sane. Without routines, life would be chaotic and overwhelming.

Consistency and routine, though, do not bode well for the bedroom. Maybe this is why variation in the sex act is identified in 42% of the recipes for this group. Some say that variety is the spice of life. If so, this woman's "Saturday night" is hot, hot, hot!

Saturday night sex with my husband prior to getting pregnant and having a child. On Saturdays we used to have a lot of energy, were able to be spontaneous, blast music, have a few drinks, and get lost in our sexual passion. We could have a lengthy period of foreplay, sexual talk, oral sex, and build up the tension toward intercourse. We would switch positions and move around the house (floor, sofa, bed, shower). And intercourse would culminate with very powerful orgasms—sometimes I could have more than one, but not always.

I think this is a dish that should be replicated, even when parenting. Part of the system of marriage should include putting the kids to bed early enough to make date night happen right in the house. Sometimes, on a Friday or Saturday night, once the kids are asleep, my husband and I order take out, have a few drinks, watch a movie, and pretend we don't have kids. We take it to the basement where we can have our treats all to ourselves. Now, that's a "staycation" for you. Married individuals need time to nurture their marriage. I can't say it enough: babysitter, babysitter, babysitter!!!

In a good marriage, things are stable, consistent, predictable and dependable. These are the things that provide a sense of safety and allow for the vulnerability that creates true intimacy. Maybe not always, but for the most part these elements should be present. If they are not, you might need to take another look at the menu or seek some guidance in the kitchen of life and love. Guidance comes in many forms: books, workshops, parents, pastors, and my personal favorite: couch time (therapy).

At the same time, who wants chicken every night? Yeah, you can count on it to be good for you, and depending on who's cookin', good to you. But, there is something about trying a new dish that invites excitement. That is why ingredient number four, newness, appears in 38% of the recipes.

Newness

Many of these experiences focused on the newness of the feelings aroused. For example, *"It was overwhelming since I never recalled these feelings with the man I had been married to for 15 years."* I imagine this is why she is no longer cooking with him. Fifty percent of the savory soliloquies pointed to the newness of the relationship, while others focused on the new feelings that came when she did. Look at this married and mothering woman's recipe:

My most sexually satisfying experience was the first time I had sex with one of my boyfriends. He came into my room and surprised me. He tied me up with handcuffs to my bed. One thing led to another and we had sex for what seemed like forever. We both had multiple orgasms. The first time was one of the best times for us... It was so satisfying because everything was so new for the two of us. We were exploring one another.

Sometimes there are many aspects of newness at once. She wrote about a very exciting sexual encounter that took place *"in San Francisco"* on *"the top of a pillar at the Palace of Fine Arts"* with someone new. She states,

I had never really done something so 'wild' (i.e., in public) and that was exciting. It was the second week or so I had been dating my now husband, and he was very attentive to my needs.

This woman was in a new place, trying something new, with someone new. I imagine she felt like a new woman. Who wouldn't?

Here is another soliloquy that delights in the experience of things being new. Her most satisfying experience included novelty, *"sexual intercourse in a shower with my husband when we first met... Because it was our first sexual encounter and my husband was very gentle and patient."* About the orgasm she wrote, *"This was the first time that I experienced this in that type of setting."* New, new, and new!

Arousal

The final ingredient, *arousal*, was identified by 35% of married women who are also mothers. Some of them spoke about their arousal in terms of *"passion." "heat,"* or *"lust."* A woman who made love *"under the stars"* said that this experience was so satisfying because of *"the thrill of it; the danger of being caught and it was very passionate."* Another woman reports that many things, such as *"intimacy, love, excitement"* and the *"feeling of being naughty"* turned her temperature to high.

Love and lust. The perfect combination. Isn't it great when he can tempt you with the taste of nuts and honey, even before you sit down for breakfast? This woman's husband knows how to make it happen.

We had sex about 5 a.m. before work. It was dark. He didn't ask, he just went straight to it. Without words we seemed to connect physically. We did it once and it was good. A few minutes later we did it again and it was wonderful". "He was tender and sweet...

I felt sexy. I felt affection towards him, love and lust. The first orgasm made me throb inside. The second one made me scream uncontrollably.

Unbridled passion tastes oh so good! Like biting into a dark plum—tender and sweet. I know that is how I like it.

Or take me like you are a ravenous savage, getting his first taste of meat in a long time. I like that, too.

Many things facilitate arousal. What makes one woman's temperature boil might extinguish another woman's flame all together. It is also true that what hits her spot tonight might turn her stomach tomorrow. Women are picky like that. Many things, including mood, timing, technique, setting, and nature of the relationship affect arousal.

So, be sure to check your list and make sure you have all of the required ingredients if you are looking for something smoking, red hot!

You won't need to use your imagination as this next married woman puts all of the ingredients of a family dinner together, including some extras, to reach her recipe for ecstasy. Anytime a mother has an opportunity to get *away* from her children, with the love of her life, is cause for celebration (mood).

I was determined to have a great time with my husband. It was his homecoming at TSU, his twenty-year fraternity anniversary, and my first time on the scene, [new]. Plus we really needed this time away. We had been beefin' off and on since one of our last trips, earlier this year with the kid. It was time to kick it and be friends [N.O.R.].

He needed to do him, I needed to do me, and we wanted to look and feel good doing it. This trip was a long time coming, so I was prepared: a new hair-do that came fully equipped with a new attitude. We had packed all of the necessary accoutrements: lingerie, fuck me pumps, smell good, music, Astroglide (personal lubricant), the bullet, blue dolphin, Vicerex (male sexual enhancement supplement), and treats (grey goose and tonic with a twist of lime). I wanted to be prepared when he released the beast on me.

My job this weekend was "to be gorgeous, cool as hell, and super fun" (a close friend reminded me), and to talk. But, not in my usual voice. I needed to tell him how beautiful he is with my action and my words. This is what he needed and wanted from me. So that is what I gave.

It started before we even got in the air, with the texting that was sure to arouse his curiosity and his cock, his beautiful cock. Charisse was calling for Wesley, and I needed to channel my inner sex-goddess, mother-whore, freak because Wesley was around and ready.

We had fun all day kickin' it at the happy hour and dinner that followed. In true fashion, shortly after we arrived at the hotel, he was off to sleep. I just knew we were done for the night. I was disappointed and borderline pissed! But, to my shock, amazement, and pleasure, around 12:30 a.m., my husband was up and ready to eat. First my lips, with passionate kisses, and then a nibble here and a nibble there; he nibbled my neck and back. That was the appetizer. He inhaled my pussy; he didn't even stop to chew. What a hungry man he was. I was so grateful for his nap. The orgasm was great because I got to shout it out, without worrying who was on the other side of the wall to hear me [setting]. And he did the same when he exploded inside of me. Now we were really hungry. After a little socializing in the lobby, it was off to get a pizza.

By 4:00 a.m., my husband's appetite had returned. I was so sleepy that I can't remember the details; all I know is that we both gave and received good head (mutuality). I came, and it was good. Who is this hungry man? Back for seconds, taking me from the back. The next thing I remember was waking up; lying in the last position he had me in. He knocked me out with the dick [satiety].

It was apparent he wanted me all weekend. Usually I am the one who is always trying to make sure that sex is on the menu. This was his weekend, his homecoming, his insatiable appetite, and that made me hot. So I followed his lead. Oh, he was sure to like that. "Big Daddy" likes it when I sprinkle a little suga on it, and make it sweet. No backtalk, that comes with its normal kick. Spicy! Just fun.

The sex just kept coming at me, like the dishes of a twenty-course meal at Per Se. We had a big delicious breakfast (real food this time), the homecoming parade, fraternity dedication, shopping, burgers and fries (gotta eat right?), tailgating, and football game. Sex was the last thing on my mind when we went back to the room for a quick change for dinner at 10:00 p.m.

We did not leave the room until 11:30 p.m. We just got it in where it fit in. As the clothes came off the temperature in the room went up. The heat probably emanated from the friction of our bodies grinding to some jams (Woozy, Give It To Me Right, just to name a few) as we stood at the foot of the bed facing the wall mirror. He wasn't even inside of me yet. I was getting so wet, looking at his lustful eyes in the mirror, as he dipped his fingers inside of me, while I gave him a lap dance on tiptoe. His fingers were the only tools that he needed to turn the temperature to hot-n-ready, but we used a little Astroglide to ease the way, and we were on our way—standing, sitting, his front to my back, straddled over the ottoman, and finally to the bed [variety]. "Head for me? I shouldn't. I'm stuffed. OKAY just a little". He gave me just enough to make me scream with pleasure, and, yes, I did scream because there were no kids around to hear my moans and groans, nor the screams of passion as I exploded from sheer satisfaction. It was his turn next. He growled with passion as he released his warm gravy inside of me. And like many times before, he started to say, "That was..." and I finished his thought, "the best orgasm I have ever had."

Indeed!

Part 4
Refining the Ingredients for Love and Ecstasy

Chapter 10
As Spicy as You Like It

From the Kitchen of: All Women

The Ingredients for Sexual Satisfaction

His Focus on Her	49%
Multiple Orgasms	49%
Sexual Abandon	46%
Variation in the Sex Act-Oral Sex	37%
Quality of Relatedness-Mutuality	19%

recipe card #5

Specialty Ingredients

This next list of ingredients will not be found at the local grocer. You may have to go to a store that specializes in gourmet delights such as Dean & De Luca, where you can find herbs and spices like pink peppercorns and lavender flowers to distinguish your dish from all others. Just as there are many herbs and spices that can be used to create your own personal taste, there are ingredients in the recipe for ecstasy that can customize your love making experience. Look beyond the shelves at the corner store. Think imported.

It is important to understand the nuances of even a subtle change in a recipe. Like the difference between sea salt, coarse salt, and iodized salt, it can change the flavor of your dish. For this reason, five additional ingredients were added to the recipe for ecstasy: His focus on her (H.F.O.H), multiple orgasms, sexual abandon, variation in the sex act: oral sex, and quality of relatedness (mutuality). While they are not considered staple ingredients, these five specialty items will turn your ordinary into extraordinary.

His Focus on Her (H.F.O.H.)

His Focus on Her was an important ingredient for single and married women with children. Surprise! Surprise! Women who have children spend an inordinate amount of time thinking about someone else's needs. It makes sense that having the tables turned would be important for them. It is one of the reasons I like to dine out, especially if the service is good. It doesn't matter whether it is Red Robin or Wolfgang Puck; it is nice to have someone who wants to service you.

This additional ingredient was identified in 49% of the questionnaires (of all the mothering women). There was particular emphasis placed on the fact that the male was not just interested in pleasing himself, but his partner, too. One single woman stated, *"He held off from having an orgasm to make sure I had as many as I could to completely satisfy me (I love that) and he even kept count with me to see how many I had."* The real men out there can delay gratification and wait until she is satisfied.

A man can also focus on her by what he chooses not to do, for example, *"the fact that he cuddled with me after and didn't just roll over like he was done with me."* Fellas, I know that once your belly gets full, going to sleep is one of the first things that comes to mind, but if you don't want to leave a woman feeling like a piece of meat, stay awake long enough for your meal to digest. Who knows, you just might make room for round two. And if you really want to make a girl feel special, save the last bite for her.

This married woman provides a delicious example of his focus on her. She reported that her partner *"licked [her] from head to toe, [and] massaged [her] from head to toe."* I think it is important to give a person what they really want, not just what you want them to have. Ladies, he is not a mind reader so be sure to put in your order, so that he can bring it right to you. And gents, if you are not sure how she takes her fixings, just ask. It is important to know how to please her. Remember that every woman is so different. And what she likes from night to night may vary, as well. So when it is your night to cook, make sure you think about her wants and needs.

When a man focuses on a woman's needs, he should consider all of her. A woman wants to know that a man is interested in her, not just trying to get inside of her. Most women like the obvious: love notes, trinkets, flowers that appear just because. Then there are the not-so-obvious things that show that he is paying attention to her wants and needs. Grocery shopping, a card just because, bathing the kids, changing a light bulb without being asked, tidying the kitchen.

Beyond Satisfied: Multiple Orgasms

Yes! Yes! Yes! What a wonderful treat. Yes! Yes! Yes! If there was ever a thing that you could not get too much of, it would have to be an orgasm. Yes! Yes! Yes! Single and married women with children identified *multiple orgasms,* as a key ingredient in their peak experience. This ingredient was present in 49% of the recipes for the mothering women. One woman wrote, *"I reached many orgasms. This was the best experience of my life."* Another woman stated that her multi-orgasmic experience was *"very fulfilling, relaxing, exhilarating, a release of energy."* No worries if this is not an ingredient that you have been able to successfully use in your recipe. Remember, this specialty ingredient is not necessary, but it sure is nice. Just like the cherry on top, the sundae still tastes great without it. But, don't give up on that cherry, it is still within your reach.

Multiple orgasms are like eating the whole pie, one slice after another. And, as with eating pie, there comes a point when enough is enough. Multiple orgasms are a series of sequential orgasmic responses that occur in quick succession. There may come a point when you reach exhaustion, but until you get there you should enjoy them while they last. It is believed that all women are physically capable of achieving multiple orgasms. This is due to the fact that women, unlike men, do not have a refractory period. The refractory period is the stage during the sexual response cycle when it is physically impossible to achieve arousal and orgasm. This is the one time we have the fellas beat. And why shouldn't we be capable of achieving multiple orgasms? We live through monthly periods for most of our adult lives, we birth the babies, and we have to work harder to have just one orgasm during the sexual experience. So, as far as I am concerned, we had this coming to us (pun intended).

Having one orgasm is dependent on getting your mind and

body in the right place at the same time. While the clitoris has the most nerve endings in the body, the most erogenous zone of the body, the brain, plays a significant role in orgasm responsiveness.

The brain is where the entire sexual experience gets processed. It is the house of fantasy, desire, arousal, anxiety and physiological response. If you are focused on what is going on in the moment (i.e. manual and or oral stimulation of the clitoris, rubbing of the G-spot, intercourse) you can use these sensations to increase the level of arousal. It is also important to understand that thinking about other things like the grocery list or what's for dinner can put the hottest flame right out.

If you mix the mind and the body together what kind of orgasm could you have? Mind-blowing, earth-moving, back-bending, multiple orgasms. If this is so, then why is it that only 15% of women have multiple orgasms, and some women can't manage to have just one? Their minds and bodies are not in the right place. A mind focused on pleasure and a body that is relaxed and open to receiving that pleasure—that is the combination for sexual satisfaction. It is important to remember that orgasms rely on the mind-body connection.

A Recipe for Orgasms: Multiple Pleasures

I always feel so sad for women when I hear the words "I have never had an orgasm." Or even worse, "I don't know if I have ever had an orgasm." Well, if you don't know, than the answer is "I have never had an orgasm" because an orgasm is an unmistakable sensation.

Women who go through the stages of arousal and never get to claim the prize at the end feel cheated, frustrated, and dissatisfied. It's like walking into a room of free samples of your favorite treats but being told, "Look but don't touch." "Touch but don't taste." "Okay, okay, taste, but don't swallow." Men need to know this is one of the most frustrating things that could happen in bed: to get her all hot and bothered and not help her go all the way. The tension that builds and never gets released is like never popping the top on expensive bottle of champagne. What a waste. An orgasm may not be expected all of the time; however, it is desired most of the time. Yes, sometimes a woman just wants to feel close to her man. But, don't get it twisted. She wants to have her cake and eat it too. We want to feel close and we also want to cum.

It is important that every woman know her own body first and foremost. You have to know what turns you on. Is it kissing, touching, and rubbing? Touch your body. That's right. See how hot the oven can get. This is one time when putting your hand in the oven won't burn. Think about the stages of the sexual response cycle. Arousal is a key ingredient to reaching orgasm. And if first you don't succeed, try, try again. Like learning to cook: it takes practice, practice, and more practice. Don't forget patience, because this might take a while. And if you get stumped ask a friend for some help. The bullet, pocket rocket, jack rabbit, and dolphin, are all friends of mine. A good vibrator could be just the tool you need to make your recipe complete.

Speaking of practice, don't forget to do your Kegel exercises. A lot of people believe that Kegeling is to be done only after childbirth or if you have a bladder problem. Wrong! Kegel exercises promote sexual health, and can be done solely for that purpose. During Kegel exercises the man or woman exercises the pubococcygeus muscle (PC muscle) of the pelvic floor. The exercises increase blood flow to the genital area. Blood flow plays an important role in arousal, and arousal plays an important role in orgasms. How do you do Kegels?

Snack on This

Kegel Exercises: A how to-guide for women (Mayo Clinic Staff, 2010)

Find the right muscles. To make sure you know how to contract your pelvic floor muscles, try to stop the flow of urine while you're going to the bathroom. If you succeed, you've got the basic move. Or try another technique: Insert a finger inside your vagina and try to squeeze the surrounding muscles. You should be able to feel your vagina tighten and your pelvic floor move upward. Then relax your muscles and feel your pelvic floor move down to the starting position. As your muscles become stronger—and you become more experienced with the exercises—this movement will be more pronounced. But don't make a habit of starting and stopping your urine stream. Doing Kegel exercises with a full bladder or while emptying your bladder can actually weaken the muscles. It can also lead to incomplete emptying of the bladder, which increases your risk of a urinary tract infection.

continued...

Once you've identified your pelvic floor muscles, empty your bladder and sit or lie down. Then, contract your pelvic floor muscles. Hold the contraction for three seconds then relax for three seconds. Repeat 10 times. Once you've perfected three-second muscle contractions, try it for four seconds at a time, alternating muscle contractions with a four-second rest period. Work up to keeping the muscles contracted for 10 seconds at a time, relaxing for 10 seconds between contractions.

To get the maximum benefit, focus on tightening only your pelvic floor muscles or isolating your pelvic floor muscles. Be careful not to flex the muscles in your abdomen, thighs or buttocks. Also, try not to hold your breath. Just relax, breathe freely and focus on tightening the muscles around your vagina and rectum. Perform a set of 10 Kegel exercises three times a day. The exercises will get easier the more often you do them. You might make a practice of fitting in a set every time you do a routine task, such as checking e-mail or commuting to work.

I cannot stress how important concentration is when it comes to cumming. Ladies, stop thinking about what's for dinner. At the moment, you are what's cooking! No matter the technique, make sure he keeps it nice and wet. The moisture keeps things from going from pleasurable to painful. No matter the tool: hand, tongue, toy, tip of the dick, or every inch of it, use rhythmic stokes. And once you have hit the spot, don't stop, don't stop...

Developing the ability to achieve orgasm can be a little frustrating and may even provoke anxiety. Just stick with it. Somewhere down the road there is this great feeling. And once you have mastered it, you can teach any man how to turn you on and turn you out.

You might find yourself feeling satisfied like this next married woman, who gives us a savory soliloquy from her wedding night. She had food on the brain as she shared her recipe, which involved, *"Partaking in oral and vaginal sex throughout the night with multiple orgasms with a distinction between appetizer, main course, and dessert."* Sounds like she had something delectable to distinguish between her courses. A lick here, some dick there, and love everywhere. She believes that her experience was enhanced by the taste of *"love"*, and that *"it was more special because it was [her] wedding night."* And those multiple orgasms were like tasting *"... ecstasy, the best a person can have with true love".*

Eat with Your Hands: Sexual Abandon

How can something be nasty, but good at the same time? *Sexual abandon* is a thorough yielding to sexual impulses, without limitations or restrictions: a complete surrender of inhibitions. Or as the layperson might refer to it, just down right dirty, freaky, nasty. You know what I am talking about. That freak shit. No, I am not talking about something that could end with handcuffs and a jail sentence, although there maybe handcuffs involved. Something like role-playing, toys, a ménage a trois, a trip to the strip club, pole dancing for your mate, talking dirty, spanking. Go out for a night on the town, where I am not me and he is not him. I'll be Charisse Harding and he will be Wesley Russell. I'll whisper in his ear, "Be sure to bring your cock, I have lots of tail. Then we can have a for sure cocktail party."

Abandon all that you are and all that you know and do. Have drinks, a great meal, with tossed salad, of course. Take a doggy bag for later, when you are sure to do it doggy style, as he spanks you because you have been a bad girl, because he wants a mother-whore not a Mother Theresa. Tonight you will have a deep throat, and you will enjoy watching "Deep Throat." Talk dirty to each other all night. Go to the strip club in vivo or give your man a lap dance to remember. There is nothing like a naked human body, set to music, performing for your own viewing pleasure, with a man right beside you to enjoy the view. If you want to be center stage, you can borrow my playlist to help you get started on your routine (See Appendix H). If you are feeling adventurous… invite a friend.

This optional ingredient, sexual abandon, was present for two groups of women, single women without children and married women with children, accounting for 46% of the recipes. A single woman wrote, *"He made me feel sexy and beautiful, so I felt freer sexually with him… I felt totally uninhibited with him."* So free, that you feel like you can do any and every thing with him.

Sexual abandon could be the product of just not giving a fuck. It is no surprise that this is an ingredient identified by many single women without children. Take this one for example:

The man I stood up with in a wedding drove me to his place. We made love for hours and continued on the next day. The day sex was great. It was on a somewhat secluded beach. I think the best part of it was he managed to think before he acted, truly fulfilling my every need. It was also exciting because neither of us knew the other one that well. I felt pretty uninhibited. I felt pretty mysterious. He didn't know me, I didn't know him, no rules!"

When you feel so safe that you can break all the rules, without worrying about the consequences, then you can have the best of both worlds: something so good, yet so bad, and feel *"... like the sexiest, most desirable, beautiful woman."* Pay attention as this woman tells us about how he made her feel. *Engendered feelings* is another ingredient, which is further elaborated upon in Chapter 12 of this cookbook. A married woman wrote that the *"spontaneity and freedom that would allow us to get totally lost in the sexual moment"* made for her most satisfying experience. She was free to test the limits without guilt or shame. Let's face it, when some people play in the kitchen they like to get dirty.

Sometimes sexual abandon is the consequence of reaching a higher level of comfort and security in a relationship. Like being married and raising children. If he has been through childbirth with you, then getting freaky should be as easy as eating with your hands. You can be vulnerable, wide open—physically and emotionally. Let it all hang out. This takes feelings of security or a lack of care and a desire to take risk and be risqué. Maybe that is why married women with children and single women without children had this ingredient, sexual abandon, on their list.

Presumably, married women, who have children, have acquired the greatest level of relationship security. They have found a man to commit to them and their children. It is this type of security that would lend itself to sexual abandon or at the same time make it necessary. Overtime many marriages become blah, and couples decide to toss the dish down the drain. Instead, add a sprig of sexual abandon and stir the pot. It is important to break the monotony that is sure to develop in a household where there are good enough parents who impose structure and routine. It is also important for individuals in a marriage to have the assurance that they can test the bounds of their relationship by openly expressing their sexuality.

On the other hand, single women without children, can be uninhibited in their sexual expression because of their lack of commitments. They are free to task risk, test the limits, and abandon all rules and restrictions because they only have to be concerned with themselves. She can have it as spicy as she likes it!

Variety is the Spice of Life: Variation in the Sex Act

I felt the need to put specific emphasis on spicing things up because, according to my research, intimacy was the best predictor of sexual satisfaction. This was found most often in a married or committed relationship. If things are to last a lifetime, there needs to be some additives and preservatives in the mix. What better way to preserve a relationship than keeping it fresh with hot new ideas?

No one wants the same meal every day of the week. And there are so many different ways to spice up a dish. The women in my study identified many possible combinations and permutations of the various ingredients. You might find some of them appetizing, while you find others appalling. Don't knock it 'til you've tried it, though.

These first two dishes call for someone with a big appetite; these women needed more than one person to satisfy their hunger. The first woman had sex with *"two men"* and simply stated, *"Knowing that I was the freak of the night"* was the most succulent aspect of her experience. The next woman *"had sex with [a] male partner and best friend, who is female"*. She enjoyed watching things get stirred up, and she wrote, *"Seeing my male partner screwing my friend and the enjoyment he received excited me."* She was totally secure with the experience, not worried about who got a bigger portion to eat. *"There was no jealousy or guilt feeling. It was an experience we both talked about and wanted to do."* And about the orgasm, she wrote,

"*Yes, I experienced an orgasm. I recall being very, very aroused. This happened many years ago, but I can recall every detail and become aroused.*" Don't you love it when just the thought of something makes you salivate? When was the last time you had a meal that you fantasized about afterward?

For this next woman, it was not about the who's, but the what's, such as "*performing oral sex on each other, then myself receiving anal sex.*" During this experience she reached "*The highest orgasm ever (anal sex).*" She did not even have a cookbook. She just put a couple of ingredients together. "*Just experimented last month. (Hate I waited so long!).*"

For some people the idea of multiple partners or anal sex might turn your stomach, but for some women it hits the spot. If you don't want to try these recipes, then there are many other spices in the rack.

Snack on This

The Banana in the Tailpipe

Be sure that if you are going to go anal that you use lubrication. Gun oil comes highly recommended. Just ask any gay man. Remember there is a right way to do things. A girl needs to be greased up before you put the meat in. This prevents tearing and unnecessary pain. Keep it clean! That means no double dipping. Once it has been dipped in chocolate, don't try dipping it in the cherry. It makes for a bad combination. Something that only a doctor can undo. This goes for toys too. Don't just go dipping in things. Clean off the ben-wah balls, pearls, dildos, and whatever else you might choose to use for multiple places of pleasure. That is, if it is going in the back door, don't try it in the front, the anus has all types of bacteria and that is not welcomed in the vagina.

Hot Sex on a Platter: Oral Sex

While it was primarily the single women with children who identified oral sex (37%) as an important ingredient for sexual satisfaction, I don't know a woman who doesn't like to be had for dinner. Head, eating the fur pie, muff diving, brain, lick 'em low lovin', eating out, cleaning the plate, cunnilingus—whatever name you give to this delicacy, be sure it is on the menu. Many women highlighted the intense pleasure associated with oral sex. There are various sensations that can be produced with the combination of tongue, saliva, lips, and for those who like it rough, teeth. To devour her is to give her the ultimate pleasure, and it is a sure way of making her quiver with satisfaction. Just listen as these women talk about the great pleasure of a hungry man eating with his face and hands, no utensils required.

One woman wrote that her most sexually satisfying experience was *"When my boyfriend performed oral sex on me; I have never had that happen before in my life."* Who has she been dining with? Somebody has been starving for attention. And once he had a taste of her, it changed things forever. She wrote, *"I [felt] good and excited all in one." "When the orgasm came it felt so good inside and I have loved him ever since."* Now I know head can be good, but, damn, the kind of head that makes you love him forever. Cum on!

Head, 'til you burning up.
Head, 'til you get enough.
Head, 'til your love is red.
Head, love you 'til you're dead.

(Prince, 1980)

One woman wrote, *"To be honest, there is not one experience that stands above the rest. But oral sex to me really adds a lot of pleasure."* For you and any other woman who can get a man's head between her legs, trust me, you are not alone. I can't say it enough. Men are not the only ones who like head. If he ain't willing to go downtown, then you might want to consider inviting someone else to dinner, because you are missing out on a real fine dining experience. If you don't believe me take it from Kate Williams, who said, "sex is like cooking a good meal in the oven, but head is like a microwave 30sec hot pocket. Bing!" It gets the job done!

The Perfect Blending of Flavors:
Quality of Relatedness & Mutuality

When the feelings are mutual, he likes you and you like him. He wants to give it to you and you want to give it to him. You relate to him and he relates to you, such that the quality of the interaction between the two results in a peak experience. Mutuality, as opposed, one-sidedness, means having a shared experience. It sits in contrast to submission and dominance, which might be on the list of ingredients, if you are in the mood for something a little spicy.

This optional ingredient, mutuality, was essential only for the married women with children. It was found in 19% of this group's recipes. One married woman suggested that, *"a great sense of mutual enjoyment, stimulation, and gratification"* contributed to her peak sexual experience. Like it feels when she gives head to him and he gives head to her. To give and receive pleasure at the same time—when he is 6 and you are a 9. Masters and Johnson (1996) agree than mutuality is important, and state that "mutual pleasure sets a seal on emotional commitment" (p. 253). They refer to commitment as the "pleasure bond." They write: "A wish to take care of someone for whom one cares creates an overpowering sense of involvement and identification, of oneness. Some people call it love and it is the original source of commitment"(p. 252). It is no coincidence or surprise that this ingredient appeared in the recipes for married women with children. These are the women who have the most invested and who should subsequently expect the most in return.

When mutuality is included, then everyone experiences sexual pleasure. There are a number of opportunities to experience mutuality in a relationship beyond sex. Outside of the bedroom, mutuality means giving someone something that they want, and expecting to get what you want in return. Like when he makes you feel special, and you make him feel understood. Or even more hands on, like taking turns meeting the never-ending demands of children. Whatever you have a taste for, you might relate to this woman who had a *"deep feeling to satisfy each other, me to him and him to me."* Remember, mutuality is a type of relatedness wherein each person gives and gets. Erikson's (1950) description of "true genitality" emphasizes the importance of mutual pleasure between a man and a woman for sexual satisfaction, as well as relationship satisfaction. Through this concept, he integrates psychoanalytic and evolutionary theory, and provides some foundation for understanding sexual satisfaction.

> Genitality, then, consists in the unobstructed capacity to develop an orgastic potency so free of pregenital interferences that genital libido (not just the sex products discharged in Kinsey's "outlets") is expressed in heterosexual mutuality, with full sensitivity of both penis and vagina, and with a convulsion-like discharge of tension from the whole body. This is a rather concrete way of saying something about a process which we really

do not understand. To put it more situationally: the total fact of finding, via the climactic turmoil of the orgasm, a supreme experience of the mutual regulation of two beings in some way takes the edge off the hostilities and potential rages caused by the oppositeness of male and female, of fact and fancy, of love and hate. Satisfactory sex relations thus make sex less obsessive, overcompensation less necessary, sadistic controls superfluous (Erikson, p. 265).

Did you get that? Erikson tells us that the experience of mutual pleasure, often found in the experience of orgasm, can take the edge off, cut down the desire to stab your mate with a fork just because they are not of a like mind. Men and women are different and this can lead to straight up beef. But good sex—not just any ole kind of good sex, but sex that is mutually satisfying—takes away the need to hate or congratulate. You just do it!

Chapter 11
Getting Dicey: Communication

Slicing and dicing can be a very useful skill when it comes to sexual satisfaction. While communication was *not* identified as a significant ingredient in my research, I felt it could not be left out of the recipe for ecstasy. Effective communication cuts right through the bull, takes you straight to the bone.

The spoken word is such a basic tool that we take it for granted. One of the first tasks that individuals master in order to get our needs met, some people abandon verbal expressive language when they need it most. Ask for what you need. Tell him what you want. Open up and share your thoughts and feelings, so that he can really understand how to please you. I don't care if it is just a booty call. Make it worth the while.

Verbal & Nonverbal

You get what you ask for. Chop it up into bite-sized pieces so that he can fully digest what is wanted. Asked for a pinch of spice here and there, mostly there (down there, to be exact). One woman had such an experience, and boy did her partner serve it up! *"A lot of foreplay, kissing, talking and love-making, oral, vaginal and anal sex for three hours off and on. Wonderful!"* Don't leave out the fact that "It was with the man that I loved." The post-ecstasy reviews? *"I'm a complete woman (sexually) now. There is nothing that we can't openly discuss when it comes to sex and I feel this was one of the things that helped."* Now, why would the ability to openly discuss things bring so much to a sexual experience?

Well, first of all the guessing game is removed from the equation.

When you can ask for exactly what you want it increases the odds that you will get it (and get it good!). Furthermore, sharing—real, intimate sharing—brings people closer. Intimacy being a significant predictor of sexual satisfaction, *every* woman should be trying to get closer to her man.

If you doubt my words, further consider the woman who gave us the above recipe, *"I felt like he was the one that I could spend forever with. I feel that he has this mysterious way of making me feel sexual and sensuous."* Do you think after all that talking there were screams of passion? Yes! *"In fact, I reached orgasm quite a few times."*

One, two, three, four…
More, more, more, more!

Do you remember the post-menopausal woman who gave us a recipe that had been cooked up after more than a year of celibacy? If not, chew on this morsel to refresh your palate:

We lay awhile, just stroking and talking. We ended up having a long, intimate conversation about sex. We shared personal histories, laughed, and reassured each other that what we were doing now was fine. We kept stroking and asking each other, 'Do you like this?' 'How does this feel?' Pretty soon I was telling him that it felt really good and we were looking into each other's eyes… Each advance, we went slowly and checked in, always feeling and talking with our eyes and faces."

From words to looks, mouth to eyes, verbal to nonverbal this woman knew how to ask for what she wanted. The outcome?

It was the first time I'd gazed into my partner's eyes while making love and knowing that he cared how I felt and wouldn't go anywhere unless it felt good to me. That wordless communication marked the rest of our sexual life together. I felt reaffirmed, desirable, and respected and liked just for myself. I loved the communication.

Soulfood vs. Sushi

When you are in a relationship, the ability to communicate is such an essential ingredient, not only for sexual satisfaction, but also for relationship satisfaction. The ability to communicate effectively can cut down on the inevitable confusion and conflict inherent in a relationship. People have differences. No greater are the differences than those between a man and a woman; like the difference between sushi and soulfood. We have divergent ideas, feelings, wishes, dreams, perspectives, goals, intentions, preferences, interests, objectives. His and hers may or may not gel together, may not even be of the same substance. People are separate; we need space to be our individual selves, especially when we are sharing our lives.

I have learned a valuable lesson from the conflict in my marriage. After a conflict, I want to talk about it, kiss, make up and, yes, make love. At that same moment, my husband can't stand the sight of me. It took me a minute to figure out that he just wanted to be alone so that he could stew in it in his "cave." Sometimes the roles are reversed; he is ready and I'm still out to lunch. Sometimes it just depends on who is willing to be vulnerable first. Other times it takes awhile for things to cool off after they have become so heated.

Since conflict is inevitable, the best that a person can do is to figure out how to resolve it. Many people loathe conflict, and thus attempt to avoid it like salmonella. But, the longer you avoid conflict, the worse it gets. Might as well deal with it while it is still manageable, before it goes from gourmet to garbage.

It is tough to be angry all of the time and stay in love. It is like putting cooking oil and water together. It doesn't mix. While you should be able to stay connected when you are angry with the one you love, you might not be able to stay in the same house. Go for a ride, take a long walk, then come back and hug it out. Staying connected means keeping each other in heart and mind. And, for us women who want to talk it out, space after a conflict may seem like torture. Just think of it like going on a diet, but instead of being off carbs, you have to be off of your man while he gets into a space where he can become mindful of you again. And just like diets, it won't last forever; when it is over you get to reunite with all of your favorites, even Mr. Goodbar.

Simmer Down

It is important to understand that different levels of conflict call for different approaches. While there are some conflicts that need immediate attention, (e.g. when there is a decision to be made), there are others that require you both to step back, put it on the back burner to simmer. For those mild irritations and frustrations, I suggest using the butter-them-up technique: pour on kindness and make room for forgiveness. This helps loosen things up and resolve conflict. Everyone knows, butter makes everything better; though don't use it as a vaginal lubricant, you might find things slipperier than you want them to be.

If you let things get too hot, someone is sure to get burned. It is simple: the less fighting the better. This does not mean that you avoid conflict. But, there can be too much and, in some relationships, not enough. Couples that never fight are in just as much trouble as couples that fight all the time. Consider the difference between over-indulgence and starving. Too much fighting is like eating too much food. It will leave a heavy feeling in your heart. If you and your partner have trouble clearing off the table, you've got piles of dirty dishes. You might want to invest in a dishwasher. You may need a professional to help you get things clean.

You can't cook in a kitchen and not leave crumbs. If there are no crumbs then you are not cooking. For those of you who never fight, your relationship is missing a key ingredient—intimacy. Working on a problem together brings two people closer. For example, a compromise brings two people, who were at totally different ends, to a place in the middle: closer. If you are not talking about the hard stuff, then you are starving your relationship. Using words to express anger can give people the chance to learn something about each other. Anger is the signal that something is wrong; maybe you and your partner can use words to fix it. Ultimately, "problems can become opportunities when the right people come together" (South, n.d.).

Even when you argue, love should still be present. Don't leave it out. Like bread without yeast, your relationship will not rise. You may not be able to take your relationship to another level if anger and love are split from each other. They must be able to coexist. Anger can be just as important as love when it comes to developing intimacy. The ability to tolerate frustration, anger, disillusionment about the most cherished love object in our lives—that is what creates richness within a person. To know that both partners can honestly experience such upset while still holding in mind their loving feelings, well that creates richness within the relationship. If not, it is like having cabinets full of fine china that you never eat on. What a waste!

Communication, even when it is angry communication, should take into account a person's values. Have any idea what that sounds like? When my values are responsibility and hard work, and his values are respect and morality, then we will both take responsibility for the health/success of our relationship. We will work hard to respect each other, and stick by what is moral when it comes to marriage. We will choose our words carefully and earnestly. Within this atmosphere, I will be able to hear him and he will be able to hear me. We will listen with the intention of understanding, as opposed to defending ourselves.

Keep tweaking your recipe. As you grow older, things change. Change generally leads to conflicts—some great and some small. People mature and evolve as they experience life demands (adulthood and parenthood). We acquire and lose taste for things. What worked before may not fit right anymore. To adjust your recipe, you will need to talk with your partner and figure out together what suits your evolving palate.

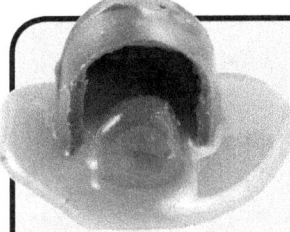

Snack on This

The Recipe for Coming Together

Combine equal parts:

    Communication

    Commitment

    Compassion

    Compromise

Mix in large quantities so your pantry never runs out.

Come together with this mix and you'll be cumming together in no time!

Chapter 12
From Caveman to Gourmet Chef: How We Evolve

Survival of the Fittest

Evolutionary theory tells us that humans evolved from earlier species. Our species continues to exist and evolve as a result of reproduction and natural selection, respectively. Natural selection is the process by which "individuals possessing characteristics advantageous for survival in a specific environment constitute an increasing proportion of their species in that environment with each succeeding generation" (The American Heritage Dictionary, p. 875). Thus, with the passage of time, society has a higher representation of genetically fit individuals. This is why faces and bodies look increasingly attractive through the generations.

Natural selection produces a phenomenon known as adaptation (Noonan, 1987). The structural, physiological, and behavioral characteristics of an organism, which contribute to its survival and reproduction, are considered to be a consequence of adaptation. Like cheese or wine, we get better with time.

As I mentioned earlier, parents pass things down from generation to generation. Recipes. Names. Genes. Behaviors. Traditions. Money. Property. Health. Disease. Genes are the most constant of these things. They are fixed. They are what allow for our continued existence.

The Pair-Bond

Evolutionary theory states that our main purpose, as a species, is to make babies. Because of this, so says the theory, women have necessarily developed adaptive strategies to ensure that the man they choose will devote his love and resources unselfishly to his partner and potential children. These adaptive strategies include requiring love, commitment, and sexual prowess from your man. These same adaptive strategies are also important in establishing and maintaining the "pleasure bond" and the pair-bond between a man and a woman.

The "pleasure bond" implies a "choice" to unselfishly devote one's self to the fulfillment of someone's emotional and physical needs. The choice is made because it gives one pleasure to fulfill in this way.

The pair-bond is a ubiquitous phenomenon, even if you are not consciously aware of it. It is the monogamous union of man and woman that supports raising a child. These are the bonds that facilitate sexual satisfaction and relationship satisfaction. At the most basic level, sex allows us to meet our needs for intimacy, pleasure and survival. It may seem obvious that reproduction and sexuality are connected. But, even more specifically, reproduction is linked to sexual responsiveness and satisfaction.

Regardless of the road taken to womanhood, there appears to be some common ground: a woman gives life and sustains life through nurturing others. We are mother, unlike any other. How we experience the mother-child relationship (the original pair-bond) sets the stage for romantic relationships.

Both psychoanalytic and evolutionary theories recognize the importance of reproduction in female sexuality. According to both theories, it is this predisposition that pushes a woman toward romantic relationships. Her goal is to find *him*, that special someone to call her own: "My husband." Evolution would dictate that women seek out physically attractive males, who are healthy, and preferably wealthy, to increase our reproductive success. Now you might say, "I am not thinking about getting married." But, the truth is, it is in our nature to seek intimacy and reproduce... to be bountiful, fruitful and multiply.

The search for a mate is driven by inborn survival instinct and is informed by the sociocultural setting. And, thus, adult women find themselves on something of a manhunt, guided by natural selection, their own pair-bond experiences, and knowledge of themselves. It is a search for a sexually attractive mate who makes you want to have his child, who makes you confident that he can provide and protect, who makes you feel more 'you' because of the way he loves you.

In monogamous species, the pair-bond involves specific acts directed toward confirming the relationship between a man and a woman. The pair-bond acts are all associated, ultimately, with reproduction: love, commitment, marriage, fathering of children, and allocation of resources. Of course, everyone who has sex is not interested in making babies. Sex is an activity that serves various functions. Sex is recreational. Sex is exercise. Sex bonds and unites. Sex is comforting. Sex passes time. Sex is fun. Sex is restorative. Morris (1967) notes that most sexually active people are not concerned with having children, but with solidifying the pair-bond through mutual reinforcement for their sexual partner.

Mutual reinforcement of the pair-bond goes a long way. There is an old colloquialism: A way to a man's heart is through his stomach. Eating certain foods does release chemicals in the brain that effect mood and feelings of pleasure. So, with good cooking you are warm, but if you go down a bit further you will turn up the temperature a notch. During sex there is an increase in the release of the neurotransmitter dopamine. Dopamine is responsible for feelings of pleasure, increased mental focus and alertness. Ostensibly, sexual pleasure motivates a man to make a commitment to you. Thus, the way to a man's heart might start in his pants.

Snack on This

Circle of Commitment

This idea is also captured by Masters and Johnson's *Circle of Commitment*: "Being together gives them satisfaction, including sex, that reinforces their decision to live together as a couple; these satisfactions, which are highly valued, must be safeguarded." "They live according to the commitment of mutual concern, and pleasure is the bond between them" (p. 254).

The pair-bond developed out of the days of hunting and gathering. A man who is a real beast knows how to track his prey, capture it, and do with it what he will. Hopefully, he will savagely devour her, so that she can taste the greatest pleasure. "The ability of the human female to experience orgasm comparable to the male enhances the reward value for both. It maximizes the utility of sexual behavior as a potent form of interpersonal bonding" (Hamburg, 1978, p. 163).

An orgasm is a powerful tool when it comes to solidifying the pair-bond. Eibl-Eibesfeldt (1975, p. 503) suggests that orgasm in the human female "increases her readiness to submit and, in addition, strengthens her emotional bond to the partner." If you are wondering how to keep your woman close, feed her lots of meat. Not just any kind of meat; make sure that it is well done. According to Masters and Johnson (1966) the "pleasure bond," depends on love, commitment, *and* sexual satisfaction. Therefore, a woman's desire for love, commitment, and orgasm guides her choice in a man. All three ingredients are key to the recipe for ecstasy.

Psychoanalytic Theory

The mystery of the "Dark Continent" has left many theorists wondering about the road to womanhood. Traditional psychoanalytic theory posits that female sexuality is initially phallocentric (male-oriented); that there is no awareness of the vagina until puberty. Thus the idea of penis envy—boys have something and I've got nothing. Well, if you mothers out there are doing your jobs, there is no way your daughter shouldn't be aware of her vagina until puberty. It should be amongst her first words.

Nonetheless, according to this theory, a female's penis envy serves as a catalyst in her psychosexual development, such that she is constantly trying to compensate for its absence by acquiring love (presumably the love of a man) and a child. Now, I don't know about you, but I like my part just fine. I love being a woman, from the kitchen to the bedroom.

In addition, psychoanalytic theory also emphasizes the primary role of the mother-child relationship in the development of female sexuality. One line of thought states that the relationship is based on anger, frustration, and disappointment, which precipitate a change in love-object from the mother to the father. As a result, the girls' focus shifts from mother to father. It first manifests as a wish to possess father (the Electra complex) and later shifts to finding someone like father. Here, the female is attempting to compensate for an insufficient love-object (mother). Thus, our psychosexual development is rooted in conflict.

Other psychoanalytic theorists contend that female sexual development is just that, inherently female in nature. They suggest that to be born female is to possess a vagina and the ability to bear children. This reality leads to conflict-free identifications with mother and the maternal image. Some also contend that there is a libidinal (loving) relationship with the father from birth, which is unique and that develops independent of the relationship with the mother.

There is enough evidence in the literature to suggest that, both, the theory of primary femininity and the concept of penis envy play vital roles in female sexuality (Freud, 1931a; Galenson, 1976; Stoller, 1976; Toronto, 1991). Both lines of thought agree: during puberty a female reworks infantile conflicts, identifies with aspects of both parents, and that directs these identifications towards finding non-incestuous love-objects (i.e., her own man).

Narcissistic Confirmation

A woman's value should be—no *needs* to be—consciously integrated as a part of the feminine ideal. Mom, that is your job. The development of positive self-esteem is related to early relationships; intimate loving relationships with parental figures should result in what psychologists call narcissistic confirmation (self validation).

Adequate support and reinforcement are needed during all phases of development. Picture an infant's first word or first step— all of the fear and anxiety that may accompany this experience, first attempts at separate self from mother. Keep this in mind as you picture adolescent recalcitrance and rebellion against parental guidelines and expectations. What is the common thread?

These behaviors are all directed at defining one's self, physically, emotionally, and sexually. They are not only directed at clarifying definition, but they are also aimed at discovery, the discovery of how to get one's needs fulfilled (with speech, movement, independent thinking). When separation and individuation have gone well as revisited throughout childhood and adolescence, the result is a narcissistically confirmed adult. (The opposite is an adult who does not know himself or herself, cannot think or act freely). The narcissistically confirmed female can enter any relationship and get her needs met. She will know who she is and what she wants; she will command these things with her words, her actions, and her presence.

In adulthood, according to psychoanalytic theory, a woman seeks narcissistic confirmation through securing a man partner with whom she can make babies. To assist in the solidification of narcissistic confirmation, this man supports the female's sense of self by making her feel loved and valued. By engendering these feelings, he then reinforces her positive self-regard. It is hard to differentiate between persons' perception of themselves (self-regard), and how they feel because of their partner's efforts (engendered feelings). Whatever the origin, it is important that these positive feelings are present.

Engendered Feelings: A Woman's Worth

It has been a long-standing belief that "women are the emotional ones." As a result of the ubiquitous gender role expectations imposed by society, women are expected to bring about feelings of warmth and love. I label this *engendered feelings*, which is to bring an emotional condition into existence or to produce an emotional condition. This ingredient did not show up in significant portions for any group of women. However, the engendered feelings are closely connected to positive self-regard, which was identified by all the surveyed women as an important ingredient to sexual satisfaction. While it is a woman's job to know her worth, her man can definitely support it by the way he makes her feel.

An example of a positive self-regard that might be rooted in feelings engendered by her partner is: *"I felt sexy, loved, wanted, excited, young, [and] energized."* Whether sourced solely by her self-esteem or by self-esteem that was boosted by investment from her partner, the result is the same: she is now in the mood for love. These women are saying, "Make me feel good and I will respond to you. Do for me and I will do for you. Kiss me here, kiss me there. Enjoy my body, enjoy me. Know my body because of how it makes you feel. Know wants, my desires and me. Indulge me. Make me feel loved and desired, and I will do the same for you."

So what feelings did he spark? I hope you brought your appetite, because here comes a mouth full:

intense intimacy, relaxed, content, tired, loved, loving, romance, connectedness, trust, well-being, excitement, fun, youthful, free, adventurous, tender, erotic, sexy, wanted, young, energized, attraction, gratification, amazed, turned on, happy, wonderful, safe, peaceful, beautiful, assertive, alive, giving, feminine, energized, together, nasty, without jealously or guilt, playful, needed, sad, kinky, overwhelmed and aroused.

More than anything a woman wants to be cherished; why shouldn't she be? She is the giver of life. What tops that? Psychoanalytic theory asserts that women are envious because we don't have dicks. Please, there is nothing more powerful than the woman. She may not know that, because of socialization to the contrary. Historically, women have not been held in esteem. She has been made to believe that she is inferior. She had to fight for the right to vote, she makes less money in the same jobs, and she is sexualized for the pleasures of man. Inferiority is something created by people who want power; if they can make you feel small then they get to feel bigger. Women need to stop falling for this trick—we are beautiful, powerful, and subordinate to no one. Pussy rules the world!

If you are being treated right, it should be all five star treatment. Five star restaurants. Five star dick. If he's not giving you five star loving, go back to the menu and find another dish. What is five star treatment? Listen to this married woman's description: *"[He] made me feel wonderful, wanted and 'together' with him."*

I think Mary Ann F. Jackson, hit the spot when she wrote "look @ me":

Look @ me
My smile is intriguing
My eyes are enticing
My walk is alluring
Unless you're blind
you'll want me because
I have my act together
I have my feet well planted
& I have my attitude in check
I'm known for treating my man well.
Chase me
For I'm priceless
and not easy to obtain
I don't go to just anyone
Once you catch me
love me right
For I have no qualm with walking away

Others lay @ my feet
waiting for me to begin my step
So be careful
Treat me like a queen
For my personality & style is one of royalty
So look @ me
For truly seeing me leads to loving me
& then you're hooked.

Sense and Sensuality

How do you know if you have found yourself a man who will commit his love, time, and resources? A true "boss," a real "big daddy," "a soldier up in here," or, as my husband refers to himself "a beast?" The responsible, dependable, man that you can trust. Take a look at your man and tell me what you see. Is he a mover and a shaker, you know, a real decision maker? The kind of man who not only can say to his woman, "Sit down and shut the fuck up. Let me handle this," but his words turn you on instead of pissing you off. You know he is going to do what he says; things will be taken care of. He is the kind of man who builds a woman's confidence in him, and provides her with the security that all women crave.

Of course a man's appeal goes far beyond his physical attractiveness. Let's start there anyway. In part, physically attractive means healthy. We are able to pick up signs of health through our senses: the eyes, ears, and nose. Certain physical characteristics are indicative of sex appeal and health. For example, a sexy face, a muscular body, and a masculine voice are indicative of the amounts of testosterone present at puberty. He not only looks good in his jeans, but he also has good genes. Puberty sets the stage for manhood. It is where the development of that man you have been searching for begins. The one with the nice round, tight ass; those kissable biceps; that deep voice, that big back and those broad shoulders; his hairy chest (not too hairy, I said hairy not scary)… but I digress. Pick the ingredients that you want; Mr. Right can be made to order just for you.

Remember to use those senses. The nose knows pheromones. Science has shown that there is a connection between our aromas and our immune system. Because no two people smell alike, the nose may give us information regarding a man's health.

Odor affects us on a subconscious level, giving us primitive information about the person to whom we find ourselves attracted (Oberzaucher& Grammer, 2010). This is likely the science behind fragrance. There is nothing like a man who looks good and smells good too. It tells us not only that he takes the time to make himself attractive and desirable, but that he could also have the biological ingredients of a good father.

Be sure to also use your mouth and ears to help you pick Mr. Right. These senses aid the conscious mind in decision-making. Ask questions about health, wealth, and whatever else comes to mind. When you are listening to his answers, don't just listen to his words, pay attention to the sound of his voice, as it, too, may hold important information regarding his health. That deep voice tells you he is all man, and when it comes to testosterone he's got it good 'n plenty. If his kisses of passion really make you wet, it could be the taste of testosterone in his saliva that serves as an aphrodisiac.

There are tell-tale signs of a man's success. Check his swagger, fancy car, big house, and his bling. If he ain't frontin', then these are sure signs of his success and resources. No, he does not have to be paid, but he needs to be able to handle his business. And if he can, you will know it. It will be in his walk, it will be in his talk. He will strut his stuff like the proud peacock, who say's "look at me" when he displays his beautiful feathers. Or like a lion, proudly exhibiting his full mane and his big "ROAR!" He will be comfortable in the role of a leader, but will know when it is time to work in tandem, as a couple. He will have a "big ego". He will be a Big Mac with cheese!

Your man might be a heavy hitter with deep pockets or a true boss, like Sonny Corinthos on General Hospital. He will put it to you, like Sonny did Claudia, when he said, "you get to flaunt your position of power to anyone who matters on my arm on my team, with your big ass ring." He could be the man in charge, with you happy to ride shotgun, as he bounces in his ride. You know, like Bonnie and Clyde. A man's ride is a sure sign of who he is. If it's a long sleek caddy, then he is sure to be big daddy.

Check out how I maxed out. I told you earlier that I wanted a handsome man. He had to be fine. This is a sign of a person's health. Ain't nothing like a six-pack to go along with that lean meat. I was not only concerned about physical attractiveness; I wanted him to be smart and successful. I almost overlooked my husband. My husband is a very attractive man, but when I met him, he was working as a personal trainer at the gym I attended. Personal trainer did not fit the bill. I wanted a professional man.

One day I over heard him with one of his clients. He was articulate and his vocabulary had some depth. That got me curious. I asked a few subtle questions, only to discover that he was a teacher who was working on his Master's degree. Personal training was a second job that he used to supplement his income. You know his hustle.

I knew just by looking and listening that he was attractive, intelligent, educated, physically fit, and hardworking. He would be mine. I had been a member at that gym for years. It never even crossed my mine to hire a personal trainer. But, I felt like he could really whip me into shape. And that's just what he did. I employed the right strategy. I looked at his label really good and discovered he had my recommended daily intake.

Sexual Prowess

Like I said, a woman can detect health, strength, intellect, and financial stability just by looking. Sexual prowess, however, is another story all together. It's complicated because it involves fertility, pleasure, planning, and the ability to integrate these things into a meaningful whole.

Baker (1996) writes that a woman uses a man's approach to foreplay and intercourse to gain information about him. A man's ability to stimulate a woman to orgasm, per Baker, suggests that he has past experience with other women who have found him attractive enough to bed. More importantly, his ability to assist in the achievement of orgasm serves a role in reproductive success. When a woman has an orgasm during intercourse it assists with sperm retention, which increases the probability that an egg will be fertilized. According to Baker (1996) this is achieved via the three following mechanisms:

(1) When a woman climaxes, her cervix "gapes." This gaping stretches the cervical mucous sideways, opening up more mucous channels for more sperm.

(2) The cervix "dips" into the seminal pool. This dipping action of the cervix mixes the seminal pool, which helps more sperm contact and penetrate the cervical mucous.

(3) This influx of sperm into the cervical mucous channels helps to neutralize acidity, making it easier for sperm

transport. It also increases the volume of semen in contact with the mucous, which also facilitates sperm transport.

Baker states that this combined gaping, dipping, and sucking of the cervix during an intercourse orgasm permits a woman to hold on to more sperm than during intercourse without orgasm.

Unfortunately, many women don't have the pleasure of orgasm. I wonder if she would work harder if she knew the role it played in reproduction? And even more importantly, would he?

A Woman's Work

A man's resources are important because from the j-u-m-p woman risk more and have more to lose. Trivers (1972) writes, the sex that invests most in offspring should be selected to exercise discretion and discrimination while choosing a mate (i.e., the female). Buss (1989) writes: "male sex cells are small compared to female sex cells, and indeed, this size difference defines which organism is male and which is female." Thus, from the moment of conception, females invest more in their children because they provide the majority of nutrients for early development. Additionally, men produce 3 million sperm a day, and women are born with all of the eggs that she will ever have. Waste not, want not! Once men start to release sperm, they can do it daily for years to come. But for us women, there is one shot every month, that magic 24-hour window when the egg is released from the ovary (ovulation). Once her biological clock starts ticking, it is just a matter of time before the kitchen timer rings, "times up!" (menopause). Fertilization and gestation usually occur internally within females, as does lactation, and this compounds the male-female investment differences. The only way to compensate for this imbalance is to secure a mate who will consistently provide parental investment in the children.

This means finding a man who is willing to put in work. He should be chompin' at the bit to serve you. Make him work for it by being kind. Make him work for it literally. J-O-B. I can't, for the life of me, understand, a woman who wants a man with no job. I know there are extenuating circumstances, like getting laid off, that may affect a man's employment. But truth be told, a man has no business stepping to a woman if he is unemployed. He should have other priorities, like eating.

Snack on This

Timing is Everything

Don't race against the biological clock when making a decision about having a baby. While a woman's age is an important factor, many other things should be considered such as the man's fitness as a father, a woman's readiness to transition into motherhood, and the stability and potential longevity of the relationship.

Once the bun is in the oven, the list of things that a mother provides is never ending. I know that for some women, pregnancy is this wonderful life altering experience. Well in my case it was life altering to be sure, wonderful, not so much. The morning to night sickness, headaches, constipation, fatigue, mood swings, vaginal odor, insatiable hunger, loss of eyelashes, feet growth, insomnia, anxiety, water retention, pain, and weight gain (that is accompanied by stretch marks to show how you have grown). The changes that your body under goes are remarkable. For some, no many, if not all, loose that body that they have become oh so at home with. It changes to something you barely recognize. What an investment. Even for those mothers out there who love pregnancy, there comes a time when she is done. Stick a fork in her, and take that bun out of the oven.

The bread has been baked, but she isn't really done, is she? There is the labor; they call it work for a reason. Once the baby arrives then the fun can really begin. There will be all sorts of fun treats: sleepless nights, crying, frequent diaper changes, that are a result of frequent feedings (bottle, breast, or both), day night confusion, colic, and diaper rash just to name a few. Please don't get me wrong. Children truly are a miracle, but they are a lot of work. And the majority of this work, traditionally, falls to mommy. The list goes on, but I think you get my point.

It is this parental investment that makes the woman so valuable in the eyes of men, but it's also what makes her vulnerable in the hands of man. Trivers (1972) defines parental investment as the "behavior of a parent toward its offspring that increases the chances of that offspring's survival (and hence reproductive success) at the cost of the parent's investment in other offspring" (p. 139). Women are looking for men who are willing to make the same type of investment. Women should thus be looking for men who won't just hit it and quit it, but men who know how to stick with it. Even after she has popped that bun out of the oven, and her body has turned into something he can't quite recognize. It takes the love of a real man, a real good man to look at her and still see her worth and still find her desirable.

If you want to become a gourmet chef you have to evolve. While our basic instincts (sex and aggression) are paramount, it is important to use the information in your conscious awareness to aid in selecting good ingredients. Don't stop at what you see; go beyond the surface and look at what's underneath. Once the right partner has been identified, together you can create a masterpiece.

Chapter 13
Hunting and Gathering:
The Recipe for Mate Selection

Good love is all about choice. As a result of a woman's ubiquitous and inherently large investment in her children, she has earned the right to pick and choose. So, ladies take your time when you are out there hunting and gathering information. Find a man who will work to get you and, once he has you, who will love you and commit to you. "The nurture that females bestow becomes a resource for which males compete. The male who wins the right to inseminate a female also wins for his progeny a share of the female's parental investment" (Daley & Wilson, 1983, p. 90). The idea that individuals of one sex (usually males) compete for mating opportunities or that individuals of one sex (usually females) choose mating partners, defines Darwin's theory of sexual selection (p. 93).

Although evolutionary theory does not directly address sexual satisfaction, Buss (1994) contends that "love" plays a central role in partner selection. He believes that women have developed psychological mechanisms that prevent them from indiscriminately choosing sexual partners. "Requiring love, sincerity, and kindness is a way of securing a commitment of resources commensurate with the value of the resource that women give to men" (p .45).

Since men are unable to bear children, women are an invaluable resource, essential to reproductive success. Requiring love for a child may be considered an even exchange. "Love may be the ultimate ruse in the reproductive game, the grandest trick of all for ensuring that humans produce babies" (Batten, 1992, p. 159). Masters and Johnson (1996) agree: "A wish to take care of someone for whom one cares creates an overpowering sense of involvement and identification, of oneness. Some people call it love and it is the original source of commitment" (p. 252).

According to this theory, women have developed adaptive strategies to secure a good man; that is a loving male who will commit his resources (genes, love, time, money, energy, knowledge etc.). In many species, offspring who have the parental investment/commitment of both the mother and father have a greater chance of survival and reproductive fitness. This is especially true for humans. Of all the primates, humans are the most helpless and vulnerable. We enter this world with an underdeveloped body and brain. It takes time for us to mature to a place where we are able to be responsible for ourselves. According to the lawmakers, it takes eighteen years— even then some of us are not ready.

Keeping all of this in mind, most women will agree that part of how they gauge the capacity for longevity in a relationship is picturing in their minds if they would consider having a child with this partner. I used this question in my study and found it to be most helpful. Indeed, there is an association between sexual ecstasy and relationship satisfaction. Likewise, supporting psychological theory, there seems to be a reciprocal relationship that a man's capacity to love and invest in a woman is reflective of his capacity to love and invest in a child, and vice versa. Consciously noticing this can help women make mindful choices about their mates, thereby increasing the odds of long-term satisfaction.

From the Kitchen of: All Women

The Ingredients for Mate Selection

Love	13%
Nature of Relationship: Committed	23%
Fitness as a Father	24%
Parental Status	26%

recipe card #6

In my study, women were asked if they had considered having children with the partner identified in their most sexually satisfying experience. Sixty percent of the women reported that they *did* consider having children with the identified partner. This tells us something about women. A man that takes the time to please his woman gives her hope. He makes her feel like sharing what evolution theorists consider her most valuable resource: the ability to reproduce.

Love & Commitment

When asked if they had considered having children with the partner identified in their most sexually satisfying experience, it is clear that these women were looking for love. One woman stated:

I felt like I was always looking for someone who would, both, be a fabulous, loving husband and father. He was very handsome, which was what first attracted me, then I could tell he was kind and loving. I saw him play with kids early on and knew he was great with them.

Another woman wrote, *"Yes. I love my partner and feel he would be a great father."* Yet another responded, *"Yes. He was the type of man that had been raised right."* What constitutes being raised right? I believe it is with love and work. *"You know the apple doesn't fall far from the tree."* She is right about that. Ladies, choose carefully, as your choice will be reflected in your child/ren. Be careful who you reproduce with!

According to evolutionary theory, being raised right means having the resources and support of two loving parents, because this is what improves a child's chances of growing into a healthy loving adult. The fruit of our loins, love, and labor don't fall from their tree. We are reflected in our children. Although you may not be consciously aware of it, the nature and nurture we each received direct our choices every day.

Love is an important ingredient when choosing a man, and even more so when it comes to parenting. It is the love that is first shown to us by our parents that affects our ability to give and receive love as adults. That is how we see them love each other and how we feel loved by them. In each case, love is such a powerful ingredient. Children need an endless supply of it. The best indicator of a man's capacity to love his children is how he loves you. Note that I said *capacity.* Just because you have the ingredients for a dish doesn't mean it will turn out as planned, though it sure increases the odds.

People have said for years that love is a crazy thing, it makes you do crazy things, you may feel crazy, or you may simply be "crazy in love." Believe me when I tell you this: making babies with someone who does *not* love you is just plain crazy. Requiring love and commitment are ways of maximizing the probability that one's sexual partner will unselfishly devote his talents to the fulfillment of sexual desire, including the attainment of orgasm. Buss (1994) states that love is one of the most important cues to commitment. And for him, "Commitment entails a channeling of time, energy and effort to the partner's needs at the expense of fulfilling one's own personal goals" (p. 43). For Masters and Johnson (1994) "to *make* an emotional commitment to someone is to be on his or her side, a steadfast ally; it is essentially an expression of loyalty. (p. 257)" "Commitments involve obligations and responsibilities but they are obligations that have been voluntarily chosen" (Masters & Johnson, p. 257).

One of the responsibilities and obligations in a romantic relationship between a man and a woman is physical in nature. It involves providing sexual pleasure, and more importantly, sexual satisfaction. Work!

> Becoming committed to someone is, by definition, to entrust one's physical and emotional well being to that person; it is an act of faith and acceptance of vulnerability. This is the opposite side of the coin of commitment. If for example, a woman has had sufficient evidence that a man has made a commitment to her, that she can trust him to be concerned about her welfare and to be there when she needs him, she will then, no matter how slowly, allow herself to become committed to him— that is, to become openly, emotionally vulnerable and sexually responsive. (Masters & Johnson, 1974, p. 257).

In a perfect world love and commitment would ensure sexual satisfaction. However, this is not the case, or is it? Not for this next woman.

Securing love and commitment were not enough to seal the deal. She responded,

I considered it due to my age and the level of love and commitment

I was comfortable that he could give. I decided not because I want my children to be able to receive educational help from my husband, and his education was minimum.

While love and commitment are scrumptiously delicious when put in the same recipe, there are some other ingredients that may need to be considered.

Nature of the Relationship

Nature of the relationship, for example, was identified by each group of women as a key ingredient to sexual satisfaction. It was also identified as part of the equation when considering a man as a potential father. Most of the relationships were characterized by love and/or commitment. Of course the type of commitment varied by group, but for all of the women it was necessary when considering baby-making. One woman simply wrote: *"Yes"* he could be her baby's daddy. *"I feel the child would be conceived out of love, not lust."* A strong foundation.

The marital unit is, without question, the foundation for the family. Thus, the nature of the relationship between the man and woman is the scaffolding for the atmosphere provided to the children. If it is a loving relationship—full of laughter, affection, compromise, adoration, honesty, appreciation, friendship, intimacy and acceptance—then the conditions are perfect for raising children. If there is drama, complaining, distance, contempt, infidelity, and conflict—well then you might want to rethink your plan. No, I am not saying that things need to be perfect; but they should be good.

Just like our appetites, relationships go through cycles. When you are committed to someone for life, you expect peaks, valleys, and plateaus. These can be managed while still holding onto the core goodness (the laughter, affection, compromise, adoration, honesty, appreciation, friendship, intimacy and acceptance) of the relationship.

Consider the cycles: ideal phases, real phases, conflictual phases, recovery phases, and phases of growth. People fall in love (ideal), they get to know, really know each other (real), they fight (conflict), they make up (recover), and they move on (growth). The relationship cannot always be in a happy phase; it cannot stay static. In a meaningful, successful relationship there is constant movement. Not by leaps and bounds, just movement. We get busy.

There is distance at times, closeness at others. The important thing is that you always get back to that space that is unique to you as a couple. What is the space in your marriage? There is a distinct feel to it. I know it when I am there with my husband. I also know when I am not.

When I fight with my husband I miss him. I want to make up so we can be close. I miss that space. There is too much space between us. This is where someone can edge in where they don't belong—the lying and cheating begins. Unlike some women, I am not so worried about the world coming between us. We will not allow that much space for too long. Nothing will come between us because we are that close. We live in this world; when we need to get away from it, we turn to each other. Intimacy: you and me. You in me. Hear him say, "I have one great love and it is you. It grew and grew until it could not grow any more. Until death do us part."

Does your relationship have fusion? A bond so tight and so strong that it cannot be broken. A fused relationship can weather the tide of rocky moments that are inevitable over the course of time. Commitment.

Fitness as a Father

Another ingredient that proved to be irreplaceable when using the prospect of fatherhood as a gauge for relationship satisfaction was a man's actual fitness as a potential father. Twenty-four percent of the sample referred to the partner's *fitness as a father,* when responding to the aforementioned question. There are many things that make a man fit to be a father. Some women consider a man's stability. That is, does he have a j-o-b? Own a home and a ride? Pay his bills on time? Other women want to know about the lessons he will teach. Will he be gentle and loving or harsh and critical?

Trivers (1972) suggests that the males who are most valuable to species survival possess some of the following characteristics: ability to fertilize eggs (e.g., sexual competence); quality of genes, including survival and reproductive potential; and quality and quantity of parent care—the willingness and ability of the person to invest resources in offspring (which may be partly heritable). In humans, these valued resources also include time, money, knowledge, and guidance. To "invest" implies that the male is willing to commit himself and his resources for an extended period of time.

Other resources that were acknowledged by the women in this study were their partner's level of education and other personal attributes such as gentleness, kindness, morality and ambition. It is important to highlight the availability of resources when choosing the right man. A man cannot give what he does not possess. A man who has numerous baby mamas has additional obligations, such as child support. If there was a previous marriage, his resources may be further compromised by alimony. I don't know about you, but the thought of my man footin' the bill for another woman makes my stomach turn. And for you single ladies out there this might be something you want to know before you get in too deep, because these obligations will reduce his cheese, and may affect your decision while you are out shopping. Girls you need to choose carefully when you are out there searching the meat department. Make sure you don't just grab any package of the shelf. You want prime rib, Angus beef, Grade A… the choice selection.

Snack on This

Read the Label

One of my male clients hipped me to something about a man's ambition. All men have something that they invest a lot of time and energy in. He said "every man has an "it" ": sports, cars, breasts, ass, golf, stocks, gambling, hanging, video games, etc... When it hit my ears I knew I had heard something. His "it", my interpretation: his passion. Many things, one of which is testosterone, drive passion. Men have this in abundance that is until age 35 when the level of testosterone starts to dip. Male menopause might be a factor if things are no longer piping hot in the bedroom. It leads to erectile dysfunction, low sex-drive, moodiness, lack of motivation. Any of this sound familiar? While a woman may be entering her sexual prime during her mid-life, her man might be slowing down. His attention and ambition may have begun to shift from her to his "it", which might not require so much effort. If you don't want your woman going out for lunch, you should rethink what you are serving up.

One of the women who did consider making babies with the man who satisfied her sexual appetite responded simply: *"Yes. He is the kind of man I would choose to father my children."* What kind of man do you want to father your children? Some women mentioned specific attributes that they felt would contribute to the partner's fitness as a father. The same woman wrote this about her man, *"He is gentle, kind, easy-going, not physically aggressive, moral and decent."* Another woman wrote, *"He would make a good father. He is caring, loving, and gentle."* These all sound like great qualities to me. I'll take one of those, to go.

Women who did not consider reproducing with the sexually satisfying partner also highlighted similar elements that fall under N.O.R. and poor fitness as father. For example, in the ideal phase of a relationship, one woman noted:

"For a quick minute in the beginning of the relationship. He was a kind man, but he thoroughly enjoyed being with different types of women. That was the downfall."

Translation: she could not get him to commit. And, to add insult to injury, the odds that he would become someone else's baby's daddy increase as his involvement with other women increases. Monogamy, although important amongst humans, is a rare concept for other mammalians. Monogamy is especially important to women because of the great demands required to raise physically and emotionally healthy babies. It is the combination of the love and work of a man and woman that increases a child's potential to grow into a productive member of society. So, mama seeks to find a man she can call "all mine." Mamma's baby, papa's maybe; that leaves a woman to raise a child alone. If papa is a rolling stone, the net outcome is fewer resources and more problems.

Parental Status

When men have children outside of the marital unit their resources (physical, emotional, and financial) get divided amongst the children. The slices of that pie get smaller and smaller. Not to mention the baby mama drama.

That's why one woman decided against considering the man in her peak sexual experience as a husband. She responded, *"No. He has nine children already."* No? Hell no! Women should run, not walk, the other way when they see this man coming. If he is being a half-decent father, then he has no money or time for someone additional. If he has money and time for you, you've got to wonder if he gives any of himself to his kids (each of the nine of them, mind you). Unless he is independently wealthy, a man with nine children is spread thin. And, who knows how many baby mamas are in the mix?!? If you ask me, he is just irresponsible. Today it is rare for a family to plan to have nine children. It is a hardship to do so.

Having many children does not ensure physical or financial survival as it did long ago. Nowadays, to have a big family means planning ahead and being resourceful. You must know how to hunt and gather if you are to be successful. Arranging and paying for education, alone, is just so costly. The parents providing this are buoyed by their relationship with each other. Doing so alone or in a high conflict atmosphere—well, while not impossible, it feels so. It is a tough road. A man who inflicts this upon his children's mother— well, he is not someone you want to be dating seriously. Ask yourself if you can honestly collude with a structure that is causing others to suffer.

Snack on This

Baby Mama Drama

Baby mama drama is real. And it must be considered when deciding whether or not this person is right for you. Ain't nothing like having your husband's ex-wife (someone he used to love and who he made a baby with) calling yo' crib, talking knowingly to yo' man. Maybe it is all the niceties that pass between them as they try to remain civil (for the kids sake, of course) or maybe it is the cussin' and fussin'. Whatever the flavor, it has a bad after taste that lingers... and lingers.

To make things even worse, sometimes you have to talk to her yourself, when all you really want to do is pretend that she doesn't exist. Like that extra 10-15 pounds that you just can't shake.

Or better still, how about the one he didn't marry? Just popped the bun in the oven and didn't bother staying for dinner. The bitter baby mama, you know, the one that likes to clown; she's always up for a good food fight. Throwing insults around and spittin' mad drama. If this doesn't sound like it is right for you, you just might need to reconsider your selection. Go back to the menu and start again. Here's a hint—find a man who does not already have mouths to feed.

A man who is willing to support the mother's efforts at nurturing their children also benefits. By helping them to develop into responsible adults, one day mom and dad can be in the back seat. It will be someone else's turn to cook, do the dishes, clean the house, wash the laundry. I can't wait until my children learn the system and figure out their role in our interdependent family structure. Grow them up and get them off my bankroll. Until then, it is love and work.

Part 5
Understanding What Tastes Good, Bad, Exotic

Chapter 14
The Mixing Bowl

Snack on This

A Little Brainteaser

After reading about these groups of women:

- Who do you think reported being the most sexually satisfied?
- What ingredient appears to be the most important for sexual satisfaction?

I conducted my research and began writing this book when I was single and child-free. I used psychoanalytic and evolutionary theories to shape my hypotheses regarding the outcome of the study. I hypothesized that married women with children would be the most sexually satisfied. I really thought that. Since both theories rely on the importance of woman as mother and her desire to secure a proper mate, I figured a woman who has been successful at both would be the most satisfied. Therefore I hypothesized:

(1) Married women would exhibit higher sexual satisfaction than single women.

(2) Being in the developmental phase of motherhood would interact with marital status in predicting sexual satisfaction; i.e. that having a child will increase sexual satisfaction in married women and decrease sexual

satisfaction in single women.

Additionally, I believed that differences among the marital and parental groups in commitment, emotional, intimacy and orgasm responsiveness would account for group differences in sexual satisfaction. Therefore I hypothesized:

(3) There would be notable differences between married versus not married and between parenting versus not parenting women in regard to their rankings of commitment and emotional intimacy, as well as in regard to their orgasm responsiveness.

(4) These three constructs (commitment, intimacy, orgasmic response) would predict sexual satisfaction, with emotional intimacy being the best predictor of sexual satisfaction.

When the data was collected, coded, and analyzed, the results were a mixed bag. While some findings were supported others were not. Now that I am married and have children of my own, the findings take on a totally different meaning.

Table 2. Mean Scores for all Measures as Mediated by Marital & Parenting Status				
	Single		Married	
	Child Free n=26	Mothering n=27	Child Free N=26	Mothering n=26
Sternberg Scale: Intimacy **	7.00	6.70	8.30	7.71
Sternberg Scale: Commitment **	6.23	6.10	8.38	8.14
Sternberg Scale: Passion	6.44	6.10	7.43	6.35
Orgasm Responsiveness Questionnaire	19.60	18.80	20.35	19.15
Index of Sexual Satisfaction (ISS) **	20.15	18.60	16.62	30.31

Note: ** = statistically significant at p<.05. ISS is an inverted scale, meaning that a high score indicates lower sexual satisfaction. Based upon statistical analysis, marital status has significant effect on intimacy scores. Higher commitment scores are due to an interaction effect of parental status and marital status.

In summary, as a whole, the married group had the highest scores on measures of intimacy, commitment, and passion. Additionally, this group reported the highest level of sexual satisfaction, as indicated by fewer areas of dissatisfaction identified on the ISS. To my disappointment and dismay, the married group's scores on all the aforementioned measures declined once children where added to the mix. There was an interaction between sexual satisfaction and parental status, but it was different from what I had hypothesized. Being a mother *decreased* sexual satisfaction in married women and *increased* sexual satisfaction amongst the single women. These findings will be discussed in Chapter 16.

The married group's scores on the Orgasm Responsiveness Questionnaire were only slightly higher than the single group's (M=19.75 vs. M=19.2), with the highest scores generated by the married and child-free group. The most significant differences in orgasm responsiveness were identified when coding the narratives; this finding will be discussed in more detail later. As hypothesized, intimacy, commitment, and orgasm responsiveness do predict sexual satisfaction, with intimacy being the strongest predictor.

In the Pantry of the Top Chefs

When it comes to sexual satisfaction, married women take the cake, but that is *without* children in the mix. This group also has the highest level of intimacy, commitment, and passion in their relationships (just as I predicted). According to Sternberg, the combination of these three ingredients is love. He calls it the Triangular Theory of Love. I call it The Recipe for Love.

Let us first consider intimacy and commitment, which have been identified as two essential aspects of relationship satisfaction by other researchers, as well (Ferguson, 1993; Stock, 1985). Passion, which has remarkable meaning for the married woman, will be put aside for a moment; it will be discussed in the next section.

Researchers have found a clear association between relationship satisfaction and sexual satisfaction (Fields, 1983; Kaplan, 1974; Maison, 1981; Parkinson, 1987). Given both married groups' higher levels of emotional intimacy and commitment as found in my study, research (Katz, 1993; Moret, 1995) would predict higher levels of sexual satisfaction for this group as a whole.

Of course I am talking about the ideal circumstances here. I know there are married couples that are not committed or close. However, for those of you who got it right, you get to have your cake and eat it too. After all, isn't that the purpose? Why waste time putting together a delicious treat, if you don't get to eat it?

When closely studied, the group differences (single versus married) in the degree of commitment and emotional intimacy were attributed to the nature and length of the relationship. In contrast to the single group, 54% of childless married women would consider becoming mothers with their most sexually satisfying partners. These women identified the nature of the relationship as an integral aspect of their most sexually satisfying experience.

The nature of a married relationship inherently means that one has an available partner who has committed to the other and to the preservation of their life together. Included in this commitment is his willingness to satisfy his wife physically, emotionally, and sexually. Without any crumb snatchers around, they can totally focus on meeting each other's needs.

In their most sexually satisfying experiences, on average, the married women had been involved with their partners for 10.75 years, while the single women were involved with their partners for 3.56 years. More time cooking together means more time to perfect their technique.

In revisiting the respective groups' recipes for sexual satisfaction, married women without children identify the same top three ingredients as married women with children: mood, nature of the relationship, and setting (See Recipe Card 7a and 7b). The married woman wants her man's focus to be on getting her in the mood, while making her feel safe and loved. The married woman wants to feel safe enough not only to ask for what she wants physically and emotionally, but also to show her husband through her own initiations. Given this opportunity she may ask to do something risqué like having sex outside. Audience potential was identified as an important aspect of setting for this group, suggesting the desire for freedom of self-expression and acceptance. She wants to do it where she wants and how she wants.

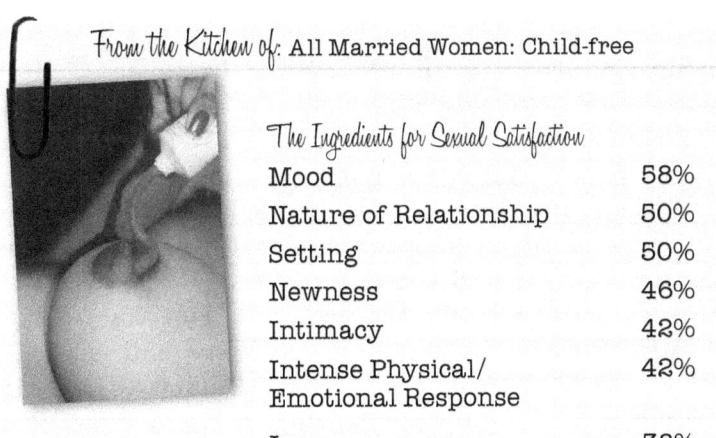

From the Kitchen of: All Married Women: Child-free

The Ingredients for Sexual Satisfaction

Mood	58%
Nature of Relationship	50%
Setting	50%
Newness	46%
Intimacy	42%
Intense Physical/ Emotional Response	42%
Love	38%

recipe card #7a

From the Kitchen of: All Married Women: Mothering

The Ingredients for Sexual Satisfaction

Mood	77%
Nature of Relationship	46%
Setting	46%
Variation in the Sex Act	42%
Newness	38%
Arousal	35%

recipe card #7b

A good man will keep his woman well fed. He needs to have stamina and ambition to satisfy her appetite. A man's ability to create a safe mood and make love to his wife to satiation is a rare treat. She will long for nothing. When she asks, she shall receive. Sometimes, her cup shall runneth over. There is nothing like starting at full and fucking 'til empty. You have nothing left to give and want nothing in return. I am talking about the type of sexual pleasure that extends over and above average, pleasure that rocks you to sleep at night. According to Freud (1905b), *"What holds good all through life, [is] that sexual satisfaction is the best soporific."* When the sex is good—and I'm talking damn good—it is just like having a full belly. All you want to do is sleep. That is, until it is time for the next feast.

The last three ingredients identified by childless married women might be considered not only as a part of her strategy to ensure sexual satisfaction, but as attributes of a good man. These married women desire one part intimacy, one part intensity of the physiological and emotional response, followed by love. Batten (1992), an evolutionary theorist, tells us that securing the love of a male partner is a strategic move on a woman's behalf. It is her way of increasing the probability that her man will unselfishly commit his parental investment. Intimacy represents one third of the recipe for love. As hypothesized, overall, emotional intimacy was the best predictor of sexual satisfaction. A feeling of closeness precipitates a woman's willingness to be vulnerable, to submit herself to her partner. And finally, what better way to express your love for someone while exhibiting your sexual prowess, than to excite her to intense levels of physical and emotional pleasure. Or as one woman wrote, *"Ecstasy: the best feeling a person can have with true love."*

I don't mean to make this sound easy by any means. Marriage is as tough as a steak when it has cooked too long. There will be conflict, and lots of it, as two people who come from different places attempt to build a life together. It requires compromise and communication, compatibility and combat-ability. Steel sharpens steel, so as long as you rely on each other's strength you will be able to cut it.

Add Kids, Mix Carefully

Many people get married with the idea of beginning a family. The married woman who prepares for motherhood is not surprised when she misses her period. She is ready to transition.

Though, as soon as children are added to the mix, married women find themselves hard-pressed to get satisfied. They move to the bottom of the barrel, last in the hierarchy of sexual satisfaction (See Table 2, ISS scores). That is a serious problem!

I looked high and low for an explanation of this finding. Was it the difference in age, education, or occupation? Nope. Not even close. The most significant difference, when considering parental status, was in the levels of passion that the respective women identified. There was a trend suggesting that women without children have higher levels of passion in their relationships (M=7.43 vs. M=6.35). Passion, according to Sternberg (1986) is that aspect of love that involves physical attraction, which ignites the desire for sexual fulfillment. Married women with kids might want to take a cooking lesson or two from the child-free women when it comes to passion. Go back to your roots. Channel the single and/or married and childless woman inside of you. She is there somewhere. Access those memories so you can spice up your love life. Stable does not mean *stale.*

After having my own children, it does not surprise me that married mothering women have trouble keeping the flame burning. Hell, we are tired! Flat out! There is a lot for a wife and mother to think about in any given day. Therefore, she does not have the time, energy, or inclination to keep things on. Kaplan (1974) wrote that a woman's love for a man is her primary motivation until they have a child. Once the baby arrives, the child takes precedence when it comes to getting fed. Babies cannot meet their own needs, but daddies can. So, he might have to fend for himself sometimes. The woman now has to negotiate between the roles of mother and wife. This task might prove to be particularly challenging if the male partner/spouse is not contributing his share of parental investment.

It is believed that parenthood places an enormous demand on the marital relationship, which subsequently affects the sexual relationship. This issue is not present for single women because, in general, they are not involved in the types of relationships that require a certain amount of parental investment from their partners. The number of ingredients identified by the respective groups supports this line of thought. As a whole, single women identified 15 essential ingredients, while the married group identified 20 essential ingredients. See Appendices (Table 4 & 5 for a complete list). This finding suggests that married women approach sexual satisfaction with greater complexity, when compared to single women. Simply put, we want more; we've earned it!

Given the fact that there is less emotional intimacy, commitment, and passion in the relationships of the single group, these women might expect less from their sexual partners. The lower the threshold of expectation the lower the level of dissatisfaction.

A Heavy Load

So, what are the high expectations? A man is expected to support the family physically and financially. This means different things in different contexts. There are the concrete aspects—a safe home, health care, and schooling. And there are the subjective aspects—care, concern, support, and keeping family members in mind. Hash all that out and you would have one hearty marriage and family. Most families are somewhere in the middle—wanting it hashed out, but not knowing how.

Who is responsible for making sure the mother's needs are met? First and foremost, *she* is responsible. This does not let her spouse off the hook. As the husband, he has the responsibility of making the woman feel appreciated, desired, valued, and, most of all, loved. These expectations are traditionally associated with the wife. Being expected, these responsibilities often go unsaid and are unfortunately not recognized nor realized. The wife, now mother, wants to be appreciated for all that she is and all that she does. The passion that may have once come naturally now requires effort.

The workload is heavy in a family with kids. Therefore, the concept of mutuality is particularly important. A wife and mother, she needs a true partner in life. It is difficult for the wife to remain excited about her sexual relationship when she is disappointed in the marital relationship. This is especially true in a relationship where a man's ingredients are missing. Is he giving time, energy, money, along with love, support, and understanding? There are many guys out there who are remiss in their duties. Read the label, it's the boys, not the men, who are falling short. It is hard to keep the torch burning while he is blowing in the wind.

The need for reciprocity in these relationships is suggested by the appearance of *mutuality* as an additional spice only for married mothering women. The ingredient mutuality was present for the other groups of women, but not in significant numbers. Mutuality characterizes the quality of relatedness between the man and woman. It suggests giving and receiving in equal amounts—not just the giving and receiving of sexual pleasure, but also of love, support, compassion and work.

Traditional psychoanalytic theory would have us believe that it is in a woman's nature to bow down to her man. Krafft-Ebing (1965) states:

In women, voluntary subjection to the opposite sex is a physiological phenomenon. Owing to her passive role in procreation and long existing social conditions, ideas of subjection are, in women, normally connected with the idea of sexual relations. They form, so to speak, the harmonies which determine the tone quality of feminine feeling. (p. 130).

Kaplan (1991) states that a woman's inclination toward subordination to men (which Krafft-Ebing conceded might be, in part at least, an adaptation to long-standing social conditions) is a normal manifestation of female sexuality. This line of thought suggests that her submission is a manifestation of an instinctual predisposition to give. A woman gives of herself, without knowing that she herself is a gift? To the contrary, on some level (instinctual) these women know they are a gift. They know that the ability to bear children is a unique and highly desired attribute. This is evidenced by the strategies that some women implement—strategies directed at finding a man who will commit to a long-term relationship and offer his resources to the family—a mate who will invest and give commensurate with all that is invested and given by a mother from her child's conception through adulthood: Mutuality.

Chapter 15
Mix Up the Flava— But Don't Spoil the Recipe

Pantry Favorites Get Stale Sometimes

A closer examination of the Index of Sexual Satisfaction (ISS) (which was used to quantitatively measure sexual satisfaction) revealed that married mothering women were dissatisfied with the level of excitement in their sexual relationship with their spouse. This brings us back to that old standard: passion. Recall that the level of passion for married child-free women was higher than for the married mothering group, M= 7.43 and M=6.35, respectively.

You got to keep it hot! Stop serving up the same boring dishes every time. In part, this lack of excitement is related to monotony in the sexual relationship as evidenced by above average scores in response to the following statement:

My sex life is monotonous.

Ouch. Adding insult to injury, it often happens that this monotony extends throughout much, if not all, of the relationship.

According to Masters and Johnson (1966), monotony is a common cause of lower levels of sexual satisfaction in women, especially older women. You know, the woman who has been there and done that! She needs for her man to bring something new to the table. Think daily special. Excitement and arousal can be used synonymously, like butter and margarine; they can both be used to grease the pan to get it ready for the meat. It is therefore not surprising that the top five ingredients identified by these married mothering women are things that clearly contribute to the level of excitement/ arousal: mood, nature of the relationship and setting, variation in the sex act, newness and arousal. How do these ingredients affect arousal? Why are these ingredients so important to the married women with children?

For a woman, the initial phases of arousal can be facilitated by her mood. Remember that one of the moods reported by this group of women was *playful*. When a woman is adequately prepared, she invites her mate inside to play. She can open up emotionally and physically. The vagina expands and lubricates to accommodate his fullness. The external genitalia (labia majora and labia minora) turn bright pink and red, and swell in preparation to envelop him. Her nipples become erect and her areola becomes enlarged. Her body signals her partner that she is ready, as if calling out to a playmate, *"Come and get it."* If she can, at the same time, open her heart and her mind and make a connection, she can also experience sexual satisfaction. She is now a playground.

Can you remember the excitement you felt at recess, knowing that all of the toys were at your disposal for a whole hour? No books, teachers, assignments. Think of how excited the married woman with children must be when she has time to play.

The opposite, of course, is also true. The anxious woman, who cannot trust her partner, may experience difficulty in areas of arousal, sexual expression, and emotional intimacy, yielding sexual dissatisfaction. The anxious woman may have insufficient lubrication and expansion, thus making intromission uncomfortable and sometimes impossible, as is the case with vaginismus. Vaginismus is recurrent or persistent involuntary contraction of the outer one-third of the vagina that interferes with penetration, including, but not limited to intercourse.

Inefficient levels of arousal can also lead to problems in subsequent phases of the sexual response cycle, such as the orgasmic phase. Female Orgasmic Disorder, a delay or absence of orgasm following the excitement phase, is another condition that affects sexual dissatisfaction. These conditions affect many women of various backgrounds, and may be related to various psychological/ emotional factors, including anxiety and relationship distress, adding credence to the importance of mood and nature of the relationship for sexual satisfaction.

Married women with children spoke of feeling relaxed and playful. One way to play might be to try new things that could be very exciting. Like sex in a "unique" place such as in the backyard in the middle of a thunderstorm. Or grab a few pieces of fruit and some Hershey's chocolate and make your self a sweet treat (pun intended), a treat that he would love to eat.

Make her feel so relaxed that she wants to get "freaky" and play a role. She can be your naughty waitress who serves you up proper. I don't know about your man, but my hubby loves it when I bring his plate to the table, hot-n-ready! The married woman wants to feel relaxed enough to lower her inhibitions, and trust that her spouse will not reject her, but respond with excitement. Like when he shows you how good it is by licking the plate. Sexual abandon was identified as an additional spice for this group of women. This further suggests that they want to let go of their inhibitions and abandon the ubiquitous role expectations and responsibilities of being a mother and a wife. These women want to feel free to express their sexuality without limitations or judgment that might be imposed by roles, society, culture, or religion.

Snack on This

Why It's So Hard to Initiate Sex

A woman's fear of rejection, disappointment, and humiliation would prevent her from being able to ask or initiate sex. She needs to be able to communicate her wants and desires and trust in his ability to understand and respond. She needs to feel safe enough to tell her husband that she wants to try something new: she want her breast caressed; she wants to be licked from head to toe; she wants to be spanked; she wants to experience an orgasm; she wants to hear him say "I love you;" she wants to be held when all is said and done. At the same time, the wife should be able to tell her husband what she does not like. Maybe he is too rough or too distant; maybe she is sleepy; maybe she really does have a headache. These women especially want their husbands to hold them in their hearts and minds in the absence of lovemaking, and always, for him to stay committed to her and her only.

This married woman has definitely abandoned the traditional, and sunk her teeth deep into the verboten, when she had *"sex with an (now) ex-boyfriend's best friend for revenge."* She wrote, *"We had been attracted to each other for a long time and then finally just let go and released all of the tension between each other."* It is important to note that this married woman's peak experience took place before she became a wife and mother, before she had to be concerned about setting an example, being a teacher, and living by certain morals and values.

For her, sexual abandon represents in many ways a former life, a life where letting go did not have consequences. What she may not be aware of is that she can still let go, be free, and get nasty in her current life: with her husband, even though she is a mother. She, like you may question, how? She does this by acknowledging and accepting her human nature, her femaleness, her sexuality, her self. By putting it all in the same pot and stirring the mixture until complete. Complete with all the trimmings, especially passion.

Mixing up the flavor is also very important to married women with children. The importance of interrupting the monotony is suggested by the presence of the ingredient "variation in the sex act." These women say that variety brings spice to their love life. For married mothering women variety means trying different positions such as sixty-nine (mutual oral stimulation of the genitals), anal sex, using accessories (e.g., baby oil, liquid virgin, chocolate frosting, blindfolds, handcuffs), and having sex in different locations, such as in the shower. These women suggest that you keep a monogamous relationship hot and new by adding something you can sink your teeth into!

Where is the Focus?

While married women with children want a little spice in their life, they are also dissatisfied with their partner's "sensitivity to their sexual needs and desires." Specifically, they identify his focus on her as an additional "spice," which appears essential to the culinary masterpiece. Where is the partner's focus if it is not on the woman, the wife? Is he thinking of himself first, bills, work, providing for the family, another woman? After a child is born, the focus may no longer be on sex (for reproduction nor pleasure). The husband is focused on providing resources for the family, while the wife is focused on being a mother. This is one tall order.

How do women learn to mother? Some have an internal experience of motherhood that directs them. They have learned how to provide care, be attentive, listen, direct, protect, guide, reward, discipline, play, comfort, and love—they have learned it from their own mothers. Others have an internal experience of motherhood that taught them fear, anger, abuse, abandonment, rejection, neglect, and hatred. Both types of women have to find and refine the mother within; this requires focus. Each must focus on who she is—woman, wife, mother, lover—and what she wants, while *at the same time* deciphering each child—separate, baby, boy, girl, dependent. This, too, requires attention and focus.

Multiple children require diffuse attention and the ability to be flexible. While one may need a diaper changed, the other may need help with homework, while yet another requires advice on boys, not to mention that in this era the wife/mother is often employed outside the home. As a result, she is also focused on providing resources.

So when does she have time to focus on her own pleasure? After the kids are asleep, when the laundry is done, and the bills are paid. This woman—this wife, mother, provider, decipherer, investor—should have a partner who remains sensitive to her needs and desires at all times, including her wish for sexual satisfaction.

A girl's primary identification is with the mother; therefore, the mother has the responsibility of teaching her daughter, at a very young age that she deserves to be loved and appreciated. She deserves her partner's focus on her, and she deserves satisfaction. The mother must command these things from her husband so her children, especially daughters, know that they deserve to be loved for just being who they are, and for what they one day may become: a lover, a wife, a mother. It is important that children have many opportunities to witness the father's admiration for the mother, and her ability to reciprocate in kind. This serves as the template for kids to learn how to love and be loved. If couples give in to monotony, their relationship will suffer and the kids will fare poorly when it is their turn to build and sustain intimate relationships.

When a woman stops asking for what she wants and needs, it should be a sign. Why doesn't my wife want to make love to me? Why doesn't she initiate sex? Perhaps she is not excited or she doesn't feel that her husband is attentive to her wants and desires. Research suggests that reduced frequency in sexual initiation by the female may be a result of sexual and/or marital dissatisfaction (Hulbert, 1991;Tavris & Sadd, 1975).

The Pot is Not Hot—
Decline in Sexual Satisfaction

Parkinson (1987) identified a decline in sexual satisfaction over time in both partners in the marital relationship. This decline in sexual satisfaction was attributed to several things, including the general enjoyability of sex and pregnancy. This, along with findings of my current research, raises questions about the effect of parenthood on sexual satisfaction. Note that, in this study, married women with children exhibit the lowest frequency and the lowest preferred frequency of intercourse, at 1.68 and 2.22 times per week, respectively. Married women without children are having sex 1.79 times per week and desires sex 2.50 times per week. Given the demands of parenthood, it logically follows that a child would decrease a woman's level of sexual involvement, thus affecting opportunities for sexual satisfaction. Research also suggests that mutuality in sexual initiation is indicative of sexual satisfaction and contentment in long-term relationships (Donaldson, 1989; Tavris & Sadd, 1975).

A woman who cannot receive libidinal satisfaction from a man who has supposedly committed himself to the fulfillment of her needs becomes angry and withdraws. She withdraws physically, emotionally, and sexually because she feels deprived, and anything but narcissistically confirmed. This is especially true of a woman who has given of herself, a woman who has given the gift of a child, for she has made an enormous parental investment, having sacrificed her body for nine months plus.

I get overwhelmed just thinking about it! Imagine how these mothers feel, and what they have earned and deserve in turn from their mates. Sensitivity to their needs and desires does not even begin to cut it.

No man can fully understand the demands of pregnancy and motherhood, but all men can show their appreciation. Men can take notice of how tired and overwhelmed a mothering woman might be—*and respond.* A sprinkle of awayness might be in order. Go away so that the focus can be on pleasure. If you are away on vacation for the weekend, or away for just an hour, the focus in not on work, school, the children, etc. Awayness does not require a physical move or change. It can be a state of mind. Like a soothing bubble bath takes you away—to a beachfront condo, making love on the Atlantic Ocean, underneath the stars—away.

Snack on This

Pregnancy

As outlined in America's pregnancy bestseller, *What to Expect When You're Expecting* (1991), women experience a plethora of physical, psychological, and emotional changes. The physical changes alone are enough to warrant a lifetime of gratitude from their male counterpart who does not have to endure them. These changes include: fatigue, frequent urination, nausea (with and without vomiting), excessive salivation, heartburn, indigestion, bloating, flatulence (gas), breast changes (fullness, heaviness, tingling, darkening of the areola, bluish lines under the skin (indicating increased blood supply), increased appetite, weight gain of approximately 30 pounds or more, constipation, headaches, faintness, dizziness, complexion problems (blemishes, acne, stretch marks), insomnia, swelling of ankles and feet, bleeding gums, nasal congestion, occasional nose bleeds, varicose veins, vaginal discharge, backaches, increased heart rate, leg cramps, engorged genitals, changes in the orgasmic response (easier, more difficult, painful, multiple), rectal bleeding, hemorrhoids, itchy abdomen, hot flashes, varicose veins, shortness of breath, leaking breasts, urinary leakage, clumsiness, and Braxton Hicks contractions (prepatory contractions).

The psychological and emotional changes are like icing on the cake. They include: depression, anxiety, low sex desire, feeling sexually undesirable, mood swings, irritability, frustration, weepiness, joy, apprehension (about motherhood, pregnancy, baby's health, labor and delivery), absentmindedness, dreams and fantasies of the baby, over-sensitivity, impatience, restlessness, and excitement.

Baker (1996) wrote that a woman uses a man's approach to foreplay and intercourse to gain information about him. Foreplay starts outside the bedroom. It starts with flowers just because; with getting up in the middle of the night to feed the baby so she can sleep; or making a phone call during the middle of the day just to say "I love you." These actions might indicate that he is still focused on her, pleasing her, loving her. It might convey that she means enough to him to put aside everything and everyone, if only for that moment. His focus might also convey that he has committed himself to the fulfillment of her sexual needs and desires. A man who is concerned about her pleasure over his, a man who licks toes, elbows and ear lobes, a man who rubs her body down, and fills her body up, a man who listens, a man who loves, has his focus in the right place: on her. What woman doesn't want this? To be treated like a queen, to be narcissistically confirmed? A husband's focus on his wife expresses his commitment to maintaining the pair-bond.

When he has his focus on her, nothing can go wrong. Remember that married women with children have the longest list of ingredients (20 items). This increased number of ingredients may suggest a degree of complexity associated with how married women approach sexual satisfaction. This complexity might be reflected in the expectations associated with the roles of wife and mother.

Wife & Mother: A Woman's Roles

While women have to be responsible for a litany of things to do as, both, a mother and a wife, we also have the responsibility of keeping things hot in the relationship. You need to be a lover. Remember, this is how you got here in the first place.

My, how things can change when you shift the focus from lover to mother. For example, she may no longer be as concerned with her physical appearance. There are obvious physical changes for a woman subsequent to childbirth, saggy breast, bigger feet, weight gain or stretch marks. These changes could affect one's sex appeal, and with that, the level of passion in the relationship. Changes in physical appearance may also include things like a decrease in a woman's attention to her makeup, hair, or style of dress (including sexy bedtime attire). There may also be postpartum physiological discomforts associated with childbirth, such as vaginal dryness or a slowly healing Cesarean section or episiotomy, which would have subsequent affects on sexual desire and level of passion.

There may also be emotional or psychological reactions experienced after childbirth, such as body image concerns, "maternity blues," or postpartum depression. The most common postpartum psychological reaction is "maternity blues," and it is characterized by crying spells, anxiety, mood swings, headaches, forgetfulness, irritation, and insomnia. These symptoms may appear any day within the first week subsequent to delivery, and may last an average of ten days to several months. Symptoms that last longer are considered postpartum major depression. This occurs in 8–15% of mothers (Bowes, cited in Gabbe et. al., 1998). Depression also effects sexual desire, which would, in turn, affect sexual satisfaction.

Role Conflict

Role conflict captures the experience of being pulled in two or more directions at once. Dissonance. Like when you really want that dessert, but also really feel like you shouldn't. Conflict produces emotional discomfort and a desire to relieve this discomfort. For some, the relief comes as a result of self-exploration, discovery, understanding, and integration; that is, by acknowledging a part of one's self and making room for its expression. But for many, the relief comes after yielding to the conflict, and renouncing a part of one's self. In terms of sexuality, it means giving up what one desires (suppression and repression of sexual urges) and thus experiencing disappointment and dissatisfaction.

Just how sexual can a mother be without experiencing feelings of guilt and shame? If she has been taught that sexuality is a normal function of the relationship, that sex is a healthy expression of affection, that sex maintains the pair and pleasure bonds, then integrating motherhood may not be so difficult. But what if the opposite is true?

If the opposite is true, married women with children may find freedom of sexual expression to be very challenging. On average, these women reported that sex is a normal function of the relationship "a little of the time." Note that this statement reflects the most problematic aspect of sexual satisfaction for this group of women. How can that be? Sex is just as normal as eating. You eat everyday, several times a day. So why skimp when it comes to sex? Could it be that some women have taken this mothering thing too far?

One spice identified by these married women with children in their peak sexual encounters was sexual abandon. All of the women who identified this spice mentioned the "freedom" that allowed them to "get lost in [their] sexual passion." One woman wrote that there was *"no need to hide feelings of pleasure."* Who is this woman hiding from? And what is she hiding? Another woman stated that there were *"no rules!"* What rules is this woman referring to? Who has imposed rules in the bedroom? Stop it!

For years, Western society has dictated what is considered socially and sexually acceptable. This lesson has been passed down from generation to generation, and has landed in the laps of mothers and fathers who have the responsibility of orienting children to sexuality. Primarily, it is the mother who has the responsibility of shaping the core feminine identity. The young girl learns from her mother's expressions of femininity and sexuality. She also learns from her father's response to her mother and to her own attempts at feminine expression (Herzog, 1994). Does she come to experience her expressions of sexuality as "beautiful, sexual, assertive, free, alive, exciting, and giving," or naughty, inappropriate, perverse, freaky, nasty (but not in a good way)?

The mother conveys to the daughter what it means to be female through her communications, both verbal and nonverbal, and through her actions, all that she does and does not do as a woman. That is how she walks and where she goes, what she says and how she says it, what she wears and how she wears it. The mother can exhibit positive self-esteem, pride, values, and excitement about her femininity and sexuality; or she can convey self-consciousness, shame, and insecurity.

At the same time, the daughter looks to the father and uses his response to the mother as a barometer of what is tasteful or desirable. Is the father excited or embarrassed by the mother's feminine wiles? The father expresses his approval or disapproval of his wife's exhibitions through his words and actions also. His reactions to the mother could provide essential information about what he, and other men, finds sexy versus crude. Does he convey his love and affection for her with terms of endearment, hugs, and kisses or does he belittle, ignore, and reject?

The Consummate Mother-Whore

The potential role conflict associated with sexuality for married women with children is captured in the idea of the consummate mother-whore. A mother is a female parent who provides nurturance, guidance, and love to her offspring. She fixes boo-boos, cooks dinner, cleans the house, checks the homework, drives the car pool, attends parent-teacher conference, etc. A whore is a woman who offers herself indiscriminately for sexual activity, especially for money. She sucks dick, does it doggy style, likes ass slappin', gets nasty, and fucks big daddy.

"Naughty," "kinky," "nasty," "freaky"—all adjectives used by women in the study to express sexual abandon. Although these descriptions are not limited to married woman with children, it is not unreasonable to presume that married women with children would experience the highest amount of role conflict,

given the number of roles they play: mother, wife, lover, teacher, keeper. It is difficult to say with any certainty whether or not the aforementioned adjectives are indicative of a positive or negative self-concept for these women. However, by definition, they carry negative connotations. For example, naughty is defined as guilty of disobedience and misbehavior or lacking in taste or propriety. Kinky, nasty, and freaky are defined as bizarre, unusual, or perverse.

The different labels used to characterize displays of male and female sexuality have indicated negative attitudes about freedom of sexual expression for females. While a man who exhibits sexual abandon is considered macho and maybe even more desirable (as suggested by evolutionary theory and societal standards), a woman who exhibits the same behavior is considered whorish or perverse. A woman who feels the need to conform to societal expectations of female sexual expression may experience conflict when developing an integrated core feminine identification. She may especially have difficulty developing a feminine idea that allows for uninhibited sexual expression. Her struggle may manifest as role conflict.

The mother and the whore have separate identities; yet these two can exist in the same woman. Some say that every man wants a consummate mother-whore (and at the same time fears her): someone to raise their children who will keep the sex hot and delicious. Yeah, this all sounds fine and good, but it's the indiscriminate part that bothers him. Her freedom of sexual expression may be threatening. It could produce fears of infidelity.

The duality of the consummate mother-whore may not be so easily integrated for the woman either. One might wonder if there could be a healthy integration of these two roles? If a woman is able to accept her whole self, the part that is mother and the part that represents lover, then, certainly a healthy integration of mother and vixen can be attained. In reality, they are one and the same because they originate from the same source: the initial mother-child bond. This relationship provides the first lessons in love and sexual satisfaction: how to both give and receive pleasure without feelings of guilt or shame.

Breastfeeding provides an excellent example of the potential for role conflict produced by the giving and receiving of pleasures. Mothers who choose this natural way of providing substance to their infant may find it difficult to go from experiencing their breasts as a food source, which supplies nurturance and gratification to the infant, to experiencing their breasts as an erogenous zone, a source of sexual excitation and pleasure for themselves and their mate.

Snack on This

A Dirty Big Secret

As a society, what are we teaching children about freedom of sexual expression when we hide sexuality because of the fear that it may over-stimulate or traumatize them?

Sex is just as natural as eating and sleeping, which we don't go keeping secret. With sex we are vigilant about keeping quiet, locking doors to ensure little ones don't stumble upon the animalistic underbelly from which they came... the primal scene. This only exacerbates inhibition. With a person's developmental age and stage considered, there must be a way to communicate the normalcy of sexual expression.

Maybe the taboo associated with unbridled sexual passion has affected the mother's ability to feel comfortable giving and receiving sexual pleasure. Specific acts such as anal sex and oral sex, which were identified by several women as pleasurable, could be experienced as shameful or dirty. Freedom of sexual expression for married women with children may feel incongruous with motherhood. This would explain why married women go from first to last in the race for sexual satisfaction with the introduction of children. Taken together, the factors that affect sexual satisfaction in the married group are related to having children. These factors may include decreased passion, difficulty getting in the mood, role-conflict, physical and emotional changes after pregnancies.

Chapter 16
Poisonous Berries: Hunting and Gathering Gone Wrong

We must decide what to do with the nature and nurture that has been given to us. If you are good at the hunt, if you gather the right ingredients, then it will be reflected in the mate you choose and in the life you create. There are many challenges that may interfere with a woman's ability to make the right selection, "right" meaning someone who will provide her with, both, relationship and sexual satisfaction.

The numbers might not be specific, but women clearly outnumber men. There is an endless supply of pussy. When the supply is high, the demand is low. Men should compete for the prize. But, there is no need to compete if a woman is too available. Why buy the cow if the milk is free?

For men, it is like being a kid in a candy store. Pick one any one and then on to the next. So, if you make a baby with him—and he is not the kind of man who will commit—then shame on you! You have just made things harder for you and that baby. A woman's reproductive success (passing on genes in a way that increases the odds that the offspring will be able to do the same), is almost always limited by the amount of resources she has to invest in her children (Noonan, 1987, p. 53). And if yo' baby's daddy ain't around, then you and yo' baby will go hungry!

A man who is not willing to commit his resources leaves a mother alone to raise their children. Being with kids all day, every day, is taxing. Even if he commits to the child via child support and visits every other weekend, what he provides as a father will benefit you very little. Keep in mind that the role of a father is different from the role of a partner. His support of that child may give you some momentary respite, but you will carry the heavy load. Mothers need help. If you don't get help, someone will get neglected. The child, the parent, the spouse, the home, the health, the well-being—all jeopardized if a mother is isolated. Neglected children are like plants that get deprived of sun and water; they fail to thrive. They suffer.

Parents cannot do it all alone. The ones who have to, single parents, they've got it hard. I don't know how single parents do it. Well, yes I do. Some, the competent ones, work hard and give all that they can; in this they still come up short. Having limited resources is part of being a single parent. Unless a woman has a great support system, her time, money, and energy will be on low supply. There are some who fail miserably, especially mothers who have planted their crops too close together, where the plants don't have the space to grow. The seedlings are all fighting for their nutrients. The harvest will be less bountiful.

What happens when a man is not interested in the investment of his resources? Lack of commitment in a relationship may result in infidelity, which increases the possibility of disease, desertion, and sexual dissatisfaction. Baker (1996, p. 57) writes:

A woman has a lot to lose from her partner's infidelity... First, there is the risk that she will have to share his wealth, time, energy, and other resources with another woman. Second, there is the danger that he will eventually leave her for the other woman, reducing his support for her still further... Third, there is the greater risk of contracting sexually transmitted diseases, because her partner is at greater risk.

Women need to feel like they have a man that they can depend on. I am not talking about a man that will take care of you, pay all the bills, and buy everything you want. Now if that is what you want and you can find a man to provide it, more power to you! However, I am talking about someone you can depend on to share your life with, especially if you have children together. You need a man who will show up and do his part. Be honest with yourself in your assessment of your partner, as this woman was when asked if she would marry the man with whom sex was most satisfying. She writes:

A series of things happened where I needed him to help me out. I was sick, I moved, etc. In each case, he was never there to help me out. What was going on for him at that time took precedence... The fact that he was repeatedly not able to be there for me made it hard to continue.

A man's behavior during dating is indicative of how he will be in a relationship. Don't think that you can change him. If you make this error in judgment you just might be left with more than boxes to move on your own. He might just desert you with mouths to feed.

According to Fisher (1930), women look for specific things in a man. Fisher posits that women who mate with men who other women find desirable, in general, will (if these preferred characteristics are a part of his genetics) have more "sexy" sons. This is the gift that will keep on giving, because women will subsequently prefer these sexy sons and produce more children. Thus, the female has more grandchildren and has increased her reproductive success. This evolutionary process is called "runaway selection," and it accounts for the evolution of sexual selection criteria once a consensus exists among females regarding preferred characteristics (Buss, 1987, p. 338). While some characteristics might vary, I think it is fair to say women have some common tastes. In the simplest of terms, we just want you to be reliably kind to us.

Still Hungry

As discussed in the Chapter 14, single mothers were second in line to be served sexual satisfaction. It is baffling that some of the hardest working people in the world have time to ensure sexual satisfaction. Not the TV dinners I would have predicted for this cohort. The single mother is well fed and savoring it. I know you are wondering why, and I can't wait to break it down to you.

The challenge: understanding how parenthood increases the level of sexual satisfaction in single women while decreasing the level of sexual satisfaction for married women. Something didn't sit right when I was trying to digest this. She is busy, and a good bone is often scarce and hard to find. Not mention feeling overwhelmed by the responsibilities of being a single mom.

Thirty-five percent of these single mothering women had a child out of wedlock. I don't know why anyone would choose this from the menu. It would be like going out to a restaurant to eat, but the catch is that you have to prepare your own meal. That defeats the purpose; it just doesn't make sense. Of course there are extenuating life circumstances that contribute to being a single mother, such as divorce or death. However, the occurrence of single motherhood is so prevalent, one must assume that there are other factors at play. Single women with children might be considered ineffectual players in the game of life and love. Or maybe they are poor strategists when it comes to mate selection, as indicated by their hierarchy of ingredients.

I found the ranking of ingredients for sexual satisfaction for this group of women curious. These women first identify variety in the sex act and then newness as essential components to their satisfaction. This is followed by the third ingredient, which has two parts, nature of the relationship and positive self-regard. The fourth ingredient also has two parts, mood and orgasm intensity. The fifth ingredient is setting. The ingredients that rise to the top are noticeably indicative of in-the-moment variables, rather than intimacy and commitment. These ingredients contradict the group's idea about sexual satisfaction in their current relationships (as indicated by their responses on the Index of Sexual Satisfaction).

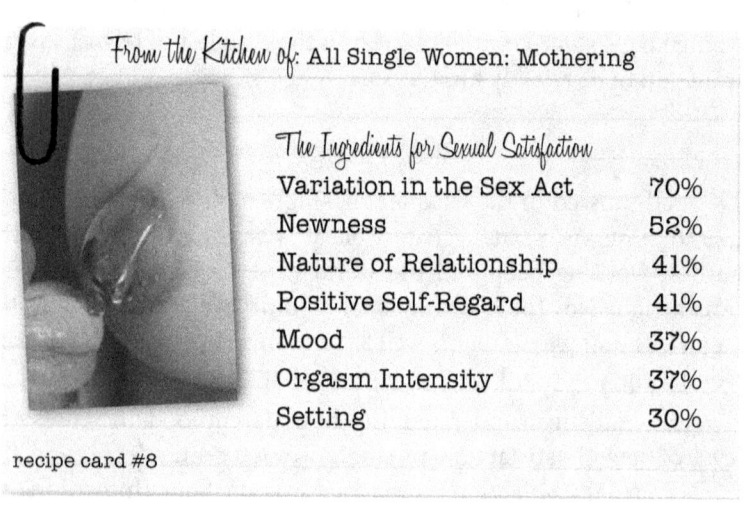

From the Kitchen of: All Single Women: Mothering

The Ingredients for Sexual Satisfaction

Variation in the Sex Act	70%
Newness	52%
Nature of Relationship	41%
Positive Self-Regard	41%
Mood	37%
Orgasm Intensity	37%
Setting	30%

recipe card #8

According to their responses on the ISS, most single women with children were dissatisfied with their sexual partners. This was indicated by the sexual problems identified on the Index of Sexual Satisfaction. These women were also dissatisfied with the role that sex plays in the relationship. More specifically, sex adds a lot to the relationship only "a little" to "some of the time." Although it sounds like a T.V. dinner to me; just something to fill that space in your belly, the kind of loving that tastes like the cardboard that it is packaged in, it seems to hit the spot for these single mothers.

For these women the sex may be delicious but the relationship is absent, and this appears to be good enough. Their satisfaction comes from the immediate gratification of their hunger. There is no nourishment. Remember, overall, the single group needed fewer ingredients in their recipes. With their lower level of expectation, it doesn't take much to satisfy their appetite. Sure, you might be able to find a TV dinner to quiet your hunger pangs, but who wants dinner out of cardboard every night?

Although these women were most dissatisfied with their sexual partners and with what sex adds to the relationship, their recipes focus on the level of excitement when identifying the essential ingredients for sexual satisfaction. The level of excitement in the sexual relationship is also lacking, as evidenced by its appearance on the list of problems identified by these women.

All of women in the study were dissatisfied with the frequency of intercourse. It was no surprise to discover that single mothers were having sex less often than any other group. Single women without children have sex on average 2.19 times per week, and desire it 2.98 times per week. Single women with children on average have sex .9 times per week, and desire sex 2.39 times per week. (Note that the differences in these frequencies between and within the groups may not be statistically significant. They are given as a point of reference.)

Given the problem areas identified by single women with children, one might expect that they would be looking for things that support the relationship. The results of my study indicate that many of these women are currently involved in casual relationships. In addition, some of them indicate that the partner in the peak experience was casual, anonymous, or experimental. For example, *"It was just a sex thing."* Just as one might suspect, the levels of intimacy and commitment in their relationships were significantly lower than those of the marital group.

Don't Fill Up On Sweets

In the absence of a strong relationship with a sexual partner, one might come to value the bond between a mother and child even more. Remember that according to psychoanalytic theory, securing a man and having his child accomplish narcissistic confirmation. Thus, the single mother has obtained one essential piece of the pie. This may account for some of this group's level of satisfaction. She has acquired a fleeting sense of narcissistic confirmation, which may manifest as an over/under investment in her child/ren. The mother who may, for example, try to overcompensate for the absence of a father by not setting appropriate limits, she overindulges, instead of teaching a child to deal with their experience of loss and/or disappointment. Relying on a child for narcissistic confirmation may help explain why having children increases sexual satisfaction in the single group, while decreasing it in the married group. *That what is food to one to some becomes fierce poison* (Lucretius, 1921/2004).

Prudence would dictate that single women with children give time and consideration to finding a man and raising a child. Many questions were raised about how these women ordered off the menu. If you are mostly dissatisfied with your man and what he brings to the table, then why are variety and newness first on your list? Shouldn't it be N.O.R or intimacy? That is, of course, unless sex is being used as a "dickstraction" from reality. On the surface, it appears that single women with children are focused on the meltaway aspects of their experience (ingredients that are considered helpful but not essential to the sexual act). Given the identified problems, why would these things take precedence over nature of the relationship and positive self-regard? Does the excitement associated with variety and newness keep the focus off what is missing in the relationship?

For many of these single moms, finding a man appeared to be important, but this was not reflected in their strategies. Forty-five percent of these women identified N.O.R. as an essential ingredient when considering their most sexually satisfying partner as her "baby's daddy," while 55% of the responses pertained to the sexual experience itself (e.g. they described the relationship as *"casual"* or *"a sex thing"*). This is in comparison to the married women with children, where only two women identified N.O.R in response to the question regarding reproduction. Most often, the women responded "no" because of things like *"He's a player,"* or because it was just a *"booty call."* The remaining responses of the married group regarding N.O.R were directed at the sexual experience itself.

The single mother also identifies positive self-regard as an important ingredient for sexual satisfaction. Again this ingredient was further down on the list, indicating some awareness about what a woman should be looking for in a mate and/or a lover. Note that it is also identified by the other women, but with less significance. So, how did these women become single mothers? What allowed them to open themselves up to the possibility of disease and desertion? I believe that it is the use of sexuality as a defense against the sadness of loss (i.e. lost love, missed opportunity, loss of time and energy, loss of esteem, lost dreams, loss of the love-object mother, and the list goes on and on…).

There has to be substantial meaning associated with being a single mother. First, take into consideration the enormity of the task of motherhood. Getting to know the subtle, yet important, nuances of a newborn baby, knowing when to feed him, clothe him, change him, or just hold him. Now picture a single mother figuring this out alone, not to mention doing this before she is an adult (i.e. teenage mothers). I imagine that a single mother's sense of self as an effective lover and mother has been challenged. Therefore, she seeks narcissistic confirmation through her sexual experiences. She, too, wants to feel "strong and very beautiful." More important, she needs to feel whole and close to someone ("one-der-full"). The teenage mother especially does not feel one-der-ful. To the contrary, she often feels empty, alone and overwhelmed. What better way to avoid this reality than immersing yourself in momentary pleasure? Sex is fun and exciting, it can distract a person from experiencing the greatest of losses. Dick for breakfast, lunch, and dinner; and don't forget to snack in between. While it may taste good, there will be no nutritional value. There will be nothing to help you grieve those losses, nothing to help you move on and grow.

A single mother's reality is clear; her baby's daddy is nowhere near. Perhaps these women's strategies are being directed at another goal all together. Instead of looking for an ideal mate, they are building the wall of denial so high as to protect themselves from being aware of their aloneness, from being aware of the disappointment of having been deserted, of knowing about the pain of separation, the shame of poor choices, loss, trauma, and feelings of rejection. This would suggest that their sexuality is being used in a defensive manner.

Psychoanalytic theory has identified sexualization as a defense mechanism in which the ego uses sexuality to struggle against painful or insufferable affect. As I wrote above, these women are using sex to protect themselves from the *awareness* of their situations. Defenses don't make painful things go away; they just hide them from us. If something is hidden from view, then it cannot be addressed. Thus, the single mother who has sex without intimacy and commitment puts herself at a disadvantage. You might feel better right after that dark chocolate candy bar; but once he's gone, the problems still exist.

Don't let the smooth taste fool you. Single women with children also want to feel "one-der-full." However, these efforts may be keeping her from feeling anything except moments of sexual satisfaction, especially if she is living and loving unconsciously.

Maybe excitement (all the newness and variety) distracts the single mother from the pain and disappointment of having been deserted (N.O.R.) or having chosen poorly (self-regard). In the end she is left hungry, longing for something to satisfy her appetite, and maybe even worse off then when she began. Posner et al., cited in Gabbe et al. (1998), suggest that being unmarried with a child and being involved with a dissatisfying partner places a woman at risk for postpartum major depression. This demographic also places a woman at risk for anger and frustration. The meal has been ordered, she waits patiently, she takes a bite—only to just want to spit it out and rid her self of its memory. Certainly would make one angry, frustrated, depressed. She is left with a nasty taste in her mouth. Pass the sorbet to clear the palette.

If this is the order, then single women with children are not making good choices. By seeking in-the-moment ingredients (like newness, variety, and excitement) without intimacy and commitment—these women are keeping themselves in a perpetual state of aloneness. There may be many possible reasons why. Such as addiction to the rollercoaster ride and/or the repeating of old patterns (see below Poisonous, Yet We Keep Picking).

Stop Shopping Down the Wrong Aisle

Something happens that interferes with a woman's ability to implement her choice well. As suggested by evolutionary theory, women should be assessing a man's ability to love and commit when looking for a mate. I know you single women are out there saying, "I was not looking for a man, I was just trying to get laid, you know have a little fun." So how did you wind up getting knocked up? Every woman knows that unprotected sex can lead to pregnancy. Yet many women knowingly take the risk. There can be a strong argument that there is no such thing as an accidental pregnancy. Unless you are like me, a person who took her birth control religiously, and fell within than small failure rate. It must have been meant to be! Otherwise you are just playing with fire. If you are trying to have fun, don't ruin it by getting pregnant, because if you are not properly prepared, you will get burned.

Single mothers need their mates to be more than just a lover, but also a parent and provider to a child who is not biologically theirs. These women seek a mate who is generous and kind, someone who will unselfishly devote his resources. These women need a man who is willing and able to help with the science project, coach the baseball team, and finance a college education.

Single women with children have the arduous task of finding a mate who will invest in an unrelated child. Her baby needs a daddy. Even if the biological father is involved, he is not in the home. He is part-time. It takes a special kind of man to raise the seed of another and not feel "cuckolded." According to biologists, a man has been cuckolded if he raises another male's offspring as if they were his own, because this does not contribute to his reproductive success (Daly & Wilson, 1983). So then, single women with children, you are looking for a unique brother. A man that is loving, unselfish, and devoted. A man who would sacrifice himself in this manner, a man who exhibits high levels of parental behavior.

The Paradox: Hungry, Yet Satiated

It may seem surprising that, in this study, single women with children have the second highest level of sexual satisfaction, particularly given the low levels of intimacy and commitment in their relationships. But, keeping in mind that dick can distort reality, then maybe it is not that far fetched. Single women with children may be protecting themselves from reality. The reality is that we are separate, and we want to be one, or at least to feel like it. Both sexuality and romantic relationships are manifestations of the human desire to feel closeness, something reminiscent of the mother-child bond. Mahler (1975) suggests that the initial symbiotic mother-child bond lays the foundation for adult relationships. Chodorow (1979) follows this line of thought: A person's early relation to her mother or his mother leads to a preoccupation with issues of primary intimacy and merging. On one psychological level, all people who have experienced primary love and primary identification have some aspect of self that wants to recreate these experiences, and most people try to do so (p. 79). Fromm (1956) contends that the strongest need of man or woman is the need to overcome separateness, and to leave the prison of aloneness. To feel so close to someone that it is hard to know where you end and he begins. If being close is the objective, than how it is that these single women find themselves alone? The hunting and gathering has gone wrong.

The Game is a perfect example of a poor strategy. By nature, it is a series of interactions between people that is characterized by lack of intimacy and commitment. Simply put, it is an immature way of relating. It is reminiscent of how children play. In the beginning it is all about fun and games. That is how dating should start out for every one: big fun. But through the developmental process, we must evolve. Just as children grow, so should relationships. Some do and some do not. And just as with small children, sometimes it is hard to know when to stop playing. In The Game, everything is an avenue for play, including your feelings, though they should not be played with. While some adults never stop playing games, others have forgotten how to play. And because life is so much work, it is important to balance work with play, without getting played.

One single mother reported that her most sexually satisfying experience was, *"A threesome: me another woman and a man."* Now there is a triangle for you. Note that it was not described as a love triangle. When further questioned about the "why" of the experience she reported that it was *"different from ordinary."* "Sexual" was the only feeling aroused, and the orgasm was described as *"different."* When asked whether or not she considered having children with the identified partner she simply responded *"No."* Although this woman's response was lacking in detail, she has shared a wealth of knowledge. There is not much to say about an experience lacking in commitment and intimacy. It comes across like something to do, and that is all.

For some, a threesome might be considered taboo; for others it may be considered adventurous, exciting, or experimental—a good way to play. Depending on the context, the experience could be very intimate. A couple may have shared personal sexual fantasies and made the decision to indulge.

But this woman does not mention any of those things. She just states that it is different from the ordinary. This raises the question: "What is ordinary?" Is ordinary for this single mother to be feeling abandoned, rejected, alone, afraid, empty, confused, bewildered, vexed, angry, hurt, helpless, hopeless, desperate, inadequate, and /or disappointed? Maybe sexual experiences like hers are used as temporary "dicktractions" from what has become all too common, regular, everyday, ordinary.

Poisonous, Yet We Keep Picking

The list of ingredients for these single mothers suggests that they are focused on the more casual aspects of their sexual relationships. Placing value in the excitement of causal sexual relationships could be the product of a repetition, with conflict originating in the phallic stage of psychosexual development. In this stage, a young girl's wish to posses the father and destroy the mother. She is envious because she does not have a penis. As you can see the stage is set for drama. Psychoanalytic theory would assert that the drama of casual sex defends against the anxiety and rage associated with having an insufficient love-object (mother) and/or with disappointment with one's own sexual make-up (e.g. when little girls, unable to be at peace with their own bodies, integrate at a young age the idea that boys are superior). If we fail to resolve this conflict, it can be repeated later in life. It may manifest as love triangles, superficial relationships, or feelings of inadequacy.

When a woman can identify when her adult-love relationships resemble those old childhood feelings of distance and disappointment, then and only then, can she prevent history from repeating itself. This is a task that may require some assistance from a professional like myself—a psychologist or someone trained in the mental health field. If you find yourself picking the same poisonous berries ask for help making a better selection.

In an adult relationship the drama is characterized by the lies and deception, things that don't mix in love. When two people are engaged in The Game, they don't acknowledge each other as a whole person. Instead they develop a superficial relationship based on objectification of the other. In other words, you are starving for love and attention, so he becomes a piece of meat, and so do you, pork chop. Kaplan (1991) wrote about a psychological strategy in which a part object is used to conceal the absence or loss of a whole object. She believes that the conscience works to make sure that the whole (the loss of what was wished for) remains unconscious. The strategy could be set into motion by the absence or loss of a sufficient love object such as yo baby's daddy.

Promiscuity or indiscriminate sexual interactions that produce excitement, guilt and/or shame are part of this strategy to ward off knowledge of loss and loneliness. According to Kaplan, this series of interactions keeps the original loss and disappointment hidden, beneath the surface. The conflict associated with early childhood's formation of gender identity remains unconscious, as do the guilt, shame, and humiliation of not getting one's needs (including narcissistic confirmation) met as a child. Thus continues the repetition, the vicious cycle, which keeps one oblivious, but also dissatisfied.

The Blacker the Berry the Sweeter the Juice

Integration requires understanding and accepting the sadness, disappointment, and humiliation associated with not getting what is wanted or needed. Some people see the sample and choose not to taste, because if they do, they have to swallow their own pain and longings, the old and the new: not getting the desired mother nor the desired lover. The pain of not being nurtured or not feeling loved by your parents is sure to find its way into this new recipe. If someone is playing The Game and focusing on the excitement of casual sexual relationships, some of their needs will continue to go unmet. Only certain aspects of the self can manifest: the side that is afraid of intimacy, commitment, and passion (the triad key to the recipe for love). While the side that focuses on variation in the sexual act and newness (instead of nature of the relationship and positive self-regard) will get gratification, the other side goes unrecognized and unsatisfied. This person is not giving love or being loved with her whole self. As a result, there may be heightened physical satisfaction in the absence of emotional or relationship satisfaction. It is a recipe that is missing essential ingredients: the awareness of you and your partner.

Full awareness of self and other allows for a complete union. Mix your ingredients with his and stir it up. When you allow yourself to know, to open up and be vulnerable, to see the clues, then you can use your psychological strategies to get the man you want, the love you want, and yes, sexual satisfaction.

So, women, put your strategies to good use and find yourself a true blackberry. As Maxwell so eloquently puts it, "let's not play The Game". Get you a mover and a shaker, a real decision maker. The kind of person that will make you say, "It has been fun playing with you boy. But I done met me a man, a real man, a real good man".

Tastes Great, Less Feeling

Single women appear to be looking for pleasure and a partner, but pleasure clearly comes first. While they have not secured a man or a child, in the race for sexual satisfaction they still managed to beat out married women with children, coming in third.

Just take a look at their recipe. When it comes to the important ingredients, single child-free women are all about arousal and setting (which, incidentally, may enhance arousal). They emphasize the fun and excitement of it all. Things like being seen by onlookers or the excitement of having sex in various locations tempts their taste buds. The single child-free woman's approach to sexual satisfaction suggests that she is able to acknowledge the urges that are primarily sexual, separate from her emotional needs.

The single child-free woman wants the setting to be right. She wants to be *"turned on by him."* And as indicated by the added spice of sexual abandon in their recipes, these women want to be *"wild"* with *"no boundaries," "totally uninhibited," "adventurous and sexy."* The priority is to make it taste good, not the nutritional value. While pleasure comes first, she is ultimately looking for someone to love and to be loved by. This is just a little further down her grocery list.

The Ingredients for Sexual Satisfaction

Setting	58%
Arousal	50%
Love	46%
Nature of Relationship	42%
Intimacy	38%
Mood	38%

recipe card #9

Being in a committed relationship that is characterized by intimacy can put one in the mood for love (lovemaking). As you cans see, the last three ingredients identified by this group are love, nature of relationship, and a mix of intimacy/mood. These women are not totally misguided in their search for a good lover/mate. There is a plan underneath the "pleasure principle," and it is guided by the "reality principle." Love is real. Taken together, these ingredients represent the emotional component of the sexual experience. And yet, why are these components further down on her list? What effect does that have on sexual satisfaction for these women?

According to developmental theories, securing the relationship would increase the likelihood of sexual satisfaction. Some of these single women (38%), when describing their most sexually satisfying experience, identified the nature of the relationship as casual (i.e. *"this partner was a fling"*). A fling is defined as a short affair, a time for pleasure or a period of self-indulgence. It is as it sounds, a fling— a fast thing.

A sexual relationship lacking in intimacy and commitment does not lend itself to sexual satisfaction. Like single women with children, these women may be making poor selections. Everyone knows that home cooking is better than fast food, any day. But instead of taking her time to pick something nutritious and delicious, maybe the single child-free woman is using her psychological strategies to distract her from the experience of being alone. Thus, when the strategies fail, she is not that satisfied in contrast to her married counterparts —be they mothering or child-free. She may be less frustrated than her single counterparts who are also mothers (because she is not as taxed), but in the end both of these groups of women are missing out because of the lack of intimacy and commitment.

Snack on This

The Psyche as defined by Freud: Id, Ego, and Superego

The id is the part of the psyche that is unconscious, irrational, impulse driven, pleasure seeking and mostly sexual in nature. It is the wild side. The ego is that part of the psyche that is in part conscious, rational, delays gratification, reality seeking, and mediates between the id and superego. The superego houses our conscience, values, and morals. It is supposed to keep us in check. It is that part of us that says, "Do you really need another piece of that delicious, mouthwatering...?" After reading some of these recipes, it is clear that the superego was out to lunch. For others however, the superego is working over-time. It won't allow a girl to have any fun. She is too full of guilt to indulge.

There were also a few things about a single woman's sexual partners that ruined her appetite (as evidenced by responses on the ISS). This includes his ability to sexually excite her, especially with his sex technique, and his experience of enjoyment in their sexual life. His ability to excite her may be dependent upon many things such as his physical attractiveness, his tool, and his technique. Nothing makes a women feel better than knowing she has satisfied her man. He should lick his fingers and smack his lips to express satisfaction and he could use these same tools to arouse her too.

Taking the time to excite a woman might not be important to a man who is just trying to satisfy his own appetite. In an ideal situation he would be interested in her pleasure, too (mutuality). A man who is strictly about his own pleasure will not think about how you like your dish prepared. He is going to give it to you based on his own longing and desires, leaving you unexcited and unsatisfied.

Simmer on Warm

The single woman wants to let her hair down. She wants to be free to express her sexuality without fears of judgment or rejection. Women who want to be sexually free (sexual abandon) need to feel safe. Winnicott (1960) suggests that a feeling of safety develops within a "holding environment." It gives you a sense that you are, and can count on, being taken care of. Your soul needs an environment that is dependable, consistent, attuned to your needs, and that provides for you in a way that is empathic to those needs (Almass, 1998). So, go ahead, cuddle after he gives you some of that warm, rich, and creamy. Remember milk does a body good.

Although the concept, "holding environment" originated to describe the experience between mother and child, it can also be applied to those who play the various roles of a woman's lover. A maintenance man should be maintaining, a pipe layer should be laying pipe, and a fuck buddy should be fucking. These jobs require consistency and dependability, so that she can be the best that she can be when she is with you. When a woman knows that she can count on a man, she feels safe. Safe enough to open up and pour out her juices so that your meat can get good and moist.

Snack on This

The Boss of the Kitchen

Just like any other job worth having, when you no call—no show, you are let go. If he is not considerate enough to call and tell you he is running late or has made other plans, you can be sure he won't be thinking about satisfying your needs, whatever they might be.

Don't waste your time and energy. Put the garbage in the disposal so that you can make room for something worth having.

Cooking Solo

Casual sexual relationships can be very exciting with all the newness and mystery. Excitement is a great way to distract from the disappointment of singlehood. Though, not all excitement is good for you. While single women are living phat-free, it can still be rather lonely. From what I remember and still hear, dating is hard work. It is full of games, disappointment and heartache. The roller coaster can be very discouraging for women. However, if you can recover from the negative experiences that are sure to come your way, you can move one step closer to satisfaction.

The demographic unavailability of a consistent and proficient sex partner may also be affecting a single woman's level of sexual satisfaction. Perhaps the single woman is the victim of circumstance. By definition, she is without a consistent partner. If there is a partner, there is no guarantee that he is a good sexual partner.

The single women in this study are specifically dissatisfied with their current partner's ability to excite and satisfy; suggesting that having a partner does not ensure satisfaction. As a result of the scarcity of men, some women may take whatever they can get. If you throw a starving woman a saltine cracker, she might mistake it for a Ritz, but sooner or later, reality will set in, and she will want the real thing baby.

These ideas about single women reflect a certain complexity in regard to being single and seeking a fit mate for marriage or sexual satisfaction. While a single woman who does not have children can be focused on her physical pleasure, she is also seeking a mate with whom she can be emotionally close and potentially develop a long-term committed relationship. The problem is that her emphasis is on physical pleasure, which may serve as an obstacle to her emotional fulfillment and sexual satisfaction. It may be that she too is using the excitement of sex to defend against being alone.

Of course there is also that woman who is not at the age and stage of life where focusing on a relationship is appropriate. Don't pick the berry before it is ripe. This woman may need to mature and focus on herself (e.g. education, career, self-esteem) before she goes berry picking. She can afford to play with her food because she has plenty of time before she needs to choose.

Single women appear to be guided by their libidos. The libido can make one feel crazy some times—crazy defined as wildly impractical, erratic. The libido can affect one's behavior, behavior specifically directed at its reduction. These physical and emotional longings can manifest as risk-seeking or indiscriminate sexual behavior. You know, acting like a ho. It could also manifest as a strategy that looks for excitement over love. Love is not crazy, although you might feel crazy at times. It is solid. If love makes you feel out of control, you need to reconsider your selection. As a matter of fact, love comforts and soothes. It can satisfy an enormous appetite, desire, or hunger.

The first love, mother, has an insatiable infant that she has to feed. These initial feedings provide the first food of life and love that teach us to bind powerful emotions so as to prepare for adulthood. Ostensibly, if you had a mother who fed you love, a mother who taught you that disappointment can be tolerated, and that gratification can be delayed, then you know how to manage the intensity of the libido—that thing that makes you feel hot, horny, hungry, and sometimes crazy.

A woman who has learned this invaluable lesson can delay gratification until she finds a man who will allow himself to be committed. I am not just talking about being in a committed relationship. I am also talking about a man who will commit to your sexual satisfaction, even if he doesn't want to spend the rest of his life with you. He can spend the night with you and leave you feeling like more than a piece of meat. If you can, wait for Mr. Right, instead of settling for Mr. Right Now. If he is Mr. Right Now make sure he has the ingredients to get it right, now. And whatever you do, don't lose perspective. If it is a sex thing, keep it strictly dickly. Don't go fallin' in love with your fuck buddy.

The Melting Pot

All of the women in this study talked about intimacy in terms of a feeling of closeness, as suggested by the following quotes: *"Emotional ties to him make the event very fulfilling," "being held in his arms when we are making love,"* and *"Without words we seemed to connect physically."* It is noteworthy that, in some instances, single and married women conceptualize intimacy differently.

Only the single women described intimacy as a type of fusion (i.e., boundarylessness). For example, *"He kissed me and our bodies just melted together,"* and *"no boundaries."* This type of intimacy appears more childlike and immature. It is suggestive of the symbiotic relationship between the mother and child, a pure derivative of the id (the id being the part of the psyche that is unconscious and guided by the pleasure principle). This type of intimacy does not take into account separation.

The single woman's description of intimacy might also capture her comfort with uninhibited sexuality as a means of expressing the level of intimacy in their relationship. Simply put, she likes to get her freak on, when she feels close to her man. There are no limits or boundaries that she won't cross, so be sure not to bite off more than you can chew.

It is important to remember the importance of separateness in the closest of bonds. This way no one gets lost in the sauce. Even in the tightest relationships each person has separate and unique feelings, thoughts, interests, desires, hopes, hang-ups, hostilities...

There is a fusion in the beginning of a new romance. When people are stuck together like white on rice. As the ideal phase gives way to the real phase, this closeness must give way to separateness: "I can do me and you can do you, and it is all good". Despite not being forever in a fused state, the relationship is able to maintain a closeness that allows for mutuality: a mature adult-love relationship where the partner's get to reap the benefits of being connected to a whole and separate other.

Chapter 17
Don't Shit Where You Eat!

There is nothing worse than the bitter taste of betrayal. Like women, a cat knows that you don't shit where you eat. But the same cannot be said for even the smartest of men. Men, like dogs, will not only shit where they eat, but will eat their own shit too. Men are obtuse. This is my nice way of saying that men are stupid ("stupid" defined as slow to understand or learn). Even the most successful, bright, and talented men can be stupid: Bill Clinton, Tiger Woods, Bill Cosby, Donald Trump, John F. Kennedy, Jesse Jackson and Martin Luther King, Jr. (just to name a few). Men just don't get it.

I have heard it said plenty of times "men are not made for monogamy;" "monogamy is unnatural." Well, not according to Selma Fraiberg (1971), she writes, "All love, even later in life, begins with a feeling of exclusiveness. You are the one who matters—only you." If this is the case, then cheating may be considered the unnatural act. It may be rooted in neglect and/or abuse, where a child did not have an opportunity to get that one-on-one with that special one (mother). He then does not know the special value of intimacy and exclusivity. Be mindful that true intimacy takes place between two people, not you, she and he. When a person is starved for attention, anyone will do. The innate response of stranger-danger is traded in for the comfort of strange pussy (no matter the cost).

I know about the research done to support evolutionary theory, which suggests that a man is not built for monogamy. In biology and psychology, the term *Coolidge effect* describes a phenomenon—seen in nearly every mammalian species in which it has been tested—whereby males and females both exhibit continuous high sexual performance given the introduction of new receptive partners

(Psychology Today, 2008). As you should know by now, I am all for something new and exciting. The more variety, the better. It is the lying and the cheating that I can't stand. I get it; guys like new pussy just as she likes new dick. I know there are some of you who would serve new pussy as a dish for your man, and some who want to watch as he eats it.

For the woman who can appreciate that variety is the spice of life, tell your man to ask for what he wants. Closed mouths don't get fed! There will always be someone or something trying to get in where they fit in. But if your relationship is airtight, like Tupperware, you can preserve the freshness. This is another reason to talk about what you crave. When people stop talking, they start acting; and sometimes they act a fool. This is often how lying and cheating find their way into the mix. These ingredients are sure to ruin your dish. You should be able to make an informed decision, remember? If he is the kind of man who has an appetite for more than one woman, he should put it on his list of ingredients. Greedy!

Couples are supposed to commit to the fulfillment of each other's needs, including the need for sexual satisfaction. Masters and Johnson (1974) assert that sexual satisfaction is related to commitment. They write:

> If either or both of them must seek sexual satisfaction with other partners, the circle of commitment will have been broken. The more satisfactions they find with other people, the fewer satisfactions do they need from each other; and the less they need from each other, the easier it is for them to go their separate ways. Beyond all rationalization, extra-marital affairs would demonstrate two things: first, that they were incapable of meeting each other's most basic physical and emotional needs, and second, that they did not consider each other unique, and therefore irreplaceable, sources of satisfaction and pleasure. (p. 254).

Given the consequences of choosing an unsuitable mate, women have necessarily developed strategies to avoid these consequences. Like finding a man who is dependable and loyal.

For the ladies who are not so risqué, but still want to satisfy their man, find some other ways to keep things hot and fresh. Research shows that when men get bored with the menu, they go somewhere else to eat. Masters and Johnson noted, "Loss of coital interest engendered by monotony in a sexual relationship is probably the most constant factor in the loss of an *aging* male's interest in sexual performance with his partner." They further note that, "such a man may be rejuvenated by having sexual intercourse with a younger woman, although the young woman may not be as adept a lover as his wife." Research suggests that the age of the other woman is less important to this effect than is her *otherness*" (Psychology Today, 2008).

The results of my research suggest that women are not different from men in this way. Above average responses were given by the entire sample to the statement: My sex life is monotonous. This is also evidenced by the importance of newness and variety in the sex act, which were identified as essential ingredients by 42% and 40%, of the 105 women, respectively. Yes, we like to keep it hot too. We know how to spice things up without fucking things up or we just know how to "dip" without getting caught.

It is my firm belief that woman are smarter than men. Pussy rules the world. You don't hear about women on the news getting caught with their hands in the cookie jar. It is not because women don't cheat every now and then. It's that she is just more cunning than he. I am not saying that being a proficient liar is a thing to be proud of. It is never good to be good at deception (unless you are working undercover). But it is what it is.

Tell your man that if he decides to lie and cheat, expect that you will eventually crack that egg, and he will be left looking like a real chicken, the coward that he is—a man who did not have the courage to say I am feeling weak, I am interested in another woman, I am just not that into you, I am feeling empty, I want out, and I just might try to disguise it with the sweet smell of pussy. Ladies if you have a man that is being honest, don't distort or disguise the facts. It its what it is, and it will not become something it is not!

People spend a lot of time trying to create the life and love that they crave. In one moment it gets trashed for a piece of ass. It is like spending all day imagining what this meal will taste like. Thinking about this meal that is going to be prepared. Thinking about the ingredients that are going to be put in each dish. You spend time at the grocery store. You spend time preparing the ingredients: chopping the onions, making the roux, marinating the meat, pasta from scratch even, and then he goes and put some off brand bullshit in it. And all of the work feels like it is for nothing; it has all been a fucking waste of time and energy. In this there is no positive self-regard.

Lying and cheating—a poisonous pair. Who put that shit in my dish? These are definitely the wrong ingredients. They have the potential to ruin any recipe and many relationships. It can take you from gourmet to garbage in a heartbeat. I say potential because I do know that many relationships survive infidelity. Yes, some people can take shit and use it as fertilizer to help things grow. But who wants the smell of shit lingering around? It places an extraordinary burden on the relationship. So to all of you reading these pages, think before you act-out and repeat something from your past; think before you tell that lie, think before you let him stick his dick in you; think before you start to confide in him; think before you ruin your life together; think before you break your partner's heart; think before you tear your family apart, think before you humiliate yourself and your-other; think before you ruin your recipe for ecstasy.

If there is one thing that is for sure, there is nothing like lying and cheating to make a woman stone cold. I am talking frigid. Ladies, if he tries to test the waters, you offer him a word of caution. Tell him, "I ain't that girl so don't you be that guy. I ain't the girl who will eat shit and tell you that it tastes like sherbet. So don't serve it up. I ain't the girl who will keep opening up the door so that you can walk all over me. I ain't the girl who will put up with your lies so don't deceive me. I am telling you right now, I ain't that girl so don't be that guy". Ladies, this means you too. Don't be the one who ruins the recipe with the poisonous pair. Don't be that girl!

I do believe that love, commitment, lots of hard work and forgiveness can turn garbage back to gourmet. However, you can't go back to being the one and only one, after you have said, "I do", if you lie and cheat. It is like loosing your virginity; cheating is another loss of innocence. Some things cannot be taken back. And she will never let you forget that. She will want to slap the taste right out of your mouth, or maybe even cut you with a knife. "Hell hath no fury like a woman scorned". This means that you have to start all over building trust and security. This is no small feat. So if you don't want things to be harder than it needs to be, don't shit where you eat!

Chapter 18
A Culinary Ménage a Trois:
Closeness, Commitment, Cumming

Just as hypothesized, with all the women in the same pot, commitment, emotional intimacy, and orgasm responsiveness predict sexual satisfaction. Among these (also as hypothesized), intimacy is the best predictor of sexual satisfaction. Kaplan (1974) contends that emotional closeness facilitates orgasm responsiveness, which would, on the face of it, affect sexual satisfaction. Consistency of orgasm responsiveness has also been identified as an important predictor of sexual satisfaction (Hullbert et al., 1993; Perlman & Abramson, 1982). This tells us that the closer two people are, and the more that they share with only each other, the greater their chances for sexual satisfaction.

My findings support existing research on sexual satisfaction. Specifically, Katz (1993) speculated about relevance of intimacy in predicting sexual satisfaction, given the high correlation between the two variables. Sternberg (1986) identified commitment as an important aspect of relationship satisfaction. Given the connection between relationship satisfaction and sexual satisfaction, it logically follows that commitment affects sexual satisfaction.

It is no coincidence that, as the level of commitment increases, the number of reported sexual problems decreases. Commitment is not solely about monogamy, which increases a woman's physical and emotional security; it is also about his commitment to her pleasure. This double dose of commitment will produce mind-blowing orgasms; she will want to reward his commitment with reciprocity.

Keep it Cumming

Despite having lower levels of intimacy and commitment, it appears that single women and married women are similar in terms of orgasm responsiveness—they cum just as hard and just as often. There was a slight decline in orgasm responsiveness as a result of adding children to the mix for, both, the single and married group. This contradicts female biology, which suggests improved responsiveness after childbirth. However, it makes total sense when you consider all of the factors that influence how a woman's body responds during any given sexual experience (i.e. physical health, fatigue, distraction, mood). Sometimes mothers have a lot on their plate and this may make it difficult to focus on pleasure.

Although there was not a significant *quantitative* difference in orgasm responsiveness for the sample, a particularly interesting difference emerged in the *qualitative* data. A closer investigation of the ingredients yielded an important finding regarding orgasm responsiveness for single and married women with children. Thirty percent of the single mothers and 19% of the married mothers reported that *multiple orgasms* were an influential part of their peak sexual experiences. This finding does support biological theory regarding female sexual development, which states that there is increased blood flow to the vagina for women who have had children, leading to increased physiological responsiveness.

As it pertains to multiple orgasms, adding children to your mix may be of benefit. If children are not in your plans, review the section: A Recipe for Orgasms, Multiple Pleasure.

Substitutions Allowed

Levels of excitement and intimacy, both, facilitate orgasm responsiveness. In the current study, the married group had higher levels of intimacy in their relationships and they placed more emphasis on the nature of the relationship. At the same time, the single group placed greater emphasis on passion and the level of excitement in their sexual relationships, which is indicated by their respective hierarchy of ingredients to the recipe for ecstasy.

Surprisingly, women in, both, the single and married groups were able to achieve orgasm with relatively similar amounts of consistency. Given the importance of intimacy *and* arousal for orgasm, maybe having *just one* of the essential ingredients is enough to ensure orgasm responsiveness. What the single woman lacks in intimacy, she makes up for in the level of excitement/arousal, therefore offsetting any difference in orgasm responsiveness that might be expected when there is a reduced level of intimacy. And vice versa, what the sexually satisfied married woman lacks in excitement is compensated for by heightened intimacy.

Given the opportunity, I would choose intimacy over excitement. But if you don't plan on becoming a regular patron, go ahead and make substitutions. Spice it up so, at the very least, your meal will be hot.

Taking Matters into Your Own Hands

Sometimes we go back for seconds even when we are no longer hungry. This is a sure sign of satisfaction. The Redbook (1975) Survey on Sexual Pleasure found a relationship between frequency of sexual intercourse and sexual satisfaction. Increased frequency of intercourse, especially with the woman as initiator, is an indication of sexual satisfaction. When she comes back for more, he has done something right. The opposite is also true; if she is not interested in more, then he is in need of a lesson on how to please her.

The women in this study were not having sex as often as they would prefer; on average they only initiated sex 40% of the time, thus suggesting areas of sexual dissatisfaction. More specifically, as a whole, the women who participated in this study are having sex with their current partners 1.63 times per week, but desire sex 2.5 times per week. This is in comparison to a preferred frequency of 3.05 times per week with the partner identified in the most sexually satisfying experience.

This offers more support for the idea that women who are sexually satisfied desire more sex and initiate more often. When a woman gets horny her body starts to talk. It says, "Feed me, please!" So ladies be clear, if you are not in the mood for seconds or if you have no problem getting up to do the laundry after being served, then there are areas of sexual dissatisfaction. Remember, sex is the best soporific. Ladies, you should be fast asleep.

The reduced frequency of sexual intercourse can, however, be in part, attributed to not having a partner. This group of women reported that the most common reason for engaging in solo sex/self pleasuring is partner unavailability (39%). Given that only 39%

of these women cited absence of lover as a cause for dining alone (solo sex), it appears that a number of women simply enjoy their own company; so they dine alone.

The second most identified reason for self-pleasuring was to reach orgasm (14.3%). Note that it is not clear whether these women were unable to reach orgasm in their sexual experience, and used solo sex as a supplement to partnered sex. However, the point that needs emphasis is that all of the women in the study had a partner (i.e., someone they were dating or a spouse). It is possible that their partners were unavailable, unable to fill them up with orgasmic pleasure, or did not take the time to make sure that she was well done. Therefore, these women remain in a state of "unpleasure" until the tension is released.

Snack on This

Self Pleasuring

Self-pleasuring is a great way for women to meet their physical needs in the absence of a partner, but it has several other uses. It can be relaxing at the end of a long day or when you need to take the edge off. There is no better way for a woman to get to know her body and how it responds than through self-exploration. This can be the first step in teaching your man what turns you on. If you are feeling adventurous, have him watch you, so that he can see first hand how you heat things up. For many women it will only take a hot minute to hit the spot, as opposed to when he is doing the pleasuring, it might take a minute. Therefore, self-pleasuring during partnered sex may also cut down on the cooking time. Whatever your pleasure, make it hot!

When the right two people put these ingredients together, sex will be one-der-full. He will enjoy your sex life and so will you. He will be pleased, and so will you. You will not only have a wonderful sex mate, but you will have a wonderful life. Sex will go far beyond a "normal function"—it will take you to ecstasy!

Pop the champagne! Join a toast to no more garbage! From here on out it is strictly gourmet.

Don't Leave Her Wanting

As a whole, this entire group of women experienced orgasm, on average, 74% of the time. Now, that is pretty damn good. However, one must take into consideration the disappointment and frustration (physical and emotional) that accompanies the experience of not reaching orgasm 26% of the time. Just as with a man, when a woman gets all hot and bothered, she needs to experience some release. The build up associated with being right on the edge, can drive a person right over the edge if they don't get to taste intense delight. If you have been paying attention to anything you have read, then you know, a man who puts in the time and effort to make a woman scream and moan might just be worth keeping. Moreover, 84% of the women reported experiencing orgasm during their most sexually satisfying experience. This indicates the importance of orgasm responsiveness for sexual satisfaction.

Freud (1905a) distinguishes between two types of pleasure. He designates one kind of pleasure as *fore-pleasure*. It is produced by the excitation of erotogenic zones. He names the other pleasure *end-pleasure*, characterized by a release or "discharge of the sexual substances." It is what I have referred to as arousal and orgasm, respectively. The difference between fore-pleasure and end-pleasure is like the difference between taking your first bite and your last. Once you have taken your first bite of something good, you can't wait until the next morsel hits your palate. And after that last bite, all you want to do is kick back and relax so you can fully digest the experience.

Freud states that this first excitation causes a build-up of tension, which necessarily involves *un-pleasure*. This unpleasure subsequently creates an urgency to release the tension, which is accomplished through pleasure. The experience associated with fore-pleasure is illustrated by this woman's statement: *"We could have a lengthy period of foreplay, sexual talk, oral sex, and build up the tension toward intercourse."*

According to Freud, the beginning aspect of pleasure is when the genitals begin to change. In women, the vagina lubricates and expands. "Mmm, mmm, that feels good." This initial pleasure can give rise to the need for more pleasure. "That's it, right there, don't stop, please, don't stop!" The final aspect, end-pleasure, is considered to be the highest in intensity. Its mechanism is different from that of the earlier pleasure. It is brought about entirely by discharge. It is wholly a pleasure of satisfaction that hinges on the tension of the libido being temporarily extinguished. "Yes! Yes! Oooh, yes!"

Many women described their orgasmic experience in terms of a release. *"It was like flying... total explosion."* and *"[It] was very fulfilling, relaxing, exhilarating, a release."* This might help us understand the immediate calmness, feeling of satiation, and the exhaustion, that accompanies or soon follows the experience of release/orgasm/end-pleasure. Moreover, the concept of the role of tension/un-pleasure and subsequent release adds support to the finding that women who do not experience orgasm during the sexual act are particularly frustrated (i.e. less satisfied).

Don't take her to a five star restaurant and tell her she can't eat.

A Mouth Full: Foreplay

Much research has focused on the importance of foreplay during the sexual act. Specifically, foreplay has been identified as a catalyst for arousal. Arousal includes the physiological changes in the genitals, and other parts of the body, which facilitate intercourse, as well as a subjective experience of being "titillated." Prolonged foreplay during intercourse has been associated with more frequent orgasms by women (Wilcox & Hager, 1980). Additionally, Davidson and Darling (1988) found that one of the most desired changes for women was "more foreplay." This early research provided areas of inquiry as I looked for reasons why the women in my study, as a whole, don't reach orgasm with greater frequency.

There are many possible answers to this question. Women can be finicky; what tempts her taste buds today may not do so tomorrow. For the mothering woman, her endless honey-do list may make sex feel like more of a chore. The partner's sexual prowess and technique may also be in question. When you boil it down, all these things translate into insufficient levels of arousal.

The Index of Sexual Satisfaction (ISS) may also shed some light on this question. It measures the magnitude of problems in the sexual relationship. It was used to assess the women's level of sexual satisfaction. The following list includes the statements that represent the problematic areas for the entire sample.

Table 3. Areas of Sexual Dissatisfaction:
Lowest Ranked Statements Among All Women Studied

Statements from the Index of Sexual Satisfaction (ISS)	Mean
I think that sex is wonderful.	1.53
I feel that my partner enjoys our sex life.	1.57
My partner is a wonderful sex mate.	1.66
I feel that sex is a normal function of our relationship.	1.72
I feel that my partner is sexually pleased with me.	1.81
My partner is sexually very exciting.	1.81
My partner is sensitive to my sexual needs and desires.	1.83
I enjoy the sex techniques that my partner likes or uses.	1.91
It is easy for me to get sexually excited by my partner.	1.94
My sex life is monotonous.	2.36
My sex life is very exciting.	2.42
I feel that our sex life really adds a lot to our relationship.	2.79

NOTE: This 25 question measure (the ISS) assesses the degree of sexual problems in a relationship. Mean scores listed here range from 1 to 5 and are listed in order from the most problematic to the least problematic.

As indicated by the scoring system, these numbers reflect the following responses: 1 = rarely or none of the time; 2 = a little of the time; 3 = some of the time; 4 = a good part of the time; and 5 = most of the time.

What do these numbers tell us? If you want to please a woman, never serve her garbage. This means keep the quality of your interactions with her high, whether you are butt-naked or fully clothed. With all of the women in the same pot, the top five areas of sexual dissatisfaction are indicated by the average responses to the following statements on the Index of Sexual Satisfaction: I think sex is wonderful (1.53); I feel that my partner enjoys our sex life (1.57); My partner is a wonderful sex mate (1.66); I feel that sex is a normal function of our relationship (1.72); I feel that my partner is sexually pleased with me (1.81), and Sex is fun for my partner and me (1.81).

When you mix it all together, two primary areas of concern stand out: pleasure/gratification and nature of the relationship. To make the dish turn out tasty women need things to be just right. She needs to be put in the mood (romantic, playful, safe, relaxed). Keep in mind that this starts outside of the bedroom, and it is often an aspect of the nature of the relationship. The closer a couple is throughout the day the better the chance for intimacy at night. Thus daytime intimacy serves as foreplay.

As a whole, the women in this study identified the level of excitement as particularly dissatisfying. Over time, the couple needs to create freshness in their relationship. Changing the setting (away, rustic, creative, outdoors) is a way to keep things new. This may cut through the monotony and can also affect passion. For each person to enjoy the sexual experience everyone's needs should be considered. Ask your sex mate what he or she enjoys so that they can use their technique to satisfy your appetite. There is no need for a special occasion to use the specialty cookbook, every day is an opportunity to go gourmet.

Remember: the oven needs to be nice and warm before the cooking begins. Ladies, make sure you and your man take the time to warm you up so that everyone can be satisfied when the cooking is done. The women in this study give us a mouth full when it comes to the things that are considered desirable during foreplay. A number of women specifically point to the duration of foreplay as being important. For example, *"It was slow and long, lots of kissing each other's bodies, oral sex, but not to orgasm."* For another woman, foreplay began hours before the bedroom:

The date consisted of a lot of foreplay which was as follows: Met at a metaphysical shop for a lecture and hugged before we left. Sat by the lake (Michigan in Chicago) and talked, kissed, and became heart to heart… Then went to my house and laid on the floor while he gave me a massage, reflexology, and he asked if I wanted intercourse.

These are two very different approaches to foreplay; however they both ended in satisfaction. Foreplay is what you want it to be. In the study, it included all of the following ways of connecting:

"intimate conversation," "sexual talk," "kissing," "touching,"

"stroking," "rubbing," "massaging," "dancing," "caressing," "stroking," "fingering," "oral sex," "looking," "listening," "exploring," "asking," "licking," "sucking", "sexting," and "fantasizing."

Did I miss anything? I don't think so. Ladies, if you want to cum, make sure that he doesn't miss anything, either.

Pantry Essentials

Some things ring true for all women no matter the age, race, education, occupation, marital status, or parental status. Women with good taste want it all. She wants to feel good and look good doing it. She wants satisfaction in and out of bed. Even though we have different tastes, there are some fundamental ingredients that remain the same in adult love relationships. To that end, I put all the women in one dish to see how the mixture would turn out. See Grocery List for All Women for the staple ingredients that every woman should have to make a sexually satisfying dish.

So, for this recipe to turn out scrum-delicious, a woman must first feel confident in her ability to produce a mouthwatering masterpiece. She must enter the pair-bond feeling narcissistically confirmed, in touch with her own fears and desires, and allow herself to open up to the enormous possibilities of pleasure, knowing that in the end she might find herself pleasingly plump (pregnant). If the above preparations have been made, a woman will find a mate who will assist her in the kitchen of life and love.

This will be a man who will reliably put her in a romantic **mood** (57%). He will create a **setting** (46%) that is playful yet safe, where **the nature of the relationship** (45%) is characterized by mutuality and commitment, allowing the couple to experience passion and **newness** (42%), such as **variation in the sex act** (40%) and a sense of awayness, while at the same time maintaining **positive self-regard** (40%) and sharing feelings of true **love** (35%). It is imperative to remember the importance of **arousal** (33%) and **intimacy** (33%), which facilitates **orgasm intensity** (27%), and which can also serve as an avenue to showcase the diversity of his **sexual technique** (24%). And of course, as with any "good meal," **timing** (23%) is crucial. If these items are put together properly, the outcome will be a recipe for ecstasy

Grocery List for All Women

The Essential Ingredients for Sexual Satisfaction

Ingredient	Frequency
Mood	52%
Setting	46%
Nature of Relationship	45%
Newness	42%
Variation in the Sex Act	40%
Positive Self-Regard	40%
Love	35%
Intimacy	33%
Arousal	33%
Orgasm Intensity	27%
Technique	24%
Timing	23%

Epilogue

Satiation

Just like any good meal, this book started with an idea: to use psychoanalytic and evolutionary theories as a premise to explore, integrate, and understand various aspects of female sexuality, with an emphasis on sexual satisfaction. I wanted to mix it up and see how things turned out. Both theories are developmental in nature and assert that sexuality cannot be understood outside of the relational context, because it is the mother-child dyad that lays the foundation for romantic relationships.

To understand a woman's sexuality you must know her body and mind, and—more importantly—her heart's desire. This requires intimacy. Intimacy requires sharing.

Intimacy is an essential ingredient in both the mother-child relationship and romantic relationships. There is no substitution for intimacy in the recipe for ecstasy.

As a psychologist, I wanted to understand the biological predispositions and developmental characteristics that contribute to a comprehensive understanding of female sexual satisfaction. Specifically, I wanted to study how female sexual satisfaction is impacted by the Oedipus/Electra conflict, primary feminine identification, mate selection, and reproduction. As a woman I needed to understand my own experience and expression of sexuality, including how it has and will continue to evolve over time.

This recipe—*The Recipe for Ecstasy*—starts with some good home cooking. Parents are responsible for teaching children how to do many things, including how to make love. That is, parents teach children how to take the right ingredients and put them together in the right order to produce something that gives a sense of fullness, of satiation.

Without lessons in love, people are left feeling empty and starved for attention. Instead of making sex a natural part of a loving relationship, it becomes the pawn in a game where every one loses. Women use it to fill the voids of loneliness and to substitute for love.

But, in any recipe, love cannot be replaced. Love is unique and necessary. Love is given to us in infancy, nurtured through childhood, so we carry it with us for the rest of our lives.

To encourage the growth process, mothers have to be tuned in, paying close attention to their children's individual needs. I think about this all the time. How does a mother nurture what each child needs, in the way each child needs? One is mastering walking; the mother needs to be there to help the child balance, to encourage the child to step away, to admire the child's motility. At the same time, her other child is mastering talking; the mother needs to help the child know that there is a word for everything, to know how to pronounce the words, to understand the garbled words, to translate to the outside world, and to admire when the words get clearer. Erna Furman called this "doing for, doing with, and standing by to admire."

Mothers know this—what one child needs as a path to master a task can be totally different than what the next child will need. Mothers of three or more children especially know about the role of temperament in personality development and, in turn, the loving flexibility required of a mother to notice, respect, and work with these differences. Mother's have the grand tasks of attending, adoring, and admonishing. And if done properly it will yield a great self-sufficient whole person.

To put in work as a parent is to give love and to nurture independence.

When children are neglected, they don't know how special they are, how lovable they are, how strong they are, how good-looking they are, how smart they are, how capable they are. Brenner (1982) calls this a "calamity of childhood." To not receive the essential scaffolding to enjoy life as it is, to trust and love others, to be at relative peace with oneself. Once grown, these children have to work harder to get there, to get to ecstasy.

But get there you will, if you love and work. Growth does not have to take place as a result of suffering, but it can. Though, this does require work. You have to work to become whole, to have a sense of self and self-worth. Yes, some kids got help with this work in their early years, but as an adult you can help yourself; it is possible to re-feed a deprived soul. Get some couch time.

This will serve as replenishment for those that are restocking their pantry and plenishment for those whose cupboards were bare. Make sure that you have done the work of introspection and maturation (e.g. feedback from peers, therapy, learning from experience) before you go shopping for a mate. Finding a mate can superficially fill a void, but finding one after seeking inner health is wiser and much more gratifying.

You must first know your own flava (your ingredients), then you must know what tempts your taste buds (his ingredients), and finally you must put them together to make *love*. My husband and I have mastered this recipe. No, things are not perfect, and as we continue to grow in love, I am sure that we will have to tweak our recipe. But, for now, we get to enjoy the fruits of our labor and our love.

What were you taught and what will you teach about life and love?

What a miracle it is to look at my children and to see myself. Those of you with children know exactly what I mean. Having an opportunity to see yourself as you were, as you would have been or as you could have been. History repeats itself through genetics and through lessons. Of course, my girls are not all me, their dad is in there, and they are clearly their own selves, too. Outside, they are a blend of us both—from their long legs to their long, naturally curly hair. Inside, you can see their unique temperaments, attitudes, intelligence, and personality all over the place. Inside and out, they are still growing; we are still feeding them, trying to have some input for the final product, as we pass down our recipe.

Some history repeats itself because it must, and with this, parts of us just get better with time. This occurs as a result of natural selection (nature). Other aspects of history repeat itself because of lessons (nurture). What will you feed your children to eat? Will you teach your children how to take care of themselves? How to love all of who they are? How to share? How to cook in and out of the bedroom? How to learn? How to live? How to earn a living? How to create a recipe for ecstasy?

Repetition is how we learn. People should practice loving and making good love. Good love and good sex are salubrious. It is all in good health. When you boil it all down, what does this all mean? Love is a primary ingredient. It is why we are here. What else is there? Oh yeah, work. If you have love and you are willing to work then you create a recipe that yields ecstasy.

I offer these ingredients as a lesson in creating a recipe for ecstasy:

love, arousal, positive self-regard, nature of the relationship (N.O.R), orgasm intensity, sexual abandon, setting, variation in the sexual act, newness, multiple orgasms, his focus on her (H.F.O.H), intimacy, orgasm intensity, mood (i.e. relaxed, playful, safe), quality of relatedness (i.e. mutuality), and intensity of the physiological and emotional response.

Make sure you have all of the ingredients to make yourself complete; make yourself a tantalizing treat. Then go out and find yourself a blackberry, remember "the blacker the berry the sweeter the juice". While he might be a breadwinner, I am not talking about someone who will just give you the dough. I am talking about a grown ass man who knows how to make his woman feel special. He will love you and commitment his resources to you and yours. He will be sweet, and your life will taste so much sweeter with him in it.

Remember that every meal you sit down to will not be a full course dinner, some men are in your life for only a morsel. Savor it. When it is time to pick someone else off of the menu, choose wisely. You want a man who will add some nutritional value, someone who has the right tools in his kitchen. Not pots and pans, but values and plans.

Things on the outside change: grey hair, wrinkles, more fat, less muscles, arthritis, dentures. But love and commitment, they stay the same. When you work, you can hold on to love. You are what you eat. I (mother/author) will feed you (child/reader) so that you can love another (man/mate) until death do you part.

Lovingly,

Myrtle C. Means, Ph.D.

Appendices

Appendix A: Demographic Information Collected

1. Age _____

2. Race _____

3. Highest Level of Education Obtained _____

4. Occupation _____

5. Primary Sexual Orientation
   a. heterosexual
   b. bisexual
   c. homosexual

6. Marital Status
   a. single
   b. married, _____ years
   c. divorced
   d. widower
   e. co-habitating (i.e. live-in partner)

7. Number of children _____; list sex and age of children from oldest to youngest.
   a. _____
   b. _____
   c. _____
   d. _____
   e. _____
   f. _____
   g. _____

8. Approximately how many times have you had partnered sex in the last year? _____

9. Approximately how many times did you experience orgasm? _____

10. How often would you like to have partnered sex? _____

11. When you have sex with a partner, what percentage of the time do you initiate sex? _____

12. Approximately how many times have you had solo sex (i.e. self stimulation, masturbation) in the past year? _____

13. Approximately how many times did you experience orgasm? _____

14. If you had solo sex, why? _____

15. Was your last sexual encounter safe? That is, did you use barrier protection (i.e. a condom)? If not, why not? _____

Appendix B: The Orgasm Responsiveness Questionnaire

Please be truthful when responding to the following statements,
as they pertain to you.

1. I have never experienced orgasm.

   True   False

   1   2

   If you have answered true to statement #1,
   STOP here; if you answered false, GO on.

2a. I experience orgasm during vaginal-penile intercourse.

low	low-mod	moderate	mod-high	high
1	2	3	4	5

2b. Rate the quality of orgasm.

low	low-mod	moderate	mod-high	high
1	2	3	4	5

3a. I bring myself to orgasm through masturbation/ self-stimulation (i.e. direct manual stimulation of the clitoris with hand, vibrator, or other).

low	low-mod	moderate	mod-high	high
1	2	3	4	5

3b. Rate the quality of orgasm.

low	low-mod	moderate	mod-high	high
1	2	3	4	5

4a. I experience orgasm with my partner during the sexual act (i.e. foreplay, afterplay), in the absence of vaginal-penile intercourse.

low	low-mod	moderate	mod-high	high
1	2	3	4	5

4b. Rate the quality of orgasm.

low	low-mod	moderate	mod-high	high
1	2	3	4	5

Appendix C: The Sternberg Triangular Love Scale

The blanks below represent the name of the person with whom you are in a relationship. Rate each statement on a 1-to-9 scale, where 1 = "not at all," 5 = "moderately," 9 = "extremely." Use intermediate points on the scale to indicate intermediate levels of feelings.

1. I am actively supportive of _____'s well being. _____
2. Just seeing _____ excites me. _____
3. I know that I care about _____. _____
4. I have a warm relationship with _____. _____
5. I find myself thinking about _____ frequently during the day. _____
6. I am committed to maintaining my relationship with _____. _____
7. I am able to count on _____ in times of need. _____
8. My relationship with _____ is very romantic. _____
9. Because of my commitment to _____ I would not let other people come between us. _____
10. _____ is able to count on me in times of need. _____
11. I find _____ to be very personally attractive. _____
12. I have confidence in the stability of my relationship with _____. _____
13. I am willing to share myself and my possessions with _____. _____
14. I idealize _____. _____
15. I could not let anything get in the way of my commitment to _____. _____
16. I receive considerable emotional support from _____. _____
17. I cannot imagine another person making me as happy as _____ does. _____
18. I expect my love for _____ to last for the rest of my life. _____
19. I give considerable emotional support to _____. _____
20. I would rather be with _____ than anyone else. _____
21. I will always feel a strong responsibility for _____. _____
22. I communicate well with _____. _____
23. There is nothing more important to me than my relationship with _____. _____
24. I view my commitment to _____ as a solid one. _____
25. I value _____ greatly in my life. _____

26. I especially like physical contact with _____.   _____

27. I cannot imagine ending my relationship with _____.   _____

28. I feel close to _____.   _____

29. There is something almost 'magical' about my relationship   _____
    with _____.

30. I am certain of my love for _____.   _____

31. I have a comfortable relationship with _____.   _____

32. I adore _____.   _____

33. I view my relationship with _____ as permanent.   _____

34. I feel that I really understand _____.   _____

35. I cannot imagine life without _____.   _____

36. I view my relationship with _____ as a good decision.   _____

37. I feel that _____ really understands me.   _____

38. My relationship with _____ is passionate.   _____

39. I feel a sense of responsibility toward _____.   _____

40. I feel that I really can trust _____.   _____

41. When I see romantic movies and read romantic books I   _____
    think of _____.

42. I plan to continue in my relationship with _____.   _____

43. I share deeply personal information about myself with   _____
    _____.

44. I fantasize about _____.   _____

45. Even when _____ is hard to deal with, I remain committee   _____
    to our relationship.

Appendix D: Index of Sexual Satisfaction

This questionnaire is designed to measure the degree of satisfaction you have in the sexual relationship with your partner. It is not a test, so there are no right or wrong answers. Answer each item as carefully & accurately as you can by placing a number beside each one, as follows:

1 Rarely or none of the time
2 A little of the time
3 Some of the time
4 A good part of the time
5 Most or all of the time

1. I feel that my partner enjoys our sex life. _____
2. My sex life is very exciting. _____
3. Sex is fun for my partner and me. _____
4. Sex with my partner has become a chore for me. _____
5. I feel that sex is dirty and disgusting. _____
6. My sex life is monotonous. _____
7. When we have sex it is too rushed and hurriedly completed. _____
8. I feel that my sex life is lacking in quality. _____
9. My partner is sexually very exciting. _____
10. I enjoy the sex techniques that my partner likes or uses. _____
11. I feel that my partner wants too much sex from me. _____
12. I think that sex is wonderful. _____
13. My partner dwells on sex too much. _____
14. I try to avoid sexual contact with my partner. _____
15. My partner is too rough or brutal when we have sex. _____
16. My partner is a wonderful sex mate. _____
17. I feel that sex is a normal function of our relationship _____
18. My partner does not want sex when I do. _____
19. I feel that our sex life really adds a lot to our relationship. _____
20. My partner seems to avoid sex contact with me. _____
21. It is easy for me to get sexually excited by my partner. _____
22. I feel that my partner is sexually pleased with me. _____
23. My partner is very sensitive to my sexual needs and desires. _____
24. My partner does not satisfy my sexually. _____
25. I feel that my sex life is boring. _____

Appendix E: Sexual Satisfaction Questionnaire

Please answer the following questions as openly and honestly as possible. Take all the time you need. Please use the paper provided and number your responses to match this sheet. If you need more writing space, ask the examiner for more paper.

1. In as much detail as possible, please describe the most sexually satisfying experience of your life.

2. What made this experience so satisfying?

3a. What was the nature of your relationship with the partner in the experience you have just described?

   a. One night-stand/Anonymous/Experimental
      [If (a), continue to Question #4.]
   b. Casual Dating
   c. Spouse/Committed Relationship
   d. Other, describe _____

3b. If you responded to question (3a) with b, c, or d, answer the following questions:

   a. How long have you been involved with this partner?

   b. How often do you have sex with this partner?

   c. How often would you like to have sex with this partner?

4. During the experience you have just described, how did you feel about yourself and how did you feel about your partner? That is, what feelings were aroused?

5. During the experience you have just described, did you reach orgasm? If so, what do you recall about that experience?

6. Have you ever considered having a child/ren with this partner? Why or why not?

Sexual Satisfaction Questionnaire Response Sheet

Please be sure to number your written responses to match the questions on the previous page.

1. _____
   _____
   _____
   _____
   _____
   _____
   _____

2. _____
   _____
   _____
   _____
   _____
   _____

3a. _____
3b. _____
   _____
   _____

4. _____
   _____
   _____
   _____
   _____
   _____

5. _____
   _____
   _____
   _____
   _____
   _____

6. _____
   _____
   _____
   _____
   _____
   _____
   _____

Appendix F: Breakup-Make Up Playlist

Sideways	Santana featuring Citizen Cope
Hangin' on a String	Loose Ends
Promise Me	Luther Vandross
Nothing At All	Santana featuring Musiq
Drink to get Drunk	Sia
Before He Cheats	Carrie Underwood
Bust Your Windows	Jazmine Sullivan
Boom	Anjulie
Lucky	Lewis Taylor
Break up	Mario featuring Gucci Mane and Sean Garrett
One More Chance/Stay With Me	The Notorious B.I.G.
Love TKO	Teddy Pendergrass
Better Love	Luther Vandross
This Place Hotel (Heartbreak Hotel)	The Jacksons
Let Not Play the Game	Maxwell
Love is	LTJ Bukem
Never Miss the Water (Til the Well Runs Dry)	Chaka Khan featuring Meshell Ndegeocello
That Feeling	Savannah Remix
Epiphany (I'm Leaving)	Chrisette Michelle
Comfortable	Little Wayne and Babyface
Regret	Letoya featuring Ludacris
Anyone Who Had a Heart	Luther Vandross
Be Okay	Chrisette Michele
Get n' Over You	Brain Culbertson
Back Together Again	Roberta Flack
Find Your Way (Back in my life)	Kem
Another Again	John Legend
Long Way	Olu
In the Morning	Ledisi
It Kills Me	Melanie Fiona
I Forgive You	Rachelle Ferrell
I Still Believe	Norman Brown featuring Michael McDonald

Appendix G: Romance Playlist

Lovely Day	Bill Withers
Don't Look Any Further	Dennis Edwards
This is For the Lover in You	Shalamar
Suitelady	Maxwell
Darlin' Darlin'	Baby Ojays
There Goes My Baby	Charlie Wilson
Island	Will Downing
Everlasting Love	Rufus & Chaka Khan
Candlelight and You	Chante Moore
Feeling the Way	Norman Brown
Purify Me	India Arie
I'll Always Love You	Booney James
No Ordinary Love	Sade
So In Love Alex	Bugnon
Love Train	Pete Belasco
Between the Sheets	Fourplay
I am Special	Rachelle Ferrell
Fantasy	Will Downing
Back Seat	Brian McKnight
No Better Love	Yung Gunz
Got To be There	Michael Jackson
Funny How Time Flies	Janet Jackson
Can't Explain It	LL Cool J
Makes Me Wanna Holler	M'Shell Ndegeocello
Love Suggestions	Will Downing
Welcome to Love	Rachelle Ferrell
Til the Cops Come Knockin'	Maxwell
Spitten' Game	Anthony David
You Were Meant for Me	Michael Franks
Nice and Slow	Usher
Do You Love What You Feel	Chaka Kahn
Soon I'll Be Loving You Again	Marvin Gaye
I Need Love	Robin Thicke

Appendix H: Pole/Lap Dance Playlist

Nasty Naughty Boy Christina Aguilera

Rope Burn Janet Jackson

Bandy Bandy Zap Mama

Like a Surgeon Ciara

Maneater Nelly Furtado

Ayo Technology 50 Cent

Lick Joi

Lollipop Lil Wayne

Candy Cameo

One in a Million Aaliyah

Gangster and Stripper Too Short

Naughty Girl Beyoncé

Get it Shawty Loyd

Wey U Chante Moore

Cater 2 U Destiny's Child

Five Star Yo Gotti

Cyclone Baby Bash featuring T Pain

Woozy Ludacris and R. Kelly

Erotic City Prince

Candy Man Mary Jane Girls

Move Ya Body Nina Sky

Your Bodies Callin' (Remix) R. Kelly

Video Phone Beyoncé

I Wanna Love You Akon

I Just Wanna Love U (Give it to Me) Jay-Z

How Do You Want It Tupac featuring K-Ci & JoJo

Wetter Twista

Come Over Jennifer Lopez

I Care For You Aaliyah

Shakin' it 4 Daddy Robin Thicke featuring Nicki Minaj

Down on Me 50 Cent

Desire Jose James

Pony Ginuwine

Appendix I: Tables

Table 4. Primary Ingredients Indentified by Each Group (N=105)

	Ingredient	Frequency
Single without Children N = 26	Setting	58%
	Arousal	50%
	Love	46%
	NOR	42%
	Intimacy	38%
	Mood	38%
Single & Mothering N=27	Variation in the Sex Act	70%
	Newness	52%
	NOR	41%
	Positive self-regard	41%
	Mood	37%
	Orgasm Intensity	37%
	Setting	30%
Married without Children N=26	Mood	58%
	NOR	50%
	Setting	50%
	Newness	46%
	Intimacy	42%
	Intensity of P/E Response	42%
	Love	38%
Married & Mothering N=26	Mood	77%
	NOR	46%
	Setting	46%
	Variation in the Sex Act	42%
	Newness	38%
	Arousal	35%

Table 5. Specialty Ingredients Indentified by Each Group (N=105)

	Ingredient	Frequency
Single without Children N = 26	Love	46%
	Arousal	38%
	Positive self-regard	35%
	NOR	31%
	Orgasm Intensity	27%
	Sexual Abandon	27%
	Setting/ Location	27%
Single & Mothering N=27	Positive self-regard	41%
	Variation in the Sex Act, Oral	37%
	Orgasm Intensity	37%
	Newness	33%
	Multiple Orgasm	30%
	His Focus on Her	30%
	Love	26%
Married without Children N=26	Love	38%
	Intimacy	35%
	Positive self-regard	31%
	NOR, Married	23%
	Newness, First Time	23%
	Orgasm Intensity	23%
	Intensity of P/E Response	19%
	Intensity Arousal	**19%**
Married & Mothering N=26	Mood	35%
	Love	31%
	Positive self-regard	31%
	Intimacy	27%
	Newness	27%
	Arousal	19%
	Multiple Orgasm	19%
	NOR, Married	19%
	His Focus on Her	19%
	Orgasm Intensity	19%
	Quality of Relationship. Mutuality	19%
	Sexual Abandon	19%
	Setting/ Location	19%
	Intenstiy of Arousal	15%
	Mood, Playful	15%

References

Abrams, P., Levy, R. Panay, A. (Producers), & Dobkin, D. (Director). (2005) *Wedding Crashers* [Motion picture]. United States: New Line Cinema.

Acker, M., & Davis, M. H. (1992). Intimacy, passion, and commitment in adult romantic relationships: A test of the triangular theory of love. *Journal of Social & Personal Relationships, 9*(1), 21-50.

Almaas, A. H. (1998). *Facets of unity: The enneagrams of holy ideas.* Berkley: Diamond Books.

Apt, C., & Hurlbert, D. F. (1992). The female sensation seeker and marital sexuality. *Journal of Sex & Marital Therapy, 18*(4), 315-324.

Baker, R. (1996). *Sperm wars: The evolutionary logic of love and lust.* New York, NY: Basic.

Barbach, L. (1980). *Women discover orgasm: A therapist's guide to a new treatment approach.* New York, NY: The Free Press.

Batten, M. (1992). *Sexual strategies: How females choose their mates.* New York, NY: G. P. Putnam's Sons.

Benedek, T. F. (1959). Sexual functions in women and their disturbance. *American Handbook of Psychiatry, 1,* 727-748.

Blos, P. (1967). The second individuation process of adolescence. *The Psychoanalytic Study of the Child, 22,* 162-286.

Blos, P. (1980). Modifications in the traditional psychoanalytic theory of female adolescent development. *Adolescent Psychiatry 8,* 8-24.

Bonaparte, M. (1953). *Female sexuality.* New York, NY: Grove.

Bowlby, J. (1969). *Attachment and loss: Vol. 1: Attachment.* New York, NY: Basic.

Bowlby, J. (1988). *A secure base.* New York, NY: Basic.

Boyatzis, R. E. (1998). *Transforming qualitative information: Thematic analysis and code development.* Thousands Oaks, CA: Sage.

Brecher, E. M. (1984). *Love, sex, and aging: A Consumers Union report.* Boston: Little, Brown.

Buss, D. M. (1987). Sex differences in human mate selection criteria: An evolutionary perspective. In C. Crawford, M. Smith, & D. Krebs (Eds.), *Sociobiology and psychology: Ideas, issues, and applications* (pp. 335-350). Hillsdale, New Jersey: Erlbaum.

Buss, D.M. (1989). Sex differences in human mate preferences: Evolutionary hypotheses tested in 37 cultures. *Behavioral and Brain Sciences, 12,* 1-49.

Buss, D. M. (1994). *The evolution of desire.* New York, NY: Basic.

Carus, T. L. (2004) On the Nature of Things. (W. E. Leonard Trans.) New York, NY: Courier Dover Publications. (Original work published

1921)

Chasseguet-Smirgel, J. (1970). *Female sexuality: New psychoanalytic views.* Ann Arbor: The University of Michigan Press.

Chodorow, N. (1974). Family structure in feminine personality. In M. Z. Rosaldo and L. Lampherere (Eds), *Women Culture and Society* (pp. 43-66). Stanford, CA: Stanford University Press.

Chodorow, N. (1979) *The reproduction of mothering: Psychoanalysis and the sociology of gender.* Berkley: University of California Press.

Crawford, C., Smith, M., & Krebs, D. (1987). *Sociobiology and psychology: Ideas, issues, and applications.* New Jersey: Erlbaum.

Crooks, R., & Baur, K. (1993). *Our sexuality.* Redwood, California: Benjamin/Cummings.

Cupach, W. R., & Comstock, R. (1990). Satisfaction with sexual communication in marriage: Links to sexual satisfaction and dyadic adjustment. *Journal of Social & Personal Relationships, 7*(2), 179-186.

Daly, M., & Wilson, M. (1983). *Sex, evolution, and behavior.* Belmont, CA: Wadsworth.

Darling, C. A., J. K. Davidson, Sr., & Cox, R. P. (1991). Female sexual response and the timing of partner orgasm. *Journal of Sex and Marital Therapy, 17*(1), 3-21.

Davidson, J. K., Sr., & Darling, C. A. (1988). The sexually experienced woman: The role of multiple sex partners and sexual satisfaction. *Journal of Sex Research, 24,* 141-154.

Davidson, J. K., Sr., & Darling, C. A. (1989). Self-perceived differences in the female orgasmic responses. *Family Practice Research Journal, 8*(2), 75-84.

Deutsch, H. (1991). *Psychoanalysis of the sexual functions of women.* London: Karnac.

Donaldson, S. (1989). Similarity in sensation-seeking, sexual satisfaction and contentment in relationships of heterosexual couples. *Psychological Reports, 64*(2), 405-406.

Downing, W. (2009) Love Suggestions. On *Classique* [CD]. California: Concord Music Group   Inc.

Eibl-Eibesfeldt, I. (1975) *Ethology: The biology of behavior.* New York, NY: Holt, Rinehart, and Winston.

Eisenberg, A. (1991) *What to expect when you are expecting.* New York, NY: Workman Publishing Company, Inc.

Erikson, E. H. (1950). *Childhood and society.* New York, NY: Norton.

Erikson, E. H. (1963). *Childhood and Society* (2nd ed.). New York, NY: Norton.

Fast, I. (1978). Developments in gender identity: The original matrix. International *Review of Psycho-Analysis. 5*, 265-273.

Fast, I. (1979). Developments in gender identity: Gender differentiation in girls. *International Journal of Psychoanalysis, 60*, 443.

Ferguson, J. (1993). Factors contributing to satisfying long-term marriages. *Dissertation Abstracts International, 54-05B*, 2808, 00130.

Fields, N. S. (1983). Satisfaction in long-term marriages. *Social Work, 28*(1), 37-41.

Fisher, R. A. (1930). The genetic theory of natural selection. 2nd Ed. New York, NY: Dover.

Fraiberg, S. (1971). How a baby learns to love. *Redbook,* ISSUE #, PG.

Freud, S. (1905a). *Drei Abhandlungen zur Sexualtheorie, Viennna.* (G.S., 5, 3;G.W., 5, 29.) [Trans.: Three Essays on the Theory of Sexuality, Standard Ed., 7, 125; I.P.L., 57.]

Freud, S. (1905b). 'Bruchstuck einer Hysterie-Analyse', G.S., 8, 3; G.W., 5, 163. (xiii, 22, 29, 31, 33) [Trans.: 'Fragment of an Analysis of a Case of Hysteria', C.P., 3, 13; Standard Ed., 7, 3.]

Freud, S. (1919). '"Ein Kind wird geschlagen"', G.S., 5, 344; G.W.,12,197. [Trans.: ' "A Child is being beaten"', C. P., 2, 172; Standard Ed., 17, 177].

Freud, S. (1923). 'Die infantile Genitalorganization', G.S., 5, 232; G.W., 13, 293. (x. 65-6) [Trans.: 'Infantile Genital Organization', C.P., 2, 244; Standard Ed., 19, 141].

Freud, S. (1931a). 'Uber libidinose Typen', G.S., 12, 115; G. W., 14, 509. (111) [Trans.: 'Libidinal Types', C. P., 5, 247; Standard Ed., 21, 215].

Freud, S. (1931b). 'Uber die weibliche Sexualitat', G.S., 12, 120; G.W., 14, 517. [Trans.: 'Female Sexuality', C.P., 5, 252; Standard Ed., 21, 223.]

Freud, S. (1962). *Three essays on the theory of sexuality.* New York, NY:Basic.

Freud, S. (1963). *Sexuality and the psychology of love.* New York, NY: Macmillan.

Fromm, E. (1956). *The art of loving.* New York, NY: Harper & Row.

Gabbe, S., Niebyl, J., & Simpson, J. L. (1998). *Obstetrics: Normal and problem pregnancies.* New York, NY: Churchill Livingstone.

Gadpaille, W. J. (1975). *The cycles of sex* (L. Freeman, Ed.). New York, NY: Scribner's.

Galenson, E., and Roiphe, H. (1976). Psychology of women: (1) infancy and early childhood, (2) latency and early adolescence. *Journal of the American Psychoanalytic Association, 24*(1) 141-160.

Gilfillan, S. S. (1985). Adult intimate love relationships as new editions of symbiosis and the separation-individuation process. *Smith College Studies in Social Work, 55*(3) 183-196.

Gilligan, C. (1993). *In a different voice.* Cambridge: Harvard University Press.

Grinnel, R. M. (1982). *Social work research and evaluation.* Homewood, IL: Dorsey.

Hamburg, B.A. (1978). The biosocial basis of sex differences. In S. L. Washburn & E. R. McCown (Eds.), *Human evolution: Biosocial perspectives* (pp. 155-213). Menlo Park, CA: Benjamin/ Cummings.

Harvey, Steve (2009). *Act like a lady, think like a man: What men really think about love, relationships, intimacy, and commitment.* New York, NY: Harper Collins.

Henry, Angela (2006). *Tangled roots.* New York, NY: Kimani Press.

Herzog, J. M. (1994). *Encountering the father in the psychoanalytic situation.* Unpublished manuscript.

Horney, K. (1926). The flight from womanhood. *International Journal of Psychoanalysis, 7,* 324 -339.

Horney, K. (1967). *Feminine psychology.* London: Routledge & Kegan Paul.

Hite, S. (1976). *The Hite report. A nationwide study of female sexuality.* New York, NY: Macmillan.

Hudson, W. W. (1982). *The clinical measurement package: A field manual.* Homewood, Il: Dorsey Press.

Hulbert, D. F. (1991). The role of assertiveness in female sexuality: A comparative study between sexually assertive and sexually nonassertive women. *Journal of Sex and Marital Therapy, 17*(3), 183-190.

Hurlbert, D. F., Apt, C., & Rabehl, S. M. (1993). Key variables to understanding female sexual satisfaction: An examination of women in nondistressed marriages. *Journal of Sex & Marital Therapy, 19*(2), 154-165.

Jackson, C., Crawford, T., Hatchett, A.R., Campbell, H. (2007) Amusement Park. 50 Cent. On *Curtis* [CD]. Los Angelos: Aftermath. (2006)

Jayne, C. E. (1983). Sexual satisfaction, relationship factors and orgasm in female sexual behavior: An evaluation of a two-dimensional model of female heterosexual responsiveness. *Dissertation Abstracts International, 44-01B,* 0290.

Johnson, B. K. (1986). The sexual interest, participation, and satisfaction, of older men and women. *Dissertation Abstracts International, 47-12B*, 4824.

Kaplan, H. (1974). *The new sex therapy.* New York, NY: Brunner/Mazel.

Kaplan, L. (1991). *Female perversions.* New York, NY: Anchor.

Katz, R. S. (1993). The psychodevelopmental achievements of identity and intimacy in males and females: relationships to marital satisfaction and sexual satisfaction. *Dissertation Abstracts International, Vol. 55-05B*, 1992.

Kestenberg, J. S. (1956). Vicissitudes of female sexuality. *Journal of the American Psychoanalytic Association, 4*, 456-457.

Kestenberg, J. S. (1968). Outside and inside, male and female. *Journal of the American Psychoanalytic Association, 16*(3), 457-520.

Kinsey, A. C., Pomeroy, W. B., Martin, C. E. & Gebhard, P. E. (1953). *Sexual behavior in the human female.* Philadelphia: Saunders.

Kinsey, A. C., Wardell, B., Pomeroy, C., Martin, E., & Gebhard, P. H. (1965). *Sexual behavior in the human female.* New York, NY: Pocket Books.

Kirkpatrick, M. (1989). Women in love in the 80's. *Journal of the American Academy of Psychoanalysis, 17*(4), 535-542.

Klein, M. (1952). Discussion of mutual influences in development of ego and id. *Psychoanalytic Study of the Child,* 7, 292-320.

Klein, M. (1975). T*he psychoanalysis of children.* New York, NY: Delacorte Press/Seymour Lawrence.

Kraft-Ebing, R. (1965). The instinct of feminine servitude. Psychopathia Sexualis, translated from the 12 German edition. New York, NY: Bell

Kulish, N. M. (1991). The mental representation of the clitoris: The fear of female sexuality. *Psychoanalytic Inquiry, 11*(4), 511-536.

Laufer, E. M. (1976). The central masturbation fantasy, the final sexual organization, and adolescence. *The Psychoanalytic Study of the Child, 31*, 297-316.

Laufer, E. M. (1981) The psychoanalyst and the adolescent's sexual development. *The Psychoanalytic Study of the Child. 36*, 181-191.

Laufer, E. M. (1982) The formation and shaping of the Oedipus complex: Clinical observations and assumptions. *International Journal of Psycho-Analysis, 63*, 217-227.

Laufer, E. M. (1986) The female Oedipus complex and the relationship to the body. *The Psychoanalytic Study of the Child, 41*, 259-276.

Mahler, M. S. (1975). *The psychological birth of the human infant: Symbiosis and individuation.* New York, NY: Basic.

Maison, S. (1982). Factors affecting the relationship between sexual and marital satisfaction. *Dissertation Abstracts International, March, 42* (9-A).

Masters, W. H., & Johnson, V. E. (1966). *Human sexual response.* Boston: Little, Brown.

Masters, W. H., & Johnson, V. E. (1974). *The pleasure bond. A new look at sexuality and commitment.* Boston: Little, Brown.

Mayo Clinic Staff (2010). *Women's Health (7)* Kegel exercises: A how-to guide for women. Retrieved from http://www.mayoclinic.com/health/Kegel-exercises/WO00119

McCathy, E. & Ewing-Mulligan, M. (1998). *Wine for Dummies.* New York, NY: Hungry Minds Inc.

Michael, R. T., Gagnon, J. H., Laumann, E. O., & Kolata, G. (1994). *Sex in America.* Boston: Little, Brown.

Miles, M. B., & Huberman, A. M. (1984). *Qualitative data analysis: A sourcebook of new methods.* Beverly Hills, CA: Sage.

Moore, B. E. (1968). Psychoanalytic reflections on the implications of recent physiological studies of female orgasm. *Journal of the American Psychoanalytic Association, 16*(3), 69-587.

Moret, L. B. (1995). Intimacy and sexual satisfaction in couple relationships. *MAI, 34-06,* 2131.

Morris, D. (1967). *The naked ape.* A zoologist's study of the human animal. London: Cape Ltd.

Morris, W. (1975). *The American heritage dictionary of English language.* Boston: American Heritage.

Noonan, K. M. (1987). Evolution: A primer for psychologists. In C. Crawford, M. Smith, & D. Krebs (Eds.), *Sociobiology and psychology: Ideas, issues, and applications* (pp. 31-60). Hillsdale, New Jersey: Erlbaum.

Oberzaucher, E., Grammer, K. (2010). Immune reactivity and attractiveness. *Gerontology, 56 (6),* 488.

Ozeil, L. J. (1978). Inconsistency of coital orgasm in women. *Medical Aspects of Human Sexuality, 11*(9), 16-28.

Parkinson, B. (1987). Sexual satisfaction in early marriage. *Dissertation Abstracts International, 49-04A,* 0964.

Patrick, J. G. (1985). Love play: The way to make your sex life more sensual—and satisfying. *Redbook 164,* 96-7.

Perlman, S. D., & Abramson, P. R. (1982). Sexual satisfaction among married and cohabiting individuals. *Journal of Consulting and Clinical Psychology, 50*(3), 458-460.

Pool, F. M. (1997). What are the relationships among sexual knowledge, sexual attitudes, intimacy, and dyadic adjustment in married couples? *Dissertation Abstracts International, 58-09B*, 4707.

Prince (1980). Head. On *Dirty Mind* [CD]. California: Warner Bothers

Reeder, H. M. (1996). The subjective experience of love through adult life. *International Journal of Aging and Human Development, 43*(4), 325-340.

Rosenzweig, J. M., & Dailey, D. W. (1989). Dyadic adjustment/sexual satisfaction in women and men as a function of psychological sex role self-perception. *Journal of Sex and Marital Therapy, 15*(1), 42-56.

Rutter, M. (1971). Normal psychosexual development. *Child Psychological. Psychiatry. 11*, 259-283.

Ryan, C. (2008) An inconvenient truth: Sexual monogamy kills male libido. Psychology Today. Retrieved from www. psychologytoday.com/blog/lust-in-paradise/200805/ inconvenient-truth-sexual-monogamy-kills-male-libido.

Seinfeld, J., Steinberg, C. (Producers), & Hickner S., Smith, S. (Directors). (2007). *Bee Movie* [Motion picture]. United States: Dreamworks.

Shaver, P. R., & Hazan, C. (1988). A biased overview of the study of love. *Journal of Social and Personal Relationships, 5*, 473-501.

South, R. (n.d.). Robert South Quotes. Retrieved from: http://www. brainyquote.com/quotes/authors/r/robert_south.html.

Sternberg, R. J. (1986). A triangular theory of love. *Psychological Review, 93*, 119-135.

Sternberg, R. J. (1987). *The triangle of love. Intimacy, passion, commitment*. New York, NY: Basic.

Sternberg. R. J. (1997). Construct validation of a triangular love scale. *European Journal of Social Psychology, 27*, 313-335.

Stock, C. G. (1985). Forming relationships in adulthood: Social dating of unmarried men and women. *Dissertation Abstracts International, 46-12B*, 4457.

Stoller, R. J. (1968). The sense of femaleness. *Journal of the American Psychoanalytic Association, 24 (Supp.)*, 59-78.

Stoller, R. J. (1976). Primary femininity. *Journal of American Psychoanalytic Association, 24*(5), 59-78.

Stoller, R. J. (1979). *Sexual excitement: Dynamics of erotic life*. New York, NY: Pantheon.

Symons, D. (1979). *The evolution of human sexuality*. New York, NY: Oxford University Press.

Tavris, C., and Sadd, S. (1975). *The Redbook report on female sexuality: 100,000 married women disclose the good news about sex*. New

York, NY: Delacorte.

Toronto, E. L. K. (1991). *The feminine unconscious and psychoanalytic theory: Psychoanalytic psychology, 8*(4), 415-438. Ann Arbor: Erlbaum.

Trivers, R. L. (1972). Parental investment and sexual selection. In B. Campbell (Ed.), *Sexual selection and the descent of man* (pp. 1871-1971). Chicago: Aldine.

Tyson, P. (1982). A developmental line of gender identity, gender role, and choice of love object. *Journal of the American Psychoanalytic Association, 30*, 61-86.

Whitley, B. (1993). Reliability and aspects of the construct validity of Sternberg's Triangular Love Scale. *Journal of Social and Personal Relationships, 10*(3), 475- 480.

Wilcox, D. & Hager, R. (1980). Toward realistic expectations for orgasmic response in women. *Journal of Sex Research, 16*(2), 162-179.

Winnicott, D. W. (1960). The theory of the parent-infant relationship. In D.W. Winnicott, *The maturational process and the facilitating environment* (pp. 37-55). New York, NY: International University Press

www.ingramcontent.com/pod-product-compliance
Lightning Source LLC
Chambersburg PA
CBHW070634290526
45790CB00001B/91